Husserl's Legacy

Dan Zahavi offers an in-depth and up-to-date analysis of central and contested aspects of the philosophy of Edmund Husserl, the founder of phenomenology.

What is ultimately at stake in Husserl's phenomenological analyses? Are they primarily to be understood as investigations of consciousness or are they equally about the world? What is distinctive about phenomenological transcendental philosophy, and what kind of metaphysical import, if any, might it have? *Husserl's Legacy* offers an interpretation of the more overarching aims and ambitions of Husserlian phenomenology and engages with some of the most contested and debated questions in phenomenology. Central to its interpretative efforts is the attempt to understand Husserl's transcendental idealism. *Husserl's Legacy* argues that Husserl was not an internalist, nor a quietist when it comes to metaphysical issues; that he assigned a fundamental importance to facticity and intersubjectivity; and that he was not opposed to all forms of naturalism.

Dan Zahavi is Professor of Philosophy at University of Copenhagen and University of Oxford, and Director of the Center for Subjectivity Research in Copenhagen. He is author and editor of more than 25 volumes including *Husserl's Phenomenology* (Stanford 2003), *Subjectivity and Selfhood* (MIT Press 2005), *The Phenomenological Mind* (with Shaun Gallagher, Routledge 2008/2012), and *Self and Other* (Oxford University Press 2014). His work has been translated into more than 25 languages. He is co-editor in chief of the journal *Phenomenology and the Cognitive Sciences*, and recently edited *The Oxford Handbook of the History of Phenomenology* (Oxford University Press 2018).

Husserl's Legacy

Phenomenology, Metaphysics, and Transcendental Philosophy

Dan Zahavi

OXFORD
UNIVERSITY PRESS

Great Clarendon Street, Oxford, OX2 6DP,
United Kingdom

Oxford University Press is a department of the University of Oxford.
It furthers the University's objective of excellence in research, scholarship,
and education by publishing worldwide. Oxford is a registered trade mark of
Oxford University Press in the UK and in certain other countries

First Edition published in 2017
First published in paperback 2019

Published in the United States of America by Oxford University Press
198 Madison Avenue, New York, NY 10016, United States of America

British Library Cataloguing in Publication Data
Data available

Library of Congress Cataloging in Publication Data
Data available

ISBN 978-0-19-968483-0 (Hbk.)
ISBN 978-0-19-885217-9 (Pbk.)

Table of contents

Preface

I have drawn on and discussed Husserl's ideas in many publications, but only a few of my books have had his work as their prime target. My very first book, *Intentionalität und Konstitution* (1992), was an analysis of some central themes in Husserl's *Logische Untersuchungen*. My dissertation, *Husserl und die transzendentale Intersubjektivität* (1996), offered an extensive interpretation of Husserl's account of intersubjectivity, and *Husserls Fænomenologi* (1997) was a general introduction to Husserl's philosophy. From the late 1990s onwards, however, and especially after publication of the English translation of the introductory book (*Husserl's Phenomenology*, 2003), I became increasingly involved in more systematic work at the interface between phenomenology, philosophy of mind, and cognitive science, and started to write on topics such as phenomenal consciousness, self-consciousness, selfhood, empathy, social cognition, social emotions, and, most recently, collective intentionality. While engaged in this systematic endeavour, I didn't entirely cease working on Husserl, but continued, on the side, to write on different aspects of his philosophy. Over the years this resulted in quite a few articles, and eventually I started to think of ways in which to pull this material together and to rework it into a book.

Husserl's Legacy: Phenomenology, Metaphysics, and Transcendental Philosophy returns in part to a theme that was already the focus of my first book: what is the relationship between phenomenology and metaphysics, and to what extent does Husserl's turn to transcendental philosophy affect that relationship? It also aligns itself with the overarching interpretation I offered in *Husserls Fænomenologi*, but deepens and expands it by drawing on and engaging with the intervening twenty years of Husserl scholarship.

I started planning the present book in 2012, and commenced writing it in 2014. While containing much new material, the book also draws on and incorporates ideas from some of my previous articles. Everything has, however, been thoroughly revised and rewritten, and none of the original articles reappears in the form of separate book chapters. Relevant previous publications include: 'À propos de la neutralité métaphysique des *Logische Untersuchungen*', *Revue philosophique de Louvain* 99(4) (2001), 715–36: 'Merleau-Ponty on Husserl: a reappraisal', in T. Toadvine and L. Embree (eds), *Merleau-Ponty's Reading of Husserl* (Dordrecht: Kluwer Academic, 2002), 3–29; 'Phenomenology and metaphysics', in D. Zahavi, S. Heinämaa, and H. Ruin (eds), *Metaphysics, Facticity, Interpretation* (Dordrecht: Kluwer Academic, 2003), 3–22; 'Mind, meaning, and metaphysics', *Continental Philosophy Review* 36 (3) (2003), 325–34; 'Phenomenology and the project of naturalization', *Phenomenology and the Cognitive Sciences* 3(4) (2004), 331–47; 'Husserl's noema and the internalism-externalism debate', *Inquiry* 47(1) (2004), 42–66; 'Killing the strawman: Dennett and phenomenology', *Phenomenology and the Cognitive Sciences* 6(1–2) (2007), 21–43; 'Internalism, externalism, and transcendental idealism', *Synthese* 160(3) (2008), 355–74; 'Philosophy, psychology, phenomenology', in S. Heinämaa and M. Reuter (eds), *Psychology and Philosophy: Inquiries into the Soul from Late Scholasticism to Contemporary Thought* (Dordrecht: Springer, 2009), 247–62; Review of E. Thompson, *Mind in Life: Biology, Phenomenology and the Sciences of the Mind*, *Husserl Studies* 25(2) (2009), 159–68; 'Phänomenologie und Transzendentalphilosophie', in G. Figal and H.-H. Gander (eds), *Heidegger und Husserl: Neue Perspektiven* (Frankfurt am Main: Vittorio Klostermann, 2009), 73–99; 'Naturalized phenomenology', in S. Gallagher and D. Schmicking (eds), *Handbook of Phenomenology and Cognitive Science* (Dordrecht: Springer, 2010), 2–19; 'Life, thinking and phenomenology in the early Bergson', in M. R. Kelly (ed.), *Bergson and Phenomenology* (Basingstoke: Palgrave Macmillan, 2010), 118–33; 'Husserl and the "absolute"', in C. Ierna, H. Jacobs, and F. Mattens (eds), *Philosophy, Phenomenology, Sciences: Essays in Commemoration of Husserl* (Dordrecht: Springer, 2010), 71–92; 'Naturalized phenomenology: a desideratum or a category mistake?', *Royal Institute of Philosophy Supplement* 72 (2013), 23–42; 'Phenomenology of reflection', in A. Staiti (ed.), *Commentary on Husserl's Ideas I* (Berlin: De Gruyter, 2015), 177–93; 'The end of what? Phenomenology vs. speculative realism', *International Journal of Philosophical Studies* 24(3) (2016), 289–309; 'Brain, Mind, World: Predictive coding, neo-Kantianism, and transcendental idealism', *Husserl Studies* 34/1 (2018), 47–61.

Husserl's Legacy was written at the Center for Subjectivity Research at the University of Copenhagen. I have profited from my interaction and discussion with both staff members and visitors. I am also grateful to the

Danish National Research Foundation, whose initial support allowed me to establish and run the research centre.

Some of the ideas found in this book were initially presented at lectures at Penn State University, the Chinese University of Hong Kong, École Normale Supérieure (Paris), Peking University, the University of Tromsø, the Catholic University of America (Washington, DC), the University of Bern, Ritsumeikan University (Kyoto), the Paris-Sorbonne University, the University of Essex, the Hebrew University (Jerusalem), the University of Freiburg, the University of Leuven, the University of Würzburg, the University of Western England, Rochester Institute of Technology, the University of Heidelberg, Charles University Prague, Boston College, Södertörn University (Stockholm), Helsinki University, the University of Vienna, and UC Berkeley. I am grateful to the various audiences for their valuable comments.

Over the years, I have profited from an ongoing discussion with various fellow Husserlians including David Carr, Steven Crowell, John Drummond, Jim Hart, Sara Heinämaa, Søren Overgaard, Tony Steinbock, and Evan Thompson. That I still owe a debt of gratitude to my former teachers Klaus Held and Rudolf Bernet should be evident from reading the book. I am also particular indebted to Liesbet de Kock, Sophie Loidolt, Louis Sass, Galen Strawson, Takuya Nakamura, and Philip Schmidt for various incisive comments on different parts of the text. I am grateful to James Jardine and Thomas Szanto for having provided invaluable help in translating some of the quotations from Husserl into English. Special thanks to Sophie Loidolt for once again organizing a workshop in Vienna where an advanced draft of most of the manuscript was discussed. Let me also acknowledge my debt to two anonymous referees for Oxford University Press who provided some very helpful comments.

Finally, thanks to Juan Toro for compiling the index and to Peter Momtchiloff for his exemplary editorship.

Introduction

How should one assess Husserl's legacy? One possibility is to study the influence he has exerted on the development of twentieth-century philosophy. That the influence has been immense can hardly be disputed. This is not to say, of course, that everybody agreed with him; but the fact that subsequent phenomenologists, including Heidegger, Ingarden, Schutz, Fink, Sartre, Merleau-Ponty, Levinas, Gadamer, Ricœur, Derrida, Henry, and Marion, as well as leading theorists from a whole range of other traditions, including hermeneutics, critical theory, deconstruction, and post-structuralism, felt a need to react and respond to Husserl's project and program testifies to his importance. We can, however, contrast this more backward-looking approach with a more forward-looking appraisal of Husserl's legacy, one that basically asks the following question: 'What are the future prospects of Husserlian phenomenology?' Or to put it differently, 'Does Husserlian phenomenology remain relevant for philosophy in the twenty-first century?' These are, of course, huge questions, and there are again different ways one might go about trying to answer them.

One option is to inquire into the way in which Husserl's work contains specific analyses of enduring value. One could, for instance, investigate whether his detailed analyses of intentionality, embodiment, time-consciousness, self-consciousness, intersubjectivity, etc. has something to offer current discussions in continental philosophy, analytic philosophy of mind, or cognitive science. In short, one way to argue for the continuing relevance of Husserl's phenomenology is by showing that there still is much to learn from his painstaking investigations of various concrete phenomena. This is a completely respectable way of approaching the question; moreover, it is an approach that is currently quite influential.

But would Husserl have been satisfied with this kind of legacy? In his eyes, would the absorption and integration of many of his specific analyses into other research programs have been sufficient to demonstrate the healthy state of phenomenology? I suspect not. I think Husserl would have been more concerned with the question of whether his phenomenological program and project continued to flourish.

In a recent critical exchange with Dennett, Siewert has defended the relevance and significance of what he calls 'plain phenomenology', which is what one is practising if (1) one is making and explaining mental or psychological distinctions, (2) one shows why those distinctions are theoretically important, (3) one relies on a source of first-person warrant, and does so (4) without assuming that first-person warrant derives from some source of third-person warrant (Siewert 2007: 202). Whatever the merits of such an enterprise, it ought to be clear that this is not what Husserl had in mind when he characterized phenomenology as the culmination and fulfilment of Western philosophy (Hua 6/195).

Rather than delving into a detailed exploration of some of Husserl's many concrete investigations of intentionality, temporality, empathy, etc., the aim of the following linked studies is to pursue a more methodological and metaphilosophical objective and offer an interpretation of the more overarching aims and ambitions of Husserlian phenomenology. What is ultimately at stake in his phenomenological analyses? Are Husserl's phenomenological analyses primarily to be understood as investigations of consciousness, and if so, must they then be classified as psychological contributions of some sort? If Husserl is engaged in a transcendental philosophical project, is phenomenological transcendental philosophy then distinctive in some way, and what kind of metaphysical import, if any, might it have? Is Husserlian phenomenology primarily descriptive in character—is it supposed to capture how matters *seem* to us, or is it also supposed to capture how things are?

The questions to be addressed are some of the most contested and debated in phenomenology. They have been discussed ever since the publication of Husserl's *Logische Untersuchungen* in 1900–1901, and as we shall see, there is still no consensus in the literature. Central to my interpretive efforts will be an attempt to understand Husserl's *transcendental idealism*. What does it amount to, and why did Husserl adopt it? Is it a metaphysical position, does it commit him to a form of (sophisticated) phenomenalism or subjective idealism, or is Husserl on the contrary engaged in a semantic or epistemological project that involves a suspension of metaphysical questions altogether?

Despite the impressive quality of recent scholarly work on Husserl, several fundamental misunderstandings are still widespread in the larger scholarly community—misunderstandings which continue to impede a sound grasp of the central aims and ambitions of his phenomenology. To mention just one example, consider as authoritative a volume as *The Oxford Dictionary of Philosophy*, where we can read that Husserl's transcendental idealism involves a bracketing of external questions and the taking of 'a solipsistic, disembodied Cartesian ego' as the starting point, and that Husserl consequently considered it 'inessential that the thinking subject is either embodied or surrounded by others' (Blackburn 2016: 229–30).

Taking issue with readings such as this, I will argue that Husserl was not a sophisticated introspectionist, nor a phenomenalist, nor an internalist, nor a quietist when it comes to metaphysical issues, and not opposed to all forms of naturalism. On a more positive note, I will argue that a proper grasp of Husserl's transcendental idealism will reveal how fundamental a role he ascribed to embodiment and intersubjectivity. Ultimately, I will argue that he has more in common with contemporary enactivism than with traditional internalist representationalism. Indeed, if anything my interpretation will seek to show that Husserl's phenomenology is as much about the world as it is about consciousness.

Husserl's Legacy is intended as a contribution to Husserl scholarship. The primary aim of the following investigations is to clarify Husserl's position and to suggest ways in which to make sense of various central claims of his. Although the aim is not to offer an independent defence of transcendental idealism, I hope to show that there are ways of interpreting the latter that will make it far more akin to dominant positions in twentieth-century philosophy than one might initially have assumed.

*   *   *

A few words about the material I will draw on are in order. I will primarily make use of texts published in the text-critical Husserliana edition. As is well known, the few books that Husserl managed to publish during his life make up only a very small part of his enormous production. Husserl had the habit of writing every day, and when he died in 1938, his literary legacy amounted to more than 40,000 pages. How these manuscripts were secretly brought to safety in Belgium before the outbreak of World War II is an exciting story in its own right (see van Breda

1959). But one of the principal tasks of the Husserl Archives in Leuven, founded in 1939, was to commence a critical edition of Husserl's works. By now, the Husserliana consists of 42 volumes, and contains not only new editions of works that were published during Husserl's life but also, and more importantly, text-critical editions of his previously unpublished works, articles, lectures, and research manuscripts.

The decision to base an interpretation partially on Husserl's research manuscripts faces a methodological objection. Is it not problematic to make use of book manuscripts or research manuscripts that Husserl kept back from publication, and which he might even have written for himself alone? Husserl's daily writing was partially an attempt to try out new ideas (Hua 13/xviii–xix), and the reason these texts were never published might precisely have been because Husserl was dissatisfied with the result. Is it consequently not better to base an interpretation exclusively on the writings published by Husserl himself?

If this reasoning seems compelling, then consider for instance what Wittgenstein scholarship would currently look like if it had focused exclusively on *Tractatus Logico-Philosophicus*, the only work that Wittgenstein published during his lifetime. If we take a closer look at Husserl's working method and publication plans, it will in any case become clear that there are many reasons why it would be unwise to adhere to the methodological principle in question.

Husserl often expressed reservations and misgivings about his published works soon after they appeared. In some cases, he spent considerable time revising substantive portions of the texts. In his *Nachlass*, one can, for instance, find revisions of both *Logische Untersuchungen* and *Cartesianische Meditationen*—revisions that have subsequently been published (see Hua 20/1–2 and Hua 15).

In his later years, Husserl made different attempts to write a definitive systematic presentation of his philosophy. Many of these attempts remained unsuccessful and did not result in published books. But the reason for this was not that Husserl was particularly dissatisfied with the results, but rather that he had difficulties maintaining focus, and kept getting distracted by and absorbed in other projects (Hua 15/xvi, lxi).

Precisely because of his recurrent problems with completing a systematic and comprehensive account, Husserl eventually started to work quite explicitly with his *Nachlass* in mind (cf. Hua 14/xix, 15/lxii, lxvii–iii). As he frequently remarked in letters to friends and colleagues such as Paul

Natorp and Adolf Grimme, his most decisive contribution was contained in the unpublished manuscripts. As Husserl wrote in 1931: 'Indeed, the largest and, as I actually believe, most important part of my life's work still lies in my manuscripts, scarcely manageable because of their volume' (Hua Dok 3-III/90, cf. 3-V/151).

The continuing publication of Husserliana has made an increasing number of Husserl's research manuscripts available, and a study of these has made it necessary to revise and modify a number of widespread and dominant interpretations. This is so not only because the new material has offered a plethora of analyses and descriptions that allow for a more precise grasp of Husserl's phenomenological core concepts, but also because they have disclosed aspects of his thinking that it would have been difficult, if not impossible, to anticipate through a study of the few works whose publication were authorized by Husserl himself.

Whereas early Husserl scholarship primarily focused on classical volumes such as *Logische Untersuchungen, Ideen zu einer reinen Phänomenologie und phänomenologischen Philosophie I, Cartesianische Meditationen,* and *Die Krisis der europäischen Wissenschaften und die transzendentale Phänomenologie,* this is no longer the case. Indeed, there is widespread consensus among Husserl scholars that it is no longer admissible to base a comprehensive interpretation on such a narrow range of publications. The focus and scope have expanded to include all of the Husserliana volumes, and, apart from the texts already mentioned, volumes such as *Ideen zu einer reinen Phänomenologie und phänomenologischen Philosophie II, Erste Philosophie II, Zur Phänomenologie des inneren Zeitbewusstseins, Analysen zur passiven Synthesis,* and *Zur Phänomenologie der Intersubjektivität I–III* have had a particular dramatic impact. This change of focus has brought about a new type of interpretation, which is not only characterized by an emphasis on the dimensions of facticity, embodiment, sociality, passivity, historicity, and ethics in Husserl's thinking; it has also enabled reinterpretations of the classical volumes, thus revealing a unity and consistency in the development of his thinking that would otherwise have remained concealed.

1

Introspection and reflection

Damit hängt die grundverkehrte Ansicht zusammen, als ob es sich
bei der Phänomenologie um eine Restitution der Methode innerer
Beobachtung handle oder direkter innerer Erfahrung überhaupt.

Ideen III

1.1 Methodological worries

Husserl starts his lecture course *Phänomenologische Psychologie* from
1925 with the following historical overview (Hua 9/3–20). During the
nineteenth century, psychology underwent tremendous development.
Through the collaborative effort of scientists like Müller, Helmholtz,
Hering, Fechner, and Wundt, psychology established itself as a truly
scientific enterprise. Although experimental psychology quickly gained
results, it was a psychology that looked to the natural sciences, especially
to physiology, for guidance. It was a psychology that—in Husserl's
words—could not withstand the temptation of naturalism. It approached
consciousness as if it were an object in the world, one that could be
investigated and explained by means of the standard methods of natural
science. This approach was soon met with criticism. Could psychology of
this kind really do justice to the experiential dimension? Was it at all able
to capture subjectivity? In *Ideen über eine beschreibende und zerglie-
dernde Psychologie* from 1894, Wilhelm Dilthey argued that psychology
had become much too influenced by the natural sciences, and that it
should to a larger extent orient itself towards the humanities. Dilthey
wished to preserve the difference between the explanation offered by the
natural sciences and the understanding provided by the humanities, and
distinguished an explanatory or constructive psychology from his own
descriptive or analysing psychology. The former was committed to the

ideals of natural science. It was atomistic and based on hypotheses and inferences. But by proceeding in such a manner, it also proved itself incapable of grasping the life of consciousness. It failed to realize that the unity of psychic life is an experienced unity and not simply an inferred and postulated one. However, Dilthey's counterattack was not altogether successful. On the one hand, his own alternative remained too wedded to an introspective methodology. It only dealt with particularities, and was unable to offer universal insights and formulate proper psychological laws. On the other hand, its criticism of experimental psychology was not sufficiently worked out, and it was countered in 1895 by a brilliant and devastating article by Hermann Ebbinghaus, who had pioneered the development of experimental methods for the measurement of rote learning and memory. At the turn of the century, the battle consequently seemed to have been won by the naturalists. Then *Logische Untersuchungen* (1900–1901) was published, and as Husserl remarks, this radically changed the situation (Hua 9/20).

Logische Untersuchungen heralded the birth of a new method for studying consciousness, a method called 'phenomenology' (Hua 9/28, 302). One of its central aims was to explore the intentionality of consciousness, the fact that our perception, thinking, judging, etc. is about or of something. The very attempt to offer a careful description of our psychological life, the very idea that intentionality must be appreciated as a distinctive feature of mental states, were however ideas already found in the work of the prominent Viennese psychologist and philosopher Franz Brentano, whose lectures Husserl had attended in the early 1880s. It is consequently natural to ask whether Husserl was not simply continuing the project commenced by Brentano. Husserl's own answer to this question is unequivocal. As he remarked in a late letter to Marvin Farber from 18 June 1937:

Even though I began in my youth as an enthusiastic admirer of Brentano, I must admit I deluded myself, for too long, and in a way hard to understand now, into believing that I was a co-worker on his philosophy, especially, his psychology. But in truth, my way of thinking was a totally different one from that of Brentano already in my first work [...]. In a formal sense, Brentano asks for and provides a psychology whose whole topic is the 'psychic phenomena' which he on occasions defines also as 'consciousness of something'. But his psychology is anything but a science of intentionality, the proper problems of intentionality never dawned upon him. He even failed to see that no given experience of consciousness can be described without a description of the correlated 'intentional object "as such"' (for example, that this perception of the desk can only be described, when I describe this desk as what and just as it is perceived). Brentano had no inkling of intentional implication, of intentional modifications, of problems of constitution, etc. (Hua Dok 3-IV/82)

In his own pioneering analysis of intentionality in *Logische Untersuchungen*, Husserl had argued (1) that every intentional experience is an experience of a specific type, i.e. an experience of perceiving, judging, hoping, desiring, regretting, remembering, affirming, doubting, wondering, fearing, etc.; (2) that each of these experiences is characterized by being directed at an object in a particular way; and (3) that none of these experiences can be analysed properly without considering their objective correlate, i.e. the perceived, doubted, expected object. Why did Husserl engage in this analysis of intentionality in the first place? Because he wanted to provide a new foundation for logic and epistemology (Hua 18/7). But why should a clarification of the former lead to an understanding of the latter? In fact, is not the very proposal that it does tantamount to some form of psychologism—the very position that *Logische Untersuchungen* is also supposed to have criticized so devastatingly?

How to characterize psychologism? Its main line of argumentation is as follows. Epistemology is concerned with the cognitive nature of perceiving, believing, judging, and knowing. All of these phenomena, however, are psychical phenomena, and it is therefore up to psychology to investigate and explore their structure. This also holds true for our scientific and logical reasoning, and ultimately logic must therefore be regarded as part of psychology and the laws of logic as psycho-logical regularities, whose nature and validity must be empirically investigated and established (Hua 18/64, 89).

As Husserl showed, this argument is flawed. For one, it does not distinguish sufficiently between the *object* of knowledge and the *act* of knowing. The birthday cake that I perceive is quite different from my perception of it. The birthday cake weighs three kilograms, can be eaten, and can be used in a clown act. My experience of the cake by contrast does not weigh anything, cannot be eaten, and cannot hit anybody in the face. And whereas the cake is not of or about anything, the perception of the cake is exactly about something, namely the cake. Such a principled difference between act and object, between the seeing and the seen, the hearing and the heard, also obtains in the case of logic. When one speaks of a law of logic or refers to logical truths, theories, principles, sentences, and proofs, one does not refer to subjective experiences with temporal duration. Although the principles of logic are grasped and known by consciousness, we are, according to Husserl, conscious of something *ideal* whose nature is quite unlike the psychical process of knowing. Despite the irreducible difference between the act and the object, however, we are still confronted with the puzzling fact that objective truths are known in subjective experiences of knowing. And as Husserl insists, it is this relation between the objective and the subjective that must be investigated and clarified, if we wish to attain a more substantial understanding of the possibility of knowledge (Hua 18/7).

Despite Husserl's criticism of psychologism, his interest in the fundamental problems of epistemology consequently made him return to consciousness. And although this move might not constitute a relapse into psychologism, it could still be suggested that phenomenology ultimately amounts to a new psychological method. Such a proposal could find some support in Husserl's own text, since in the first edition of *Logische Untersuchungen* he chose to characterize phenomenology as a 'descriptive psychology' (Hua 19/24 [I/176]).

In its investigation of intentional consciousness, phenomenology highlights the significance of the first-person perspective. But is that not precisely what the introspectionist psychologists were also doing? So perhaps phenomenology ought to be classified as a form of introspectionism. As Husserl remarks in a manuscript entitled *Phänomenologie und Psychologie* from 1917, by then this line of thought had become so widespread that the very term 'phenomenological' was being used in all kinds of philosophical and psychological writings as a label for a direct description of consciousness based on introspection (Hua 25/103).

This usage lives on. Consider, for instance, the assessment of Dennett, who in explaining the difference between Husserl's phenomenology and his own heterophenomenology has insisted that, whereas he himself seeks to determine the notional world of another from the outside, the classical phenomenologists sought to gain access to their own notional world by some special 'introspectionist bit of mental gymnastics' (Dennett 1987: 153). Indeed, as Dennett puts it in an often-quoted passage from *Consciousness Explained*, the aim of the philosophical tradition founded by Husserl was to:

find a new foundation for all philosophy (indeed, for all knowledge) based on a special technique of introspection, in which the outer world and all its implications and presuppositions were supposed to be 'bracketed' in a particular act of mind known as the epoché. The net result was an investigative state of mind in which the Phenomenologist was supposed to become acquainted with the pure objects of conscious experience, called *noemata*, untainted by the usual distortions and amendments of theory and practice. Like other attempts to strip away interpretation and reveal the basic facts of consciousness to rigorous observation, such as the Impressionist movement in the arts and the Introspectionist psychologies of Wundt, Titchener, and others, Phenomenology has failed to find a single, settled method that everyone could agree upon. (Dennett 1991: 44)

Why is the phenomenological methodology unreliable, and why did it fail to generate a consensus? One reason is that introspection, according to Dennett, is less a matter of observation than of theorizing. In fact, it is precisely because there is so little to see that there is so much room for fabrication and confabulation (Dennett 1991: 68, 94; 1982: 173). In addition, Dennett has repeatedly characterized classical phenomenology as an 'autophenomenology' (Dennett 1987: 153). For classical phenomenology, the subject and the object of the investigation coincide, since the autophenomenologist, rather than investigating the mental life of others, is concerned with his or her own mental life. In fact, classical phenomenology is ultimately committed to a form of 'methodological solipsism'—a term originally coined by Putnam (1975: 220) to designate a position according to which no psychological state presupposes the existence of any individual other than the subject to whom the state is ascribed. Classical phenomenology considers the subject a detached and self-sufficient existent and thereby fails to recognize, for instance, to what extent consciousness is language-dependent. The phenomenologists have consistently emphasized the importance of the first-person perspective, and have tried to develop a first-person science; but in the end their introspectionist and solipsistic method does not qualify as a sound scientific method, since proper science requires a third-person method (Dennett 1991: 70; 1987: 154–8). A real scientific investigation of consciousness should focus on the actual goings-on in the brain, and those subpersonal mechanisms are not introspectively available, but are only accessible from the outside.

Dennett's treatment of the phenomenological tradition can hardly count as thorough and exhaustive. In fact, it does not really add up to more than a few scattered comments. This has not prevented him from dismissing the tradition rather categorically, however. In his view,

Husserlians are deeply into obscurantism for its own sake, and reading their works is consequently largely a waste of time (Dennett 1994). But how familiar is Dennett with the topic of his criticism? Somewhat surprisingly, on more than one occasion he has called attention to what he sees as his own Husserlian heritage. He studied Husserl and other phenomenologists with Dagfinn Føllesdal as an undergraduate, and learned about phenomenology from his graduate adviser, Gilbert Ryle, whom Dennett considers a masterful scholar of phenomenology (Dennett 1994). In reply to those who have accused him of ignoring the resources of classical phenomenology, Dennett has consequently had a ready reply: 'it is precisely because my disregard has *not* been complete that it has been, and continues to be, so confident' (Dennett 1994).

But Dennett has not only stressed his familiarity with the phenomenological tradition, he has also defended the accuracy of his own Husserl interpretation quite explicitly, and even argued that if his reading should turn out to be wrong, it would be so much the worse for Husserl (Dennett 1994). This is in many ways a puzzling claim. Given that Dennett keeps insisting that Husserl has been employing a fatally flawed unscientific methodology, it is difficult to see why Dennett's interpretation should particularly benefit Husserl.

Dennett is not alone in assessing Husserl's phenomenological method in such bleak terms, however. In *Being No One*, Metzinger argues in a similar fashion and concludes that 'phenomenology is impossible' (Metzinger 2003: 83). What kind of argument does Metzinger provide? The basic argument seems to concern the epistemological difficulties connected to any first-person approach to data generation. If inconsistencies in two individual data sets should appear, there is no way to settle the conflict. More specifically, Metzinger takes data to be things that are extracted from the physical world by technical measuring devices. This data extraction involves a well-defined intersubjective procedure, takes place within a scientific community, is open to criticism, and constantly seeks independent means of verification. The problem with phenomenology is that first-person access to the phenomenal content of one's own mental states does not fulfil these defining criteria for the concept of data. In fact, the very notion of first-personal data is a contradiction in terms (Metzinger 2003: 591).

Whereas some interpreters have claimed that Husserl's phenomenological method amounts to a form of introspectionism in order thereby to discredit his research program, there are others who have likewise argued that 'there are no major differences in acts between phenom- enological "reflection" and psycho-phenomenological introspection' (Vermersch 2009: 25), but for whom this amounts to praise, since they consider Husserl 'a great unrecognized psychologist' (Vermersch 2011: 22). This particular interpretation has recently gained traction due to the work of advocates of the so-called 'elicitation interview method'—a method pioneered by Vermersch (Vermersch 1994; Depraz et al. 2003), and further developed by Petitmengin and Bitbol (Petitmengin 2006; Petitmengin and Bitbol 2009).

In his *Textbook of Psychology*, which offers a classical exposition of the method of introspection, Titchener provided a description of what he felt when reading the sentence 'Infinity broods over all things': 'The most prominent thing in consciousness was a blue-black, dense arched sky, which palpated, as if with immense wings, over a solid convex surface' (Titchener 1910: 517–18). A page later, he also offered the following description of the imagery evoked by the meaning of 'meaning': 'the blue-grey tip of a kind of scoop, which has a bit of yellow above it (presumably a part of the handle), and which is just digging into a dark mass of what appears to be plastic material' (p. 519). I hope that nobody would seriously propose that there is any relevant similarity between these kinds of descriptions and the analyses provided by Hus- serl. But consider an example given by Petitmengin and Bitbol:

I am in a *café*, absorbed in a lively philosophical discussion with my friend Paul. At the beginning of the conversation, my attention is completely focused on the content of the ideas. But as the discussion goes on, my mode of attention progressively changes and I start to become aware of other dimensions of my experience. I first realize that we also speak with our hands, and that I was initially unaware of our gestures. I then realize that I am feeling many emotions triggered by the ideas we are exchanging, that these emotions are experienced in several parts of my body (especially my chest and my throat), and that I was not clearly aware of this. Suddenly, I also become aware of a vague and diffuse, yet intense and specific feeling which is likely to have been within me from the very instant I was in Paul's presence: the energy, the rhythm, the special 'atmosphere' that emanates from him, his highly personal way of being present. At the moment I become aware of this feeling, I keep on participating in the conversa- tion, but the field of my attention is now broader and defocused. I do not try to capture this feeling but it imposes itself on me. It is as if instead of trying to fetch it, I am allowing it to come to me, to pervade me. While I adopt this open and receptive form of attention, I am present and awake but lightly so, effortlessly and without tension. (Bitbol and Petitmengin 2011: 33)

Should phenomenology concern itself with reports of this kind? As Bitbol and Petitmengin argue, any reader of a phenomenological description should not accept this description solely on Husserl's or anybody else's authority, but should instead seek to re-enact the process that led to the description in question. It is precisely this re-enactment, this 'anchoring in singular experience', that on their view makes up the 'true difference between an abstract hermeneutical work and an active, lively, and embodied phenomenological discourse' (Bitbol and Petitmengin 2011: 36). Should we consequently appreciate Husserl's phenomenological work as a collection of fine-grained descriptions of thin time-slices of experiences, as Petitmengin and Bitbol seem to claim (2013a: 271, 273)? Will a technique (like the elicitation interview) that allegedly broadens our field of attention in such a way as to allow us to discover hitherto unreflected and unnoticed aspects and details of lived experience (Bitbol and Petitmengin 2013b: 181, 194) make us into better phenomenologists? Is the aim of the phenomenological method ultimately to 'detect laterally occurrences that are not in the main focus of attention' (Bitbol and Petitmengin 2013b: 179)? Is it about revealing the margins 'of our experience that are overlooked as long as exclusive concern for objects prevails' (p. 179)?

Let us for a moment respect the phenomenological dictum and return to the things themselves, which in this case are Husserl's actual writings. *Logische Untersuchungen* is a recognized milestone in twentieth-century philosophy and indisputably a work of phenomenological philosophy. In fact, it constituted what Husserl himself took to be his 'breakthrough' to phenomenology. What kind of analysis does one find in this book? In addition to Husserl's attack on and rejection of psychologism, one also finds a defence of the irreducibility of logic and the ideality of meaning; an analysis of pictorial representations; a theory of the part–whole relation; a development of a pure grammar; a sophisticated account of intentionality; and an epistemological clarification of the relation between concepts and intuitions, to mention just a few of the many topics treated in the book. Is this a work of introspective psychology? Does it primarily contain refined descriptions of inner experiences? I think anybody who has actually read the book would answer no. Should we then conclude that the book is after all not a work in phenomenology, or should we reconsider our hasty identification of phenomenology and introspective psychology? I think the answer ought to be straightforward.

It is no coincidence that Husserl categorically rejected the attempt to equate the notion of phenomenological intuition with a type of inner experience or introspection (Hua 25/36), and even argued that the very suggestion that phenomenology is attempting to restitute the method of introspection (*innerer Beobachtung*) is preposterous (*grundverkehrt*) (Hua 5/38). It is significant that Husserl's stance on this issue was fully shared by the other phenomenologists, who all openly and unequivocally denied that they were engaged in some kind of introspective psychology and that the method they employ was a method of introspection. Not only did Heidegger (to take one example) deny that his own analysis of the existential structures of Dasein is a psychological analysis (Heidegger 1996: 42–7), he also wrote that the attempt to interpret Husserl's investigations as a kind of descriptive psychology completely failed to do justice to their transcendental character. In fact, as Heidegger added, phenomenology will remain a book sealed with seven or more seals to any such psychological approach (pp. 15–16).

Phenomenological disputes as well as disputes among phenomenologists are philosophical disputes, not disputes about introspective findings. Although it would be an exaggeration to claim that Husserl's analyses in *Logische Untersuchungen* found universal approval among subsequent generations of phenomenologists, I do not know of any instance where Husserl's position was rejected because of an appeal to 'better' introspective evidence. On the contrary, his analyses in this milestone work gave rise to an intense discussion among phenomenological philosophers, and many of the analyses were subsequently improved and refined by thinkers like Sartre, Heidegger, Levinas, and Derrida (cf. Zahavi and Stjernfelt 2002). Compare this to Metzinger's claim that the phenomenological method cannot provide a method for generating any growth of knowledge, since there is no way one can reach intersubjective consensus on claims like 'this is the purest blue anyone can perceive' vs 'no it isn't, it has a slight green hue' (Metzinger 2003: 591). But such claims—or claims concerning, say, the precise shape of the visual patterns one sees with one's eyes closed—are simply not the type of claims that are to be found in works by phenomenological philosophers; and to suggest so is to reveal one's lack of familiarity with the tradition in question.[1]

Phenomenology is indeed interested in experiential consciousness, in the first-personal dimension of consciousness, but its goal has never been to offer descriptions of idiosyncratic experiences—'here and now, this is just what I experience'. Phenomenology is not concerned with factual claims such as 'I am currently feeling slightly nauseous' or 'when tasting Amarone, I am always reminded of my first visit to Venice'. Phenomenology is not interested in qualia in the sense of purely private data that are incorrigible, ineffable, and incomparable; it is not interested in your specific experience, or in my specific experience, but in invariant structures of experience and in principled questions concerning, say, the presentational character of perception, the structure of temporality, or the difference between empathy and sympathy.

A likely conclusion to draw at this point might be that there is indeed more to phenomenology than simply a compilation of introspective reports, since the aim of phenomenology is to contribute refined and sophisticated analyses of the eidetic and a priori structures of consciousness: what do essentially characterize acts of perceiving, imagining, remembering, judging, etc., and how are these different acts related to each other? This is also pointed out by Bitbol and Petitmengin, who then urge us not to forget that any intersubjective agreement on the invariant structure of experience has to involve and rely on the individual's access to his or her own lived experience (Bitbol and Petitmengin 2011: 36).

To suggest that we now have a grasp of what is distinctive about phenomenology and of how it differs from psychology would, however, amount to yet another misunderstanding. As Husserl writes,

---

[1] Thomasson has also rejected Dennett's claim that Husserl's phenomenological method should employ introspection, and that phenomenological knowledge is based on an inner observation of our mental states (2005: 116). Her argument proceeds differently from mine, however. Although Thomasson rightly highlights the importance of the phenomenological reduction and the cognitive transformation it effects, she also argues that Husserl's account of phenomenological method has much in common with the account of self-knowledge developed by Sellars and Dretske (Thomasson 2005: 116). I am not persuaded by this latter claim (for a criticism of Dretske, see Zahavi 2014: 24–5), nor by the claim that Husserl's phenomenological descriptions are simply the result of an analysis of various logical and conceptual entailments (Thomasson 2005: 133). In either case, the distinct first-personal character of phenomenology is overlooked.

The eidetic analyses of experiential consciousness, of outer experience and of every kind of experience, and in continuation hereof, the eidetic analyses of every kind of consciousness might be carried as far as possible: We will still remain at the level of psychology. (Hua 25/104)

In other words, if all phenomenology could do was to contribute refined eidetic analyses of consciousness, phenomenology would not differ from a certain kind of eidetic psychology. But where then is the difference between phenomenology and psychology located?

It is undeniable that phenomenology has affinities with psychology insofar as both disciplines are interested in consciousness. But although the distinction between a phenomenological and a psychological investigation of consciousness can be difficult to draw, and might at first even appear to be an unnecessarily subtle distinction, we are, as Husserl insists, in the end confronted with a crucial nuance that is fundamental to the very possibility of doing philosophy. We should realize

that every historically available scientific discipline and even part of what normally belongs to philosophy, including formal logic, psychology and ethics, conduct their research in a natural—though in a certain way necessary—naivety. All their questions refer to a world which is given to us—with an obviousness belonging to life—prior to all science, but they fail to notice that this pre-givenness conceals a true infinity of enigmatic problems, which are not even noticed from within the natural perspective. I am referring to the transcendental problems, and it is only the truly scientific philosophy which has made their disclosure possible. (Hua 32/7)

For Husserl, the main difference between phenomenology and psychology is that whereas the latter accepts a number of commonsensical metaphysical presuppositions, the former is engaged in a transcendental investigation of those very presuppositions.

Why does Husserl's phenomenology merit the name 'transcendental'? Husserl's standard answer is that the concepts 'transcendence' and 'transcendental' are correlated, and that phenomenology is transcendental because its aim is to clarify the constitution of transcendence (Hua 17/259, 1/34, 65). Positive science cannot be faulted for making the metaphysical assumptions it does, for simply presupposing the mind-independent existence of the objects it seeks to investigate. But if philosophy is to deserve its credentials as a form of radical questioning, if it is to engage with the fundamental epistemological questions, it cannot simply prejudice the answer beforehand. Rather than simply naively accepting the ready-made character of the objective world, we need to understand how the world for us comes to acquire its character of true, valid, and objective. How is it that the world which we only have access to in virtue of our first-person perspective can appear to us as being independent of that perspective? How can something be given in experience as transcending that very experience? Husserl concedes that traditional Cartesian epistemology has also been engaged with the problem of transcendence; but in its traditional form, the problem has been posed as the question of how we can ever get beyond our starting point, the inner mental realm (Hua 1/115–16). As Husserl insists, however, this framing of the problem is wrongheaded. It presents us with a pseudo-problem, which only arises if we forget the true lesson of intentionality and conceive of the mind as an isolated, world-detached entity.

In *Phénoménologie de la perception*, Merleau-Ponty would echo this characterization by declaring phenomenology to be distinguished in all its features from introspective psychology, and by arguing that the difference in question is a difference in principle. Whereas the introspective psychologist considers consciousness as a mere sector of being, and tries to investigate this sector in the same way the physicist tries to investigate his, the phenomenologist realizes that an investigation of consciousness cannot take place as long as the absolute existence of the world is left unquestioned. Consciousness cannot be analysed properly without leading us beyond commonsense assumptions and towards a transcendental clarification of the constitution of the world (Merleau-Ponty 2012: 59–60).

Husserl's and Merleau-Ponty's remarks call for further clarification. The simplest way to understand both of them is by acknowledging that phenomenology—despite all kinds of other differences—is firmly situated within a certain Kantian or post-Kantian framework. One way to interpret Kant's revolutionary Copernican turn is by seeing it as amounting to the realization that our cognitive apprehension of reality is more than a mere mirroring of a pre-existing world. Thus, with Kant the pre-critical search for the fundamental building blocks of reality was transformed into a transcendental philosophical reflection on what conditions something must satisfy in order to count as real. What is the condition of possibility for the appearance of empirical objects? What does it mean for the world to count as real and objective? With various modifications, this idea was picked up by Husserl and subsequent phenomenologists.

Phenomenologists share the conviction that the critical stance proper to philosophy necessitates a move away from a straightforward investigation of objects to an investigation of the very framework of meaning and intelligibility that makes any such straightforward investigation possible in the first place. Indeed, rather than taking the objective world as the point of departure, phenomenology precisely asks how something like objectivity is possible in the first place. How is objectivity constituted? How is it that the world can be manifested or revealed to us in the first place?

I will in later chapters return in more detail to these issues and also discuss to what extent Husserl's project is similar to and different from Kant's; but let us for the moment continue our exploration of Husserl's methodology by considering his use of reflection, since this will give us a better grasp of the scope of his phenomenology.

1.2 The scope of reflection

In *Ideen I*, Husserl states that reflection is the name for an act that allows us to analyse other experiences, and also the name for the more general method employed by phenomenology (Hua 3/162). He also writes that one of the distinct tasks of phenomenology is to explore the contribution of reflection in a more systematic fashion. It has to engage in a kind of meta-reflection (Hua 3/165–7). But is 'reflection' not simply another term for introspection, and don't Husserl's assertions consequently provide support for the introspectionist interpretation? Doesn't Husserl's systematic employment of reflection show that the latter reading is after all correct and that his main objective is to provide accurate and faithful descriptions of our inner mental states? Indeed, isn't his complicated methodology precisely introduced in order to allow for a supposedly undistorted grasp of the pure experience—one that in no way is tainted or altered by interpretation and language? Isn't Spaulding exactly right when she claims that phenomenologists have insisted that the attempt to 'verbally express one's phenomenology is to defeat the purpose of phenomenology? To verbalize one's experiences is to impose a linguistic, cultural framework on the experience, which thwarts the goal of studying the experience itself' (Spaulding 2015: 1070). To settle this question, and show why Spaulding happens to be quite wrong, let me offer a brief comparison of Husserl's view with that of Bergson.

In his doctoral dissertation *Essai sur les données immédiates de la conscience*, Bergson argued that although reason can isolate, immobilize, and spatialize the flow of lived experiences and thereby make them accessible to verbal description and analytic reflection, the true life of consciousness cannot be caught in our conceptual network. It will always overflow our artificial demarcations and distinctions. Any intellectual, reflective, or analytic attempt to comprehend the flow will necessarily distort and petrify that which by nature is dynamic and processual (Bergson 1910: 219, 229). Reflective consciousness 'delights in clean cut distinctions, which are easily expressed in words, and in things with well-defined outlines, like those which are perceived in space' (p. 9), but that is precisely why it is incapable of revealing the true nature of consciousness. In further support of his claim, Bergson considers the relation between mind and language, and writes that our perceptions, thoughts, and emotions can occur under two aspects: one clear and precise but impersonal, the other personal but ever-changing and inexpressible. As soon as we try to describe our conscious states, as soon as we try to analyse and express them in words, the conscious states that by nature are deeply personal will change character. They will be transformed into impersonal elements that are externally related to one another (p. 163). This problem is not merely due to the fact that language employs general concepts, denoting, and thereby missing, the delicate shades of the ever-fluctuating states with simple uniform words (p. 164). The problem is also that language as a whole makes us operate with sharp and precise distinctions, thereby imposing the same kind of discontinuities between our experiential episodes as exist between material objects (p. xix). But as soon as we introduce such clear-cut distinctions, as soon as we isolate and identify a conscious state, we distort the processual character of our experiential life (p. 132). Language cannot get hold of consciousness without arresting its protean character and without fitting its irreducible individuality into a Procrustean uniform of general concepts. Indeed, for Bergson, language is simply not able to convey or render the subtleties of our experiential life but is only able to capture lifeless shadows (pp. 13, 132–3). In the end, Bergson denies that there is any common measure between mind and language (p. 165).

Later phenomenologists have occasionally praised Bergson's analysis. Sartre devoted a substantial part of the second chapter of his *L'imagination* to a discussion of Bergson, and according to his own testimony, it was *Essai sur les données immédiates de la conscience* that inspired him to study philosophy (Sartre 1981: 6). Schutz has on occasion compared Bergson's description of how, through a strenuous effort, we can turn our attention away from the world of objects and towards our own inner stream of consciousness with Husserl's notion of phenomenological reduction (Schutz 1967: 36). In my view, however, what a comparison between Bergson and Husserl will reveal is not their similarity, but their difference.[2]

Compare, for instance, Bergson's suspicion of language, his conviction that the distinctions it sets up are misleading, with the rather different attitude expressed by Husserl in the very first paragraph of his introduction to the second part of *Logische Untersuchungen*:

Linguistic discussions are certainly among the philosophically indispensable preparations for the building of pure logic; only by their aid can the true *objects* of logical research—and, following thereon, the essential species and differentiae of such objects—be refined to a clarity that excludes all misunderstanding. We are not here concerned with grammatical discussions, empirically conceived and related to some historically given language: we are concerned with discussions of a most general sort which cover the wider sphere of an objective *theory of knowledge* and, closely linked with this last, the *pure phenomenology of the experiences of thinking and knowing*. [...] This phenomenology must bring to pure expression, must *describe* in terms of their essential concepts and their governing formulae of essence, the essences which directly make themselves known in intuition, and the connections which have their roots purely in such essences. (Hua 19/6 [I/165–6])

Bergson is certainly right in claiming that language can mislead us. Consider, for instance, the three following statements: 'I see a cat', 'I hear a violin', 'I feel a pain'. All three have the same structure. But whereas in the two first cases it makes good sense to distinguish the perceptual experience from the object of perception, it is far less obvious that in the case of pain we can make an equally neat distinction between the experience and that of which it is an experience. Indeed, to attribute

---

[2]   Husserl does not engage in any elaborate criticism of Bergson. His sparse references to Bergson, which are found mainly in various letters, are almost all references to a dissertation entitled *Intuition und Intellekt bei Henri Bergson* that Roman Ingarden wrote under Husserl's supervision. At the beginning of the dissertation, Ingarden thanks Husserl for having provided him with many important insights (Ingarden 1994: 1), and it is not unreasonable to suppose that Husserl shared Ingarden's critical appraisal of Bergson.

such a subject–object structure to pain experience is arguably a serious mistake. So again, Bergson is right in claiming that language can mislead us—though we should not forget that language also enables us to identify, articulate, and criticize the mistake in question. Furthermore, Bergson is also right in claiming that language cannot replace intuition. There is an irreducible difference between reading about the aurora borealis and seeing and experiencing it in all its splendour, but one can concede this without endorsing the view that language, rather than pointing us towards the phenomenon in question, consistently points away from it, which seems to be Bergson's view. Finally, while accepting the irreducibility and superabundance of intuition, one should not overlook that there are forms of experience which rather than being deformed or corrupted by language are made possible by it. Consider, for instance, the thinking of the thought 'all profit results from an exploitation of labour' or a feeling of patriotism. It is hard to imagine the existence of either experience in non-linguistic creatures.

Bergson's position also confronts him with a methodological dilemma. Throughout his dissertation, Bergson does precisely what he warns us against. He uses language and concepts in order to articulate and describe a dimension of consciousness that on his own account is inexpressible. He even admits to the problem himself (Bergson 1910: 122). Husserl's approach is again significantly different.

In *Ideen I*, Husserl acknowledges that every reflection inevitably modifies the experience reflected upon (Hua 3/167; see also Hua 25/89). But, as he then continues, it is absurd to propose that experiences as a result of being reflectively scrutinized are transformed beyond recognition. Indeed, initially Husserl even insists that one ought not to let oneself be confused by or concerned with refined sceptical arguments of this kind, but that it is enough to stay true to the findings of pure intuition (Hua 3/169).

Husserl seems to have had some doubts about the cogency of this advice, since in the following paragraph he engages argumentatively with a sceptical objection raised by H. J. Watt. The basic concern of Watt concerns the veracity and validity of the phenomenological descriptions. The aim of phenomenology is allegedly to capture the experiential structures in their pre-theoretical immediacy, but what it delivers is inevitably the experiences as reflectively known objects. Why should we believe—indeed, how could we possibly ascertain—that those known objects match the experiences when they are not known, but simply lived through (Hua 3/170–71)?[3]

Husserl's reply to the worry that a linguistically articulated reflection necessarily distorts whatever it makes appear is that the scepticism in question is self-refuting. To say, 'I doubt the epistemic validity of reflection' is to make a reflective statement. In order for the statement to be valid, the utterer must reflectively know something about his doubt. At the same time, knowledge about unreflected experiences is also presupposed (in order to substantiate the claim that reflection distorts them). But such knowledge about the unreflected domain is precisely what is being called into question. In short, had the scepticism really been valid there would have been (1) no reason to believe in the existence of unreflected experiences, (2) no reason to believe in the existence of an act of reflection, and (3) no reason to believe that reflection transforms or distorts the lived experience (Hua 3/174).

It is important at this point not to misunderstand Husserl. His rejection of the sceptical worry does not commit him to the view that reflection is always trustworthy; all he is saying is that reflection cannot always be untrustworthy. Our attentive examination of a bottle does not change the bottle beyond recognition, so why should the attentive examination of an experience of a bottle necessarily change the experience beyond recognition? For Husserl, reflection is constrained by what is pre-reflectively lived through. Reflection is answerable to experiential facts and is not constitutively self-fulfilling. To deny that the reflective self-ascription of intentional states is based on any experiential evidence whatsoever is implausible. As Sartre would later write in *L'être et le néant* apropos reflection: 'It implies as the original motivation of the recovery a pre-reflective comprehension of what it wishes to recover' (2003: 178).

---

[3] Reacting to a related criticism formulated by Natorp, Heidegger resolutely rejected the idea that experiential life should be a mute, chaotic, and basically incomprehensible principle (Heidegger 1993: 148). Rather, our experiences are imbued with meaning, are intentionally structured, have an inner articulation and rationality, and, last but not least, are in possession of a spontaneous and immediate self-understanding. Experiential life is comprehensible because it always spontaneously expresses itself, and because experiencing is, itself, a preliminary form of understanding, a pre-understanding (Heidegger 2010: 127). Thus, Heidegger argued that there is an intimate connection between *experience, expression,* and *understanding* (Heidegger 2010: 129) and spoke of philosophy as a continuation of the *reflexivity* found in life (Heidegger 2010: 120). For a more extensive discussion, cf. Zahavi (2003b).

At the same time, however, Husserl recognizes that reflection qua thematic self-experiences does not simply reproduce the lived experiences unaltered. That is, he recognizes that reflection, rather than merely copying or repeating the original experience, transforms it, or as he explicitly states, *alters* it (Hua 1/72, 25/89). But this is precisely what makes reflection cognitively valuable. To put it differently, had reflection simply reproduced the original experience faithfully, reflection would have been superfluous.

But what kind of inevitable transformation is it that Husserl has in mind? On the one hand, he speaks of reflection as a process that in the ideal case simply disentangles, explicates, and articulates components and structures that are already inherent in the pre-reflective experience (Hua 24/244, 11/205, 236). In addition, however, he also talks of reflection as entailing a kind of doubling, or fracture, or self-fission (Hua 8/89–90, 111, 306). Why should this feature be philosophically significant? Consider that one of the distinguishing marks of rationality is the capacity to subject our own beliefs and actions (and emotional reactions) to critical assessment. Reflection is a precondition for such self-critical deliberation. If we are to subject our different beliefs and desires to a critical, normative evaluation, it is not sufficient simply to have immediate first-personal access to the states in question. Rather, we need to deprive our ongoing mental activities from their automatic normative force by stepping back from them. As both Korsgaard and Moran have argued, this stepping back is a metaphor of distancing and separation, but also one of observation and confrontation. It is the reflective self-distancing or self-division, which allows us to relate critically to our mental states and put them into question (Korsgaard 2009: 213; Moran 2001: 142–3). We find similar ideas in Husserl, who also emphasizes the importance of critical self-assessment and speaks of the evidence-based self-responsible life that phenomenology makes possible (Hua 8/167). To live in the phenomenological attitude is for Husserl not simply a neutral impersonal occupation, but a praxis of decisive personal and existential significance (Hua 6/140)—one that Husserl links to the Socratic ideal:

Socrates' ethical reform of life is characterized by its interpreting the truly satisfying life as a life of pure reason. This means a life in which the human being exercises in unremitting self-reflection and radical accountability a critique—an ultimately evaluating critique—of his life-aims and then naturally, and mediated through them, his life-paths and his current means. Such accountability and critique is performed as a process of cognition, and indeed, according to Socrates, as a methodical return to the original source of all legitimacy and its cognition—expressed in our terminology, by going back to complete clarity, 'insight,' 'evidence'. (Hua 7/9)[4]

By emphasizing the critical potential of reflection, Husserl is already indicating that his methodological employment of reflection serves other purposes than simply the compilation of some introspective reports. He is even clearer about the more overarching philosophical accomplishments of reflection in §76 of *Ideen I*, where he makes several important statements regarding the impact and scope of the phenomenological enterprise. After having stated that the most fundamental ontological distinction (*dieser radikalsten aller Seinsunterscheidungen*) is the one between the being of consciousness and the being of that which reveals itself for consciousness—i.e. between transcendental and transcendent being (Hua 3/159)—Husserl goes on to argue that this radical difference does not prevent the two types of being from being essentially related. Indeed, an *objectively* oriented phenomenology has as its main theme intentionality, and any proper investigation of intentionality must include an investigation of the intentional correlate. As Husserl would later write in the lectures *Phänomenologische Psychologie* from 1925:

The specific experience of this house, this body, of a world as such, is and remains, however, according to its own essential content and thus inseparably, experience 'of this house,' this body, this world; this is so for every mode of consciousness which is directed towards an object. It is, after all, quite impossible to describe an intentional experience—even if illusionary, an invalid judgment, or the like—without at the same time describing the object of that consciousness as such. (Hua 9/282)

External perception, the lived experience streaming on, contains as inseparable from it the appearing object as such. Perceiving of a spatial thing is nothing at all other than a having it there bodily before one, but always from this or that side and, in harmonious continuation in ever new sides, having the same object as existing. Now if we say rightly, the spatial thing is something perceived in the perception, belongs inseparably to it, and is evidently to be noted in it, nevertheless this intentional object is not immanent to the perception. (Hua 9/172)

---

[4] Much has been made of Husserl's notion of 'presuppositionlessness'. But we should understand this as an ideal to strive for, i.e. as a realized life in critical self-responsibility, rather than as a starting point (Hua 8/196, 244, 5/139, 1/53).

To employ some of Husserl's distinctions from *Ideen I*, there is not only a hyletic phenomenology and a noetic phenomenology, but also a phenomenology that deals with the constitution of the objects of consciousness (Hua 3/196). Or, as he puts it later in that text, there is a hyletic, a noetic, and a noematic form of reflection (Hua 3/349). Husserl's distinction between these different types of reflection relates to his more general understanding of what a proper investigation of consciousness must include. It should target the hyletic content, e.g. the bodily and perceptual sensations, which lack intentionality of their own; it should examine the proper bearers of intentionality, the noeses, i.e. the meaning-giving, sense-affording or animating apprehensions; and finally, it should investigate the noematic correlate of consciousness (Hua 3/192, 194, 203). Although phenomenology according to Husserl is able to offer far richer analyses of the noetic than of the hyletic dimension, he also stresses that the greatest and most important problems in phenomenology are related to the question of how objectivities of different kinds, from the prescientific to those of the highest scientific dignity, are constituted by consciousness (Hua 3/196). Indeed, 'investigating, in the most all-encompassing way, how objective unities of every region and category are "constituted in keeping with consciousness" is what counts' (Hua 3/198). It is for this very reason that Husserl can write that there is not only a phenomenology of natural scientific thinking, but also a phenomenology of nature (qua correlate of consciousness) (Hua 3/159). To think otherwise is to seriously misunderstand the nature and purpose of phenomenological reflection.

Phenomenological descriptions take their point of departure in the world we live in. How do we go about describing the difference between tasting coffee and tasting cocoa, between hearing a clarinet and seeing a dove, or between affirming and denying that the Eiffel Tower is older than the Empire State Building? Do we do so by severing our intentional link with the world and by turning our gaze inwards (*introspicio*)? No, we discover these differences, and we analyse them descriptively by paying attention to how worldly objects and states of affairs appear to us. This is precisely why there is something quite misleading about the view that the only way we could become aware of an experience would be by way of some mental gymnastics, where we turned our attention inwards and replaced the ordinary object of experience with a mental object, namely the experience itself. What this proposal overlooks is the object-directed and -presenting character of experience. It is by intending the object of experience that I can attend to the experience of the object.

By adopting the phenomenological attitude, we pay attention to the givenness of public objects (trees, planets, paintings, symphonies, numbers, states of affairs, social relations, etc.). But we do not simply focus on the object; rather, we investigate the object qua experienced as well as the structure of the respective object experience. That is, by attending to the objects precisely as they are given, we also uncover the subjective side of consciousness, thereby becoming aware of our subjective accomplishments and of the intentionality that is at play in order for the objects to appear as they do. We analyse the intentions through which we experience things, and we describe the things as presented in these intentions. We thereby also disclose ourselves as datives of manifestation, as those to whom objects appear. The topic of the phenomenological analyses is consequently not a worldless subject, and phenomenology does not ignore the world in favour of consciousness. Rather, phenomenology is interested in consciousness because it is world-disclosing. It is in order to understand how the world appears in the way it does, and with the validity and meaning it has, that phenomenology comes to investigate the disclosing performance of intentional consciousness.

To sum up. Phenomenological reflection does not only target experiential structures. It also investigates the object of experience, and the correlational a priori that holds between the experienced object and the different modes of givenness:

The task that now arises is how to make this correlation between constituting subjectivity and constituted objectivity intelligible, not just to prattle about it in empty generality but to clarify it in terms of all the categorial forms of worldliness, in accordance with the universal structures of the world itself. If we accept the premise that the constitutive functions of consciousness, both active and passive, are actually to be brought to light, functions which make evident to us the meaning and self-verifying being of a world we accept as valid, then this task is manifestly a totally different one from that of all positive sciences—and, as compared with all of them, is completely new. For all of these sciences, the intelligible existence of a world is presupposed, and its fundamental knowability, also, to no less a degree. Yet both presuppositions remain for them non-thematic. (Hua 9/336–337, translation modified)

Indeed, as Husserl would later write in *Krisis*, looking back at his life's work:

The first breakthrough of this universal a priori of correlation between experienced object and manners of givenness (which occurred during work on my

Logical Investigations around 1898) affected me so deeply that my whole subsequent life-work has been dominated by the task of systematically elaborating on
this a priori of correlation. (Hua 6/169–70 [166])

So, we are back to the question of why Husserl was interested in
consciousness in the first place. His focused investigation of subjectivity
and experience was not a goal in itself, nor was it motivated by the
relatively trivial insight that we need to include the first-person perspective if we wish to understand mental phenomena. Rather, the analysis is
transcendental-philosophical in nature. The reason why Husserl was so
preoccupied with describing and analysing the fundamental features of
consciousness was because he was convinced that a thorough philosophical understanding of the world that we experience and live in must
include an investigation of subjectivity. Not in the sense that in order to
investigate the world we will have to first investigate subjectivity in order
then, indirectly, to reach the world. His contention was rather that if we
wish to understand how physical objects, mathematical models, chemical
processes, social relations, cultural products can appear as they do and
with the meaning they have, then we will also have to examine the
subject to whom they appear. When we encounter perceived, judged,
evaluated objects, a thorough philosophical examination of these objects
will lead us to the experiential structures with which these modes of
appearance are correlated. We will be led to the acts of presentation,
perception, judgement, and valuation, and thereby to the subject (or
subjects) in relation to which the object as appearing must necessarily be
understood. Although we normally tend to ignore such subjective acts,
the task of phenomenology was from the beginning to break with the
naivety of daily life and call attention to and investigate the correlation
between act and object, between *cogito* and *cogitatum*.

In rejecting the attempt to align Husserlian reflection and introspection, I am not disputing that we are first-personally acquainted with our
ongoing experiential life, nor am I denying that our ability to reflectively
articulate first-person reports on this basis is epistemically significant.
But the question is what we should conclude from this. It doesn't follow
that phenomenology is primarily an exploration of more and more
subtle aspects of experience. Indeed, amassing experiential descriptions
is a poor substitute for the systematic and argumentative work of
phenomenological philosophers like Husserl. The former is certainly
not sufficient for the latter. Even if a certain amount of noetic description
might be necessary, a too minute investigation would merely derail the

philosophical investigation and make us lose our proper focus. It would not allow us to elucidate questions of philosophical significance, such as the relation between perceptual intentionality and scientific rationality or the link between evidence and truth, or engage with the spectre of global scepticism. It is no coincidence that Husserl (and also, perhaps slightly more surprisingly, Scheler) dismissed a purely descriptive endeavour devoid of systematic ambitions as mere 'picture-book phenomenology' (Spiegelberg 1965: 170; Scheler 1973: xix).

At the famous 1958 Royaumont meeting, Gilbert Ryle, J. L. Austin, W. V. O. Quine, Bernard Williams, and Peter Strawson met with phenomenological notabilities such as Jean Wahl, Maurice Merleau-Ponty, and H. L. Van Breda (Overgaard 2010). The meeting was not a success. As Charles Taylor, who was also in attendance, subsequently reported, it was 'a dialogue that didn't come off [. . .]. [F]ew left it much wiser than they came—at least as far as the subject of the conference was concerned' (Taylor 1964: 132–3). At one point during the meeting, P. F. Strawson expounded his own view of what the principal task of philosophy is, and insisted that language use is the only experimental datum philosophers possess if they want to inquire into the way in which our thoughts and concepts work (Strawson 1992: 324). This proposal was resisted by Van Breda, who interrupted Strawson with the outburst: 'But you have to distinguish what you are doing from what the philologist does!' (quoted in Strawson 1992: 327). Van Breda's criticism was based on a misunderstanding. Strawson's philosophy is to be conflated neither with philology nor with sociolinguistics. But it is a revealing mistake, especially since it mirrors the criticism of Dennett and Metzinger. Why are both criticisms mistaken? Because they both overlook the transcendental philosophical agenda of the targeted positions.

But wait a second, the critics might object. This attempt at exonerating Husserl is proceeding too fast and concluding prematurely. You claim that Husserl's method is not some kind of inward-looking procedure; but how does that square with Husserl's use of the epoché and reduction, and with his repeated claim concerning the importance of immanence? In *Ideen I*, Husserl argues that we as phenomenologists should 'lay claim to nothing other than what we are essentially able to make transparently evident to ourselves in consciousness itself, in pure immanence' (Hua 3/127). In *Cartesianische Meditationen*, he highlights the importance of an '*all-embracing self-investigation*' (Hua 1/182), and even ends the book by quoting approvingly Augustine's words: 'Do not go out, return to yourself; truth dwells in the inner man' (Hua 1/183).

Indeed, our journey has only just started. To understand what Husserl is up to, we need to engage in a more careful examination of his transcendental methodology, and eventually also confront his alleged internalism and (methodological) solipsism. Let us take one step at a time, and first consider the relation between phenomenology and metaphysics.

2

Metaphysical neutrality

What is the relation between phenomenology and metaphysics? Is phenomenology metaphysically neutral, is it without metaphysical bearings, is it a kind of propaedeutic to metaphysics, or is phenomenology on the contrary a form of metaphysics, perhaps even the culmination of a particular kind of metaphysics (of presence)? A moment's consideration should make it clear that no easy and straightforward answers to these questions are forthcoming. The term 'metaphysics' is simply too equivocal. Even among phenomenologists, the term is used and understood in quite different ways, and the answers to the questions vary accordingly. Consider the following examples:

- Many of Heidegger's writings in the decade after *Sein und Zeit* carry the term 'Metaphysics' in their title: *Was ist Metaphysik?*, *Kant und das Problem der Metaphysik*, *Die Grundbegriffe der Metaphysik*, and *Einführung in die Metaphysik*. Some have even dubbed this period Heidegger's 'Metaphysical decade', and suggested that Heidegger turned to the language of metaphysics in order to complete the phenomenological project of *Sein und Zeit* (Crowell 2001: 225, 229). Later on, Heidegger became more critical towards metaphysics, and described it as a thinking of identity, i.e. as a thinking that seeks to annul the ontological difference between being and beings. Either metaphysics understands being as the totality of beings, or (and more frequently) being is thought of as the ground of beings (be it in the form of logos, idea, energeia, substantiality, subjectivity, will, etc.). In either case, being is still thought of as something ontic. In the end, Heidegger would seek to substitute the conceptual apparatus of metaphysics for a more authentic type of thinking (Heidegger 1998: 185, 188, 224).

- In *Totalité et infini*, Levinas criticizes Heideggerian phenomenology for remaining too subservient to ontology. For Levinas, ontology is a totalizing enterprise. It is a philosophy of power characterized by a relentless movement of absorption and reduction. It absorbs the foreign and different into the familiar and identical. It reduces the other to the same (Levinas 1969: 42–3). In contrast, metaphysics is defined as an openness to otherness, as an acknowledgment of the infinite. In fact, metaphysics is nothing but a movement of transcendence, namely the very relation to the absolute other (Levinas 1969: 43). Given this distinction between ontology and metaphysics the question then arises: what has priority? In *Totalité et infini*, Levinas' answer is unequivocal: 'Ontology presupposes metaphysics' (Levinas 1969: 48).

- In the conclusion of *L'être et le néant*, Sartre discusses the metaphysical implications of his preceding analyses and defines metaphysics as 'the study of individual processes which have given birth to *this* world as a concrete and particular totality. In this sense metaphysics is to ontology as history is to sociology' (Sartre 2003: 639). Whereas ontology describes the structure of a being, metaphysics seeks to explain an event, namely the upsurge of the for-itself (p. 641).

- As for Derrida, he is known for having argued that phenomenology, in spite of itself, remains a kind of metaphysics (Derrida 1982: 157). Despite its attempt at a new beginning, phenomenology uncritically took over a series of metaphysical core concepts and categories, and thereby remained caught in the very frame of thought that it sought to overcome. Among these concepts, the notion of presence looms large. Traditional metaphysics defined being as identity in presence. But although Husserlian phenomenology attempted to move beyond this framework, it never really succeeded, but remained convinced that identity is more basic than difference, proximity more original than distance, and presence prior to every kind of absence and negativity (Derrida 1982: 34). As for the Heideggerian destruction of metaphysics, Derrida also has his doubts, since he argues that any criticism of metaphysics necessarily presupposes that which it seeks to contest (Derrida 2001: 354). For Derrida, we will have to remain satisfied with a perpetual problematization. A radical new beginning is not possible.

In the following, I do not intend to investigate all of these different phenomenological proposals. Rather, I will return to Husserl's own view on the matter. To be more specific, in this chapter I will consider Husserl's view on the relation between phenomenology and metaphysics as it is articulated in his pre-transcendental descriptive phenomenology. In the next chapter, I will then do the same for his later transcendental phenomenology. As we shall see, Husserl's effectuation of the transcendental turn occasions an important shift, one that very much plays havoc with the idea that the purpose of the former is to bring about a suspension of questions related to existence and being in order to make phenomenology metaphysically neutral.

2.1 Metaphysics in *Logische Untersuchungen*

In the preface to *Logische Untersuchungen*, Husserl describes his overall project as an attempt to establish a new foundation for pure logic and epistemology (Hua 18/6). He is in particular interested in the status of logic and in the conditions of possibility for scientific knowledge. More specifically, Husserl takes the cardinal task of a theory of knowledge as consisting in determining and articulating the conditions of possibility for objective knowledge. The task is not to determine whether (and how) consciousness can attain knowledge of a mind-independent reality. Husserl rejects this very type of question, as well as the question of whether there is an external reality in the first place, as *metaphysical* questions that have no place in epistemology (Hua 19/26). But what then does Husserl mean by metaphysics? In *Logische Untersuchungen*, he considers metaphysics a discipline that investigates and assesses the metaphysical presuppositions of those sciences that deal with *reality*. More specifically, its main task is to answer questions concerning the nature and existence of external reality. In contrast, the scope of a theory of science (*Wissenschaftslehre*) is much broader. It is concerned with the conditions of possibility for all types of sciences, including ideal sciences such as mathematics, which are disinterested in questions concerning existence (Hua 18/27). It is in light of this distinction that Husserl then claims that a theory of science constitutes the real foundational discipline, and that it has a clear priority over metaphysics (Hua 18/226).

Logische Untersuchungen contains numerous passages affirming this dissociation from metaphysics. In the introduction to the second part,

Husserl describes phenomenology as a neutral investigation (Hua 19/6), and claims that epistemological concerns precede every metaphysics (Hua 19/27). He then emphasizes that all six ensuing investigations are characterized by their metaphysical presuppositionlessness (Hua 19/27–8).

In the 2nd Investigation, Husserl brusquely rejects the metaphysical definition of the being-in-itself as something that is transcendent to and independent of consciousness, and argues that all metaphysical definitions of reality should be set aside (Hua 19/129; cf. 19/201). Later, in the 5th Investigation, he explicitly stresses the difference between the metaphysical and the phenomenological endeavour, and goes on to say that the descriptive difference between experience and object is valid regardless of one's take on the question concerning the nature of the being-in-itself. In fact, it is a difference that precedes every metaphysics (Hua 19/401). Finally, in the 6th Investigation, Husserl criticizes Kant for not having managed to stay clear of a metaphysically contaminated epistemology, and then claims that metaphysical theories are uncalled for when it comes to an understanding of the relation between the laws of nature and the laws of reason. What is needed is not *explanations*, but phenomenological *clarifications* of meaning, thinking, and knowing (Hua 19/729, 732).

In light of these statements, it is fairly straightforward to establish a solid link between the descriptive nature of phenomenology and its metaphysical neutrality. The task of phenomenology is to describe and analyse structures of givenness, rather than to engage in metaphysical constructions and speculations.

2.2 Realism—idealism

Husserl advocates a kind of metaphysical neutrality in *Logische Untersuchungen*. But what exactly does this imply? What kinds of questions or problems are suspended due to this neutrality? Given that Husserl regards the question concerning the existence of an external reality as a metaphysical question that is irrelevant to phenomenology, it is not difficult to provide the answer. Metaphysical realism and metaphysical idealism are metaphysical positions that phenomenology has no stake in.

Let me expand on this assessment, since it is not uncontroversial. After all, it was not only Husserl's Göttingen students who read *Logische*

Untersuchungen as a realist manifesto. Prominent scholars like Levinas and D. W. Smith have defended similar interpretations. In *Théorie de l'intuition dans la phénoménologie de Husserl*, Levinas argues that Husserl's early theory of intentionality can be taken in support of a realism (Levinas 1995: 91). And more recently, Smith has argued that Husserl in *Logische Untersuchungen* endorsed a kind of Aristotelian realism: the world around us exists independently of us, and through perception and judgement we come to know the essence of mind-independent things (Smith 2013: 161).

Can such a realist interpretation of Husserl's early theory of intentionality withstand scrutiny? In the 5th Investigation, Husserl is careful to point out that the intentional relationship between the act and the object is exactly intentional, and neither real nor causal. Moreover, he famously argues that intentionality is an intrinsic feature of consciousness, and not something that appears or disappears depending on whether or not the intentional object really exists. As he writes,

> In real [*reell*] phenomenological treatment, objectivity counts as nothing: in general, it transcends the act. *It makes no difference what sort of being we give our object, or with what sense or justification we do so, whether this being is real* (real) *or ideal, genuine, possible or impossible, the act remains 'directed upon' its object.* If one now asks how something non-existent or transcendent can be the intentional object in an act in which it has no being, one can only give the answer we gave above, which is also a wholly sufficient one. The object is an intentional object: this means there is an act having a determinate intention, and determinate in a way which makes it an intention towards this object. This 'reference to an object' belongs peculiarly and intrinsically to an act-experience and the experiences manifesting it are by definition intentional experiences or acts. *All differences in mode of objective reference are descriptive differences in intentional experiences.* (Hua 19/427 [II/120])

> It makes no essential difference to an object presented and given to consciousness whether it exists, or is fictitious, or is perhaps completely absurd (Hua 19/387 [II/99])

Given these unequivocal statements, it seems mistaken to look for some kind of counterpart to Kant's refutation of idealism in Husserl's early theory of intentionality. Husserl is not arguing that on the basis of the object-directedness of consciousness one can infer that if intentional consciousness exists then there must necessarily also exist something mind-independent towards which it is directed.

Occasionally, another aspect of Husserl's theory of intentionality has been taken to favour a kind of realism, namely his strong criticism of representationalism. We are *'zunächst und zumeist'* directed at real existing objects, and this directedness is not mediated by any intra-mental objects. The textual basis for this interpretation has typically been a passage in the 5th Investigation, where Husserl ridicules the attempt to distinguish between the intentional object on the one hand and the real and transcendent object on the other (Hua 19/439). The argument has been that since Husserl denies this distinction, the implication must be that he does in fact take us to have real, transcendent, mind-independent objects as our intentional objects, for which reason he must be a realist. This conclusion is premature, however. First, it is important to keep in mind the difference between direct realism (in philosophy of perception) and metaphysical realism. The two do not necessarily go together. Although there are forms of idealism that deny both, there are also forms of idealism that accept the former. Indeed, as we shall later see, one of Husserl's reasons for criticizing metaphysical realism was that on his view it was not sufficiently amenable to direct realism. To put it differently, Husserl's turn to transcendental idealism was partially motivated by his commitment to a non-representationalist account of perceptual intentionality. Secondly, Husserl's identification of the intentional object and the real object must be seen in a particular context, namely as a criticism of Twardowski's triadic theory of intentionality, and merely entails that the intentional object is the real object of the intention, i.e. that there is no difference between the intentional object and the intended object. In his *Zur Lehre vom Inhalt und Gegenstand der Vorstellungen* from 1894, Twardowski had claimed that our directedness towards the real intended object is mediated by an intra-mental intentional object that represents the real object (Twardowski 1982: 24–5). By contrast, Husserl claims that the only object that we can be directed at is the object of our intention, i.e. the intentional object:

It need only be said to be acknowledged *that the intentional object of a presentation is the same as its actual object, and on occasion as its external object, and that it is absurd to distinguish between them.* The transcendent object would not be the object of *this* presentation, if it was not *its* intentional object. This is plainly a merely analytic proposition. The object of the presentation, of the 'intention', *is* and *means* what is presented, the intentional object (Hua 19/439 [II/127]; see also Hua 3/207–8)

This is not to say that all intentional objects are real, but only that if the intended object really exists, then it is this real object, and no other, which is our intentional object. In other words, the distinction to maintain is not the one between the intentional object and the real object, but the one between the merely intentional object and the real and intentional object.

'The object is merely intentional' does not, of course, mean that it exists, but only in an intention, of which it is a real [*reelles*] part, or that some shadow of it exists. It means rather that the intention, the reference to an object so qualified, exists, but not that the object does. If the intentional object exists, the intention, the reference, does not exist alone, but the thing referred to exists also. (Hua 19/439 [II/127])

As long as the object does not exist, it has no mode of existence at all, it is only intended (*vermeint*) (Hua 19/386). If the object exists, however, it is not only intended but also (in principle capable of being) *given*. To put it differently, Husserl's distinction between mere intentional objects and existing intentional objects is a descriptive distinction. It carries no metaphysical weight. When speaking of an existing object, we are talking about an object in a pre-eminent mode of givenness and not about an object that possesses mind-independent reality. The object in itself (*das Ding an sich*), i.e. the real object, is consequently *not* to be contrasted with the intentional object. If it is to signify anything at all in a phenomenological context, it must, according to Husserl, be understood as that which would fulfil the sense of the perceptive intention (Hua 19/589). This is also why Husserl often characterizes the perceptual givenness of the object as the self-appearance of the object (Hua 19/614, 646). As the last sentence in *Logische Untersuchungen* has it: 'One must not forget, of course, that "actual" [*wirklich*] does not here mean the same as "external to consciousness", but the same as "not merely putative"' (Hua 19/775 [II/348]).[1]

So much for a realist interpretation of Husserl's early theory of intentionality.[2] The attempt to read the work in an idealistic vein has

---

[1] Although Husserl's assertion is contextually related to a discussion of the sensations, it has a wider application. See for a comparison his parallel discussion in the 2nd Investigation (Hua 19/139).

[2] After the publication of the *Prolegomena*, Husserl was accused of being a Platonist. If he really were, wouldn't this commit him to some form of realism? As Husserl subsequently insisted, however, he had been engaged in a defence of the validity of ideality and was not

been less widespread. Perhaps because Husserl himself unequivocally condemns phenomenalism:

It is the fundamental defect of phenomenalistic theories that they draw no distinction between appearance [*Erscheinung*] as intentional experience, and the apparent object (the subject of the objective predicates), and therefore identify the experienced complex of sensations with the complex of objective features. (Hua 19/371 [II/90])

Philipse, however, has been unpersuaded by critical remarks like this and has insisted that Husserl, in *Logische Untersuchungen* as well as in later works is a phenomenalist and reductive idealist (Philipse 1995). Philipse admits that Husserl explicitly repudiates phenomenalism if the position is taken to amount to the claim that the material world consists in nothing but actual and possible sensations in the mind. But he then points to a passage in the first edition of *Logische Untersuchungen* (a passage which was changed in the second edition), where Husserl claims that 'the things of the phenomenal world, that is to say all their characteristics, are constituted out of the same stuff which, as sensations, we consider to belong to the content of consciousness' (Hua 19/764). For Philipse, this passage confronts us with an interpretational challenge. How can we reconcile Husserl's claim that the perceived object (and the phenomenal world in its entirety) is transcendent to consciousness with his insistence that it is 'constituted out of *the same stuff* as sensations' (Philipse 1995: 265)? According to Philipse's interpretation, Husserl subscribes to the *principle of immanence*, i.e. the principle that holds that 'the primary data of outer perception are really immanent in consciousness' (Philipse 1995: 258), and in addition Husserl also endorses a projective theory of perception. The conjunction of these two theoretical commitments can then explain how Husserl metaphysically speaking can be a phenomenalist, while at the same time insisting on the descriptive or phenomenological difference between the object and the experience. What really exists is consciousness and its internal elements and components. But according to Husserl's matter–form schematism, perceptual intentionality involves the apprehension or interpretation of sensory content or matter by an objectifying intentional form. As a result

trying to argue for the existence of ideal objects in a separate supernatural realm. In short, he was advocating a logical and not an ontological platonism (Hua 22/156).

of this objectifying and externalizing interpretation of the immanently occurring sensations, the latter are posited outwards and endowed with an illusory transcendence. The perceived object is, in short, a mental projection, and Husserl's central notion of constitution simply refers to such a projective interpretation (Philipse 1995: 263–5).

Philipse is aware of Husserl's descriptive ambitions and of his explicit bracketing of metaphysical concerns and presuppositions in *Logische Untersuchungen*, and he writes that this might lead to the conclusion that Husserl in his early work is an epistemological rather than metaphysical phenomenalist (Philipse 1995: 269–70). But Philipse then argues that such a conclusion is premature, since it ignores Husserl's discussion of the *Ding an sich* in the 6th Investigation, where it is defined as a possible intentional object (Philipse 1995: 274). Given that Husserl did deal with the *Ding an sich* in *Logische Untersuchungen*, his phenomenalist position was not metaphysically neutral, but already then, contrary to the views of his early realist followers, committed to a full-blown form of reductive idealism (Philipse 1995: 276, 286).[3]

As Hardy has recently pointed out, Philipse's Husserl interpretation might be impressively detailed, but it is also 'completely wrongheaded' (Hardy 2013: 177). I tend to agree. To show why, let us consider in some detail Philipse's arguments. Why, to start with, should we ascribe to Husserl the view that the primary data of outer perception are immanent to consciousness? One central passage that Philipse takes to support this view is a passage found in §41 of *Ideen I*. After having argued that the perceived thing (as well as every part, side, aspect, and property of the thing) transcends the perception of it and is not contained in it, Husserl continues by arguing that the process of perceiving contains 'a multifaceted system of continuous manifolds of appearances and adumbrations', and he then writes that these adumbrations (*Abschattungen*) 'may be reckoned among the "data of sensation"' (Hua 3/85). But as Philipse argues, if material objects are always perceived in adumbrations, i.e. perspectivally, such that when 'we walk around a house, the different

---

[3] What is then the difference between Husserl's early and later works? According to Philipse, primarily a change in the status of consciousness. Whereas Husserl in *Logische Untersuchungen* still considered consciousness part of nature, he later on came to argue that the constituting ego is not part of the natural world, but something that can exist independently of everything else (Philipse 1995: 280).

adumbrations of the house succeed each other in an ordered manner' (Philipse 1995: 257), and if the adumbrations are identified with the sensations, which are non-spatial immanent parts of the stream of consciousness, then the primary data of outer perception are indeed immanent to consciousness (Philipse 1995: 258). The problem with this line of reasoning is that it runs afoul of the very equivocation that Husserl warns against a few lines later in the text. There he admonishes us to sharply distinguish the sensations which perform the function of adumbrating or presenting colour, smoothness, or shape from the colour, smoothness, or shape of the thing itself, just as he warns us not to conflate the adumbration or appearance of the shape, which is a non-spatial experience, with the appearing or adumbrated shape, which is spatial (Hua 3/86). To put it differently, the notion of 'adumbration' is equivocal. Sometimes the term is used to refer to an aspect of the experience of the object, i.e. to an aspect of its perceptual appearing, and sometimes to an aspect of the object that appears. When Philipse talks of the different adumbrations of the house succeeding each other, he is using the term in the latter sense. When Husserl speaks of the adumbrations being reckoned among the data of sensation, he is using the term in the former sense.

Already in *Logische Untersuchungen*, Husserl repeatedly warned against this and other similar equivocations. In the 2nd Investigation, for instance, he points to the confusing use 'of the same words to refer to the sensuously apparent determinations of things, and to the presentative aspects of our percepts' such that we 'at one time speak of "colour", "smoothness", "shape" etc., in the sense of objective properties, and another time in the sense of sensations' (Hua 19/134 [I/252]). Indeed, as Husserl also writes,

Sensations, animated by interpretations, present objective determinations in corresponding percepts of things, but they are not themselves these objective determinations. The apparent object, as it appears in the appearance, transcends this appearance as a phenomenon. (Hua 19/134 [I/252])

Objects of intuitive presentation, animals, trees etc., conceived as they appear to us [. . .] cannot be allowed by us to be complexes of 'ideas', and therefore themselves 'ideas'. They are not objects of possible 'interior perception', as if they constituted a complex phenomenological content in consciousness, in which they could be picked out as real data. (Hua 19/134 [I/252])

In an extensive further discussion of the same issues in §2 of the 5th Investigation, Husserl distinguishes the perceptual appearing (*Wahrnehmungserscheinung*) of the coloured object from the perceived coloured object. Whereas the latter is precisely perceived and not lived through, the former is an intrinsic part of my perceptual experience, and is not perceived, but immanently lived through. If I am looking at a red tomato, then it is this external object, and not my visual act or its sensations, that I perceive (Hua 19/165, 387, 424). When perceiving, the latter are never that which are intended, are not the primary data of outer perception, are never that of which the act is conscious:

Sensations, and the acts 'interpreting' them or apperceiving them, are alike experienced, *but they do not appear as objects*: they are not seen, heard or *perceived* by any sense. *Objects* on the other hand, appear and are perceived, but they are not *experienced*. (Hua 19/399 [II/105])

The colour-sensation, i.e. a part of the experience, and the perceived colour, i.e. the colour of the object, are sometimes confounded, although they are crucially different. The reason for this confusion is once again the ambiguity of the term 'sensation', which can refer to both the sensing and the sensed. On Philipse's interpretation, Husserl is a reductive idealist since he holds that the object metaphysically speaking is nothing but a complex of immanent sensations, although due to our objectifying interpretation or treatment it comes to possess an illusory externality. Here is what Husserl says about such a proposal:

It is phenomenologically false to say that the difference between a conscious content in perception, and the external object perceived (or perceptually intended) in it, is a mere difference in mode of treatment. (Hua 19/359 [II/83])

However we may decide the question of the existence or non-existence of phenomenal external things, we cannot doubt that the reality of each such perceived thing cannot be understood as the reality of a perceived complex of sensations in a perceiving consciousness. (Hua 19/764–5 [II/342])

In short, the appearing of the thing is not the thing which appears, and what is predicated of the thing's appearing is not predicated of the thing that appears (Hua 19/358–60). Now, there are indeed well-known difficulties connected to Husserl's early account of sensations. Various objections have been raised against his matter–form (content–apprehension) schema. The suggestion that our sensory experiences only become intentional after being subjected to an objectifying interpretation has, for instance, been criticized with the argument that it is quite unclear how such non-intentional and meaningless sensations are supposed to guide or constrain our interpretation. But, although some of this criticism is certainly justified (cf. also p. 109 below), Husserl's proposal that an object is brought to givenness when a certain complex of sensations is subjected to a specific interpretation, i.e. through the joint collaboration of sensible intuitions and intentions, doesn't commit him to Philipse's principle of immanence or to some kind of projective theory of perception. When in the first edition of *Logische Untersuchungen* Husserl writes that the 'things of the phenomenal world [...] are constituted out of the same stuff [...] as sensations' (Hua 19/764), the phrase 'constituted out of' should not be read as 'composed of', but as 'constituted by'.

What then about Philipse's claim that Husserl's reference to the *Ding an sich* entails that his account in *Logische Unterschungen* is no longer metaphysically neutral? I would dispute this interpretation, which contradicts all the places where Husserl affirms the neutrality in question. A far more straightforward reading is the one I offered above. Even within the constraints of Husserl's descriptive phenomenology, it is permissible to employ the notion of the *Ding an sich*. But the notion has no metaphysical weight; it simply refers to that which would fulfil the sense of the perceptive intention.

2.3 Liberation or restriction

Is Husserl's metaphysical neutrality to be regarded as a weakness or a strength? In his book *Phénoménologie, sémantique, ontologie* Jocelyn Benoist opts for the second conclusion. In his view, the decisive merit of *Logische Untersuchungen* is its discovery of a new, non-mentalistic notion of phenomenon and appearance. This discovery once and for all situates the phenomenological enterprise not only beyond every kind of representationalism and phenomenalism but also beyond any dispute between idealism and realism:

One cannot be more clear: the 'metaphysical problem' of knowledge, that is, the very choice between realism and idealism is suspended by phenomenology. This is so because, by adopting a purely descriptive attitude, phenomenology deconstructs the very conditions for the problem [...]. That which appears, precisely as it appears, is neither within nor without, neither me, nor not-me. It is a pure 'phenomenon', a pure 'given'. (Benoist 1997: 228)

According to Benoist, it is consequently crucial not to misinterpret the phenomena mentalistically or psychologically. Phenomenology is not engaged in an introspective survey of the mental inventory, but in a fundamental investigation of the nature of givenness—one that precedes and makes possible any subsequent discussion of issues like reality, ideality, subjectivity and objectivity (Benoist 1997: 285).

Benoist's interpretation and appraisal has the virtue of making *Logische Untersuchungen* into a more interesting philosophical work. It would be wrong to see Husserl's metaphysical neutrality as a mere expression of impotence. Metaphysical neutrality does not entail an incapacity to criticize certain metaphysical positions, and as we have just seen, Husserl is unequivocal in his rejection of phenomenalism. Let me in the following, however, voice three concerns and objections. First of all (and this is also acknowledged by Benoist), not everything in *Logische Untersuchungen* supports his interpretation. Secondly, there is an unresolved tension in Benoist's interpretation. Finally, even if one accepts Benoist's reading, Husserl's metaphysical neutrality will continue to entail some problematic implications.

1. Back in 1919, Heidegger observed that Husserl's original self-interpretation in *Logische Untersuchungen* was quite inadequate, and that it was consequently necessary to distinguish between Husserl's meta-reflections and his actual analyses (Heidegger 1993: 13–15). One reason for this critical remark was Husserl's own characterization of phenomenology as a descriptive psychology (Hua 19/24). This was a characterization that Husserl was to regret and reject already in 1903 and with good reasons, since it failed to capture what was going on in *Logische Untersuchungen* (Hua 22/206–8, Hua 18/12–13). Why mention this initial blunder? Because it does not match very well with the interpretation just presented. To interpret the phenomenological investigation of the structure of appearance in psychological terms is, as Benoist himself admits, a mentalistic relapse back into metaphysics (Benoist 1997: 215).

This is not the only internal tension in (the first edition of) *Logische Untersuchungen*, however. In the introduction, Husserl also identifies phenomenology with an analysis of the immanent (*reell*) content of mental acts, and asserts that one has to turn the theoretical interest away from the objects and towards the acts (Hua 19/14, 19/28). This methodological restriction is repeated in the 3rd and 5th Investigations, where Husserl not only equates the immanent and the phenomenological content of the act and contrasts it with the intentional content (Hua 19/237, 19/411) but also stresses the importance of discounting the intentional object when describing the act, because of the latter's transcendence (Hua 19/16, 19/427). In other words, if one looks at Husserl's programmatic statements, he seems to exclude both the intentional *content* as well as the intentional *object* from the sphere of research (Hua 22/206). All that is left to phenomenology is analyses of the immanent content, i.e. what would later be called hyletic and noetic analyses.

Already in the very same introduction, however, we can find statements that point in a rather different direction. Husserl declares that the intentional act possesses both a proper (immanent) content and an ideal intentional content (Hua 19/21), and insists that the objective reference is a descriptive feature of the intentional experience itself (Hua 19/25). Husserl's last comment is confirmed in the subsequent analysis of intentionality found in the 5th Investigation, where he constantly refers to both the intentional object and the intentional content in his analysis.

Given that Husserl as a matter of fact does investigate the correlation between act and intentional object in *Logische Untersuchungen*, he is contradicting some of his own methodological guidelines. That *Logische Untersuchungen*—or at least Husserl's own methodological reflections— had been far too noetically oriented was something that had become abundantly clear to Husserl by the time of the second edition of the work. As he adds in a new footnote in the 5th Investigation:

In the First Edition I wrote 'real *or* phenomenological' for 'real'. The word 'phenomenological' like the word 'descriptive' was used in the First Edition only in connection with *real [reelle]* elements of experience, and in the present edition it has so far been used predominantely in this sense. This corresponds to one's natural starting with the psychological point of view. It became plainer and plainer, however, as I reviewed the completed Investigations and pondered on their themes more deeply—particularly from this point onwards—that the description of intentional objectivity as such, as we are conscious of it in the concrete act-experience, represents a distinct descriptive dimension where purely intuitive description may be adequately practiced, a dimension opposed to that of real *[reellen]* act-constituents, but which also deserves to be called 'phenomenological'. These methodological extensions lead to important extensions of the field of problems now opening before us and considerable improvements due to a fully conscious separation of descriptive levels. Cf. my *Ideen zu einer reinen Phänomenologie*, Book I, and particularly what is said of *Noesis* and *Noema* in section III. (Hua 19/411 [II/354]. Cf. Hua 18/13, 3/296)

At this point, it might be natural to ask whether Husserl's alleged expansion of the scope of phenomenology to include intentional object-ivity (*Gegenständlichkeit*) in its field of research is not in tension with Husserl's simultaneous emphasis on the importance of immanence? When Husserl in *Ideen I* writes that we as phenomenologists should 'avail ourselves of nothing but what we can make essentially evident by observing consciousness itself in its pure immanence' (Hua 3/127), is he not simply reaffirming the noetic and inward-directed orientation already found in the first edition of the *Logische Untersuchungen*? A look at Husserl's 1907 lectures *Die Idee der Phänomenologie* can suggest an answer. There Husserl insists that we need to distinguish two quite different notions of immanence. On the one hand, he speaks of immanence when referring to that which is really immanent to con-sciousness, i.e. that which is a part of and makes up, say, a certain experiential act. This is then contrasted with that which is transcendent to consciousness, i.e. that which is not really contained in the experiential act, say, the object of experience. Thus, we should not forget that the object, for Husserl, is *for* and not *in* consciousness. This pair of concepts is then contrasted with another, entirely different sense of immanence and transcendence, where the notions refer in turn to that which is evi-dentially given (intuited, directly apprehended) and that which is merely posited and not itself given (Hua 2/35). To adopt Crowell's terminology, one might designate these two notions of immanence as a psychological vs a normative notion respectively (Crowell 2008: 346). Importantly, these two notions do not overlap. To suggest that they do, to think that only that which is immanent in the first sense can be immanent in the second sense, to think that only that which is inherent in and contained in the experiential act can be evidentially given, is, as Husserl remarks, 'a fatal mistake' (Hua 2/36). Even transcendent objects can be characterized by an evidential or 'intentional' (Hua 2/57) immanence, i.e. can be given intuitively in person. So when Husserl in various of his later writings urges us to focus on that which is immanent, he is in fact not repeating and reaffirming the mistake of the first edition of the *Logische Untersu-chungen*, but merely saying that phenomenologists ought to focus on that which is evidentially accessible from the first-person perspective (see also Boehm 1968: 141–85).

2. It is quite difficult to appraise the phenomenological project in *Logische Untersuchungen* without taking a stand on its relation to Husserl's later

works. According to one interpretation of the relationship between Husserl's early descriptive phenomenology and his later transcendental phenomenology, this development constitutes a problematic turn from metaphysical realism to metaphysical idealism (Findlay 1972: 243). As we have already seen, this interpretation fails for the simple reason that Husserl did not advocate a metaphysical realism in *Logische Untersuchungen*.

Another interpretation argues that Husserl's transcendental turn must be welcomed, since it represents an attempt to overcome some of the shortcomings of *Logische Untersuchungen*. In other words, it was in order to solve problems inherent in his descriptive phenomenology that Husserl was forced to adopt a transcendental standpoint. This reading is very much in line with Husserl's own account of the matter. If one looks at texts written in the years following *Logische Untersuchungen*, one will find frequent remarks regretting its flaws. In a letter to Hans Cornelius from September 1906, for instance, Husserl writes that his reflections on the nature of phenomenology in the introduction contained a very inadequate expression of the actual method and sense of the Investigations (Hua Dok 3-II/29; see also Husserl 1939: 109, 124, 329). And in the lecture course *Einleitung in die Logik und Erkenntnistheorie* from 1906–7, Husserl argues that it is necessary to leave the project of a descriptive phenomenology behind in favour of a transcendental phenomenology if one wishes to truly clarify the relation between the act, the meaning, and the intended transcendent object (Hua 24/425–7).

Occasionally, Husserl himself insisted that *Logische Untersuchungen* did in fact contain (proto-)transcendental elements (Hua 24/425, 2/91). A claim the young Heidegger also seemed to share. Thus, in the lecture course *Grundprobleme der Phänomenologie* from 1919/20 Heidegger criticized '*die Lippschen Schule*' for taking *Logische Untersuchungen* as a work in descriptive psychology, thereby overlooking the 'actually stimulating transcendental motive' (Heidegger 1993: 15).[4]

---

[4] This assessment is slightly surprising since it contradicts Heidegger's later, better-known interpretation, according to which the descriptive project in *Logische Untersuchungen* was preferable to Husserl's later work, exactly because it was not yet contaminated by any transcendental concerns. As Heidegger formulates it in *Zur Sache des Denkens*: 'Husserl himself who came close to the true question of Being in the *Logical Investigations*—above all in the VI—could not persevere in the philosophical atmosphere of that time. He came under the influence of Natorp and turned to transcendental phenomenology which reached its first culmination in the *Ideas*. The principle of phenomenology was thus abandoned' (Heidegger 1972: 44).

Does Benoist's interpretation of *Logische Untersuchungen* proceed along the same lines? Does it offer us a transcendental reading of the work? The distinctiveness of Benoist's interpretation might become clearer if one compares it to the one offered by De Boer. De Boer has argued that Husserl in *Logische Untersuchungen* firmly believed in the existence of an objective reality (the world of physics) behind the world of the phenomena, but that Husserl regarded this belief as a metaphysical presupposition that his own *psychological* analysis of intentionality could be isolated from (De Boer 1978: 195–7). This reading certainly represents a non-transcendental interpretation of *Logische Untersuchungen*. Not only does De Boer interpret Husserl's metaphysical neutrality very differently from Benoist—Husserl is not metaphysically neutral because he questions the legitimacy of metaphysical questions, but because he takes metaphysical issues to lie beyond the scope and realm of phenomenology—but De Boer also takes Husserl to be engaged in descriptive psychology. By contrast, Benoist's claim that the major contribution of *Logische Untersuchungen* consists in its elaboration of a new notion of givenness—a givenness that is taken to be so fundamental that it constitutes the framework within which discussions about issues like reality, ideality, subjectivity and objectivity can take place—sounds distinctly transcendental. Something similar might be said about Benoist's insistence that Husserl's account of intentionality in *Logische Untersuchungen*, rather than simply amounting to an investigation of consciousness, is also a clarification of the phenomenological status of the object, since a proper investigation of intentionality must necessarily span both sides of the correlation (Benoist 1997: 281). In short, it seems natural to consider Benoist's reading of Husserl's metaphysical neutrality as a transcendental reinterpretation of *Logische Untersuchungen*.

However, this is not at all how Benoist sees it. Although he concedes that Husserl himself tended to interpret his own transcendental turn as a more radical rethinking of the project that was launched in *Logische Untersuchungen* (Benoist 1997: 208), he insists that Husserl's early descriptive phenomenology remains untainted by any form of transcendentalism. As he puts it in one place:

The idea of the correlation is thus already there—it is constitutive of phenomenology as such, insofar as it is a showing *of* something—and it is certainly not in need of being interpreted transcendentally, as if it concerns a 'subjective' foundation or deduction. At this point, one remains within the framework of pure description. (Benoist 1997: 298)

Given the overall thrust of Benoist's interpretation, I find this attempt to block a transcendental interpretation of *Logische Untersuchungen* somewhat odd, but I suspect that it is in part motivated by Benoist's rather narrow Kantian definition of the transcendental (Benoist 1997: 298). As I will argue in Chapter 4, however, Husserl's notion of transcendental philosophy does not coincide with Kant's. To put it differently, I fully concur with Benoist if the point he wishes to make is that the project defended by Husserl in *Logische Untersuchungen* differs significantly from Kant's project. However, I think something similar holds true even after Husserl's transcendental turn, and in that case there is no reason to emphasize *Logische Untersuchungen* at the expense of Husserl's later works.

3. Let me finally turn to my last and most important reservation. One way to test whether the metaphysically neutral conception of phenomenology that is developed in *Logische Untersuchungen* is liberating or restrictive is to ask whether there are any important philosophical issues that it is in principle incapable of addressing. We have already seen that Husserl rejected the question as to the existence of an external reality as a metaphysical question that is irrelevant to phenomenology. One can react to this rejection in various ways:

- One might consider the rejection of metaphysics and metaphysical issues a liberating move, for the simple reason that this traditional framework and the questions it gives rise to has already spellbound and mislead philosophers for far too long.

- One might claim that it behoves phenomenology finally to acknowledge that it is merely a descriptive enterprise, and not the universal answer to all questions. In other words, there is a difference between phenomenology and metaphysics, and although the first might prepare the way for the latter, it does not contain the resources to tackle metaphysical issues, and should therefore keep silent on that about which it cannot speak.

- In contrast to these first two reactions, which for different reasons welcome Husserl's metaphysical neutrality, one might finally also simply regret it. One might concede that metaphysical problems are real problems, but also think that phenomenology has an important contribution to make in this area, and therefore deplore Husserl's metaphysical neutrality as a self-imposed and unnecessary straitjacket.

I have sympathy for all three reactions. In fact, I think they are less incompatible than one might assume at first glance. Thus, it could very well be argued that there are a variety of different metaphysical questions, and that some fall into the first category, some into the second, and some into the third, i.e. there are metaphysical pseudo-problems that phenomenology is wise to abandon, metaphysical questions that are beyond its reach, and metaphysical questions that it can address. But even if one wholeheartedly went for the first, rather Wittgensteinian response, this would not remove all the difficulties.

We have already seen that Husserl holds the view that phenomenology should disregard the question of whether or not the intentional object has any mind-independent reality. As Husserl also says—with a formulation that has subsequently been much misunderstood—the *existence* of the intentional object is phenomenologically irrelevant, since the intrinsic nature of the act is the same regardless of whether or not its object exists (Hua 19/59, 360, 387, 396). This stance, which seems to follow rather directly from Husserl's metaphysical neutrality, entails some important implications. One of them is that phenomenology is incapable of distinguishing between hallucinations and perceptions (Hua 19/358). Thus, according to Husserl's position in *Logische Untersuchungen* there is no phenomenologically relevant difference between a perception and a hallucination of a blue book. In both cases, we are dealing with a situation where the intentional object is *presented* in an intuitive mode of givenness. Whether or not this object also truthfully exists is, however, a question that is methodologically bracketed. Is this outcome philosophically satisfactory? Regardless of one's attitude towards metaphysics, if one wants to reserve a space for phenomenology in epistemology—and as pointed out above, this was very much Husserl's ambition—the answer ought to be negative. A theory of knowledge that is incapable of distinguishing veridical and non-veridical perceptions is wanting.

2.4 Metaphysics and theory of science

The lecture course *Einleitung in die Logik und Erkenntnistheorie* contains some of Husserl's first reflections on transcendental phenomenology. His very first use of the notion of phenomenological reduction can be found in the famous *Seefelder Blätter* from 1905, but his earliest attempt to employ the method of reduction in an effort to radicalize the project of phenomenology can be found in these lectures from 1906 to 1907 (see Hua 24/212). In addition, the lectures also contain important considerations on the status of metaphysics—considerations that are more elaborate than the sparse comments found in *Logische Untersuchungen*.

Husserl still operates with a distinction between metaphysics (which is concerned with reality, i.e. with spatio-temporal being) and theory of science (or formal ontology), which covers a much vaster area, since it deals with every type of being, not only real being but ideal being as well—i.e. basically everything that can be the subject of predication, including numbers, concepts, propositions, theories, aesthetic ideas, etc. But Husserl also employs a distinction between two different types of metaphysics. On the one hand, we have an empirically founded, a posteriori, material metaphysics, and on the other, an a priori, formal metaphysics. According to Husserl, it is the first type of metaphysics, which he also calls the 'radical science of being' or the 'science of ultimate being', which constitutes metaphysics in the proper sense of the word, whereas the second type could just as well (or even better) be called an a priori ontology (Hua 24/99–102). Importantly, however, the former kind of metaphysics does not only presuppose the work of the empirical sciences; it also presupposes a phenomenologically clarified epistemology:

> If metaphysics is the science of real existents in the true and ultimate sense, then theory of knowledge is the prerequisite of metaphysics. Theory of knowledge is formal science of being, so far as it disregards being as it shows itself factually in the inquiry into being of the specific sciences and investigates being in general in conformity with its essential meaning. We could directly call the critique of knowledge resting on pure logic *formal metaphysics* (ontology), while, on the basis of this formal metaphysics, metaphysics in the authentic sense establishes what is then factual in the categorial sense, what pertains to real being, not only in general and as such, but *de facto* in terms of the results of the specific sciences of being. (Hua 24/380)

Husserl further insists that the deepest problems of knowledge are inextricably linked to the transcendental philosophical problems, which are the most difficult and important problems of all. And as he then adds, only a solution to these problems will make a scientific metaphysics possible (Hua 24/139, 178, 191). Why is this statement significant? Because whereas Husserl in *Logische Untersuchungen* considered metaphysics to be something that is independent of and unrelated to phenomenology, he now explicitly argues that it presupposes and requires a transcendental phenomenological clarification. To use a pair of concepts employed by Husserl in the much later *Encyclopaedia Britannica* article: whereas transcendental phenomenology is *first philosophy*, metaphysics is *second philosophy* (Hua 9/298, Bernet et al. 1993: 229). Metaphysics is 'the proper science of reality' (Hua Dok 3-VI/206); it is concerned not with ideal possibilities, but with actuality, and is preceded and enabled by transcendental phenomenology qua eidetic science. But, of course, to say that phenomenology might pave the way for a metaphysics is still different from saying that phenomenology and phenomenological analyses are directly concerned with metaphysics.

3

The transcendental turn

Schließlich möchte ich, um kein Mißverständnis aufkommen zu lassen, darauf hinweisen, daß durch die Phänomenologie nur jede naive und mit widersinnigen Dingen an sich operierende Metaphysik ausgeschlossen wird, nicht aber Metaphysik überhaupt.

Die Pariser Vorträge

3.1 The phenomenological criticism

We have seen that Husserl's pre-transcendental phenomenology is metaphysically neutral, but what about his later work? One important difference between *Logische Untersuchungen* and *Ideen I* is that Husserl in the intervening years came to realize that certain methodological steps—the notorious epoché and transcendental reduction—were required if phenomenology were to accomplish its designated task. Whereas both notions were absent in *Logische Untersuchungen*, they came to play a decisive role after Husserl's transcendental turn. Indeed, as he repeatedly insisted, if one considers the epoché and the phenomenological reduction irrelevant peculiarities, one will have no chance of comprehending what phenomenology is all about (Hua 5/155, 3/200). But what exactly do the effectuation of the epoché and the reduction amount to? Are the epoché and the reduction something that phenomenology cannot do without, are they methodological tools that make phenomenology be what it is, or do they simply reveal Husserl's commitment to some form of methodological solipsism?

It is undisputable that the majority of latter-day Heideggerians and Merleau-Pontians have had trouble seeing the necessity and relevance of the epoché and the reduction. Indeed, it is no exaggeration to say that Dennett's and Metzinger's critical assessment of Husserlian phenomenology is more than matched by the dismissal we find among some post-Husserlian phenomenologists. They, as well, have argued that we do not really need to read Husserl any more, since his philosophical vision and the program he offers us is so outdated that the most charitable course of action is to bury it in silence. Although these phenomenological critics do not take Husserl to be engaged in introspective exercises, they often accuse him of being committed to a radical and problematic inward-turn. We even find Dreyfus and Kelly suggesting that Dennett's heterophenomenology might be an improvement on and better alternative to Husserlian phenomenology (2007: 47). Let us examine the criticism in more detail.

Consider first the account provided by Taylor Carman. In *Heidegger's Analytic: Interpretation, Discourse and Authenticity in Being and Time*, Carman dwells on Heidegger's relation to Husserl and quotes the two notorious remarks that Heidegger made to Karl Löwith in 1923. On 20 February 1923, Heidegger wrote:

> In the final hours of the seminar, I publicly burned and destroyed the *Ideas* to such an extent that I dare say that the essential foundations for the whole [of my work] are now clearly laid out. Looking back from this vantage point to the *Logical Investigations*, I am now convinced that Husserl was never a philosopher, not even for one second in his life. He becomes ever more ludicrous. (Quoted in Carman 2003: 57)

On 8 May 1923, Heidegger again wrote to Löwith, this time to say that in his lecture course that semester—a course entitled *Ontologie: Hermeneutik der Faktizität*—he

> strikes the main blows against phenomenology. I now stand completely on my own feet.... There is no chance of getting an appointment. And after I have published, my prospects will be finished. The old man will then realize that I am wringing his neck—and then the question of succeeding him is out. But I can't help myself. (Quoted in Carman 2003: 58)

Carman considers the substance of both letters—i.e. Heidegger's appraisal of Husserl's philosophical status—to be accurate. Carman claims that Husserl's and Heidegger's philosophy are worlds apart in both style and substance, that their respective aims and aspirations are profoundly different (Carman 2003: 54), and he consequently insists that 'Heidegger's fundamental ontology cannot be understood as a mere supplement or continuation, let alone "translation," of Husserl's philosophy' (Carman 2003: 62). On the contrary, Heidegger has shown that Husserl's phenomenology is at once uncritical and incoherent: uncritical in its appropriation of the Cartesian conception of the subject and the Platonic-Aristotelian interpretation of being as presence (*Anwesen*); incoherent because it purports to ground those prejudices in a rigorous philosophical method that can itself be made intelligible only by taking them for granted. Husserl's project is thus caught in a vicious circle, for its results presuppose its methods and its methods presuppose its results. Neither genuinely radical nor free of substantive presuppositions, Husserl's phenomenology is simply not the 'rigorous science' it claims to be. (Carman 2003: 54)

Thus, on Carman's reading, the hermeneutic phenomenology of *Being and Time* amounts to a wholesale rejection of Husserl's transcendental phenomenology (Carman 2003: 62), with all its Platonism, mentalism, and methodological solipsism (p. 56). It is consequently not surprising that Carman also claims that Heidegger rejects the core element of Husserl's methodology, i.e. the transcendental reduction, since Heidegger takes it to represent a failure to acknowledge the hermeneutic constraints on any adequate understanding of human being as being-in-the-world (2003: p. 56). But how then does Carman interpret the phenomenological reduction? Here is what he says:

The transcendental reduction [. . .] consists in methodically turning away from everything external to consciousness and focusing instead on what is internal to it. The reduction thus amounts to a special kind of reflection in which the ordinary objects of our intentional attitudes drop out of sight, while the immanent contents of those attitudes become the new objects of our attention. (Carman 2003: 80)

For Carman, Husserl's transcendental reduction essentially amounts to a form of methodological solipsism. Intentionality is internal, consciousness is self-sufficient, and how the external world is, makes no difference to one's mental states (pp. 83, 86).

Carman's interpretation has many affinities with the one we find in Dreyfus. Dreyfus also argues that Husserl's transcendental methodology commits him to a form of methodological solipsism that ignores the world and brackets all questions concerning external reality in order to focus on the internal structures of experience and on the mental representations that supposedly make intentionality possible (Dreyfus 1991: 50). By employing a methodological procedure that separates mind from world, Husserl does not only lose the world from sight, he also remains unable to recapture it. For similar reasons, he becomes incapable of providing a satisfactory account of intersubjectivity and embodiment.

Given the criticism voiced, a frequent suggestion has been that we ought to abandon Husserl's transcendental phenomenology and turn to Heidegger and Merleau-Ponty instead. Only the latter phenomenologists took the topics of intersubjectivity, sociality, embodiment, historicity, language, and interpretation seriously, and in doing so they decisively departed from the Husserlian framework.

There is, however, something slightly puzzling about this pairing of Heidegger and Merleau-Ponty. Both Heidegger and Merleau-Ponty refer to Husserl, but the presentation they give is so utterly different that one might occasionally wonder whether they are referring to the same author. Thus, nobody can overlook that Merleau-Ponty's interpretation of Husserl differs significantly from that of Heidegger. It is far more charitable. In fact, when evaluating the merits of respectively Husserl and Heidegger, Merleau-Ponty often goes very much against the standard view. This is not only the case in his famous remark on the very first page of *Phénoménologie de la perception*, where he declares the whole of *Sein und Zeit* to be nothing but an explication of Husserl's notion of lifeworld, but also—to give just one further example—in one of his Sorbonne lectures, where Merleau-Ponty writes that Husserl took the issue of temporality more seriously than Heidegger (Merleau-Ponty 2012: lxxi; 2010: 336).

Given Merleau-Ponty's persistent and rather enthusiastic (though by no means uncritical) interest in Husserl—an interest that lasted throughout his life, and increased rather than diminished in the course of time—how come that many Merleau-Pontians refuse to take seriously his interpretation of Husserl?

In his book *Merleau-Ponty's Ontology*, for instance, we find Dillon discussing Merleau-Ponty's late essay 'The Philosopher and his Shadow', where Merleau-Ponty attempts to unearth the implications of Husserl's late philosophy and to think his 'unthought thoughts'. But as Dillon then writes: 'Just as he finds his own thought in the unthought of Husserl, the Husserl Merleau-Ponty finds reason to praise is frequently an extrapolation of his own philosophy' (Dillon 1988: 27). Dillon consequently questions whether the text should be read as a genuine Husserl interpretation and not simply as an exposition of Merleau-Ponty's own thoughts. If Husserl had rigorously pursued the ontological implications of the notion of the lifeworld, which he set forth in *Krisis*, 'he might have altered his own transcendental idealism (with all its latent solipsism) and arrived at a position similar to Merleau-Ponty's. But the fact is that Husserl never abandoned the reductions or the idealism to which they inevitably lead' (Dillon 1988: 87).

A similar interpretation can be found in the work of Dreyfus and Rabinow, who argue that recent research has shown that the Husserl Merleau-Ponty was writing about was basically Merleau-Ponty's own invention. Merleau-Ponty was simply reading his own ideas back into the posthumous works of his master (Dreyfus and Rabinow 1983: 36).

It is not difficult to find further examples, but let me just mention one more. In *Sense and Subjectivity: A Study of Wittgenstein and Merleau-Ponty,* Dwyer writes that, although Merleau-Ponty occasionally tries to make excuses for Husserl and even distorts his doctrine in order to make it more palatable, the fact remains that for the most part, Husserl's work was antithetical to Merleau-Ponty's (Dwyer 1990: 33–4). And as Dwyer then concludes: 'In my view, what, for the most part, Husserl meant by and practiced as "phenomenology" can only be described as giving new meaning to the word "muddled." The less said about the details of Husserl's philosophy the better' (Dwyer 1990: 34).

But why this certainty that there is an abyss between Husserl on one side and Heidegger and Merleau-Ponty on the other? The reason seems to be that many scholars are convinced that Husserl's transcendentalism, his effectuation of the epoché and reduction, led him to idealism and solipsism—regardless of Merleau-Ponty's (desperate) attempt to prove otherwise.

As Husserl bitterly complained towards the end of his life, many of his critics had been more concerned with what his former students had to say about his philosophy than with the study of his own writings:

From the start one thinks one knows what it is all about [. . .]. In the best case one has read my writings; more often, one has sought advice from my students who, having been taught by me, are supposedly able to provide reliable information. Thus one is guided by the interpretations of Scheler, Heidegger, and others, and thereby spares oneself the admittedly very difficult study of my own writings. Protests against this are met with a ready answer: the old man is stuck in his established train of thought and is unreceptive to any refuting criticism. (Hua 6/439)

By contrast, consider Merleau-Ponty, who was well aware of the importance of reading Husserl's own writings, including the unpublished research manuscripts. Indeed, when arriving in Leuven in April 1939, he was the very first foreigner to visit the newly established Husserl

Archives. As he would write in a letter from 1942: 'After all, Husserl's philosophy is almost entirely contained in the unpublished manuscripts' (quoted in Van Breda 1992).

Merleau-Ponty, I think, got it exactly right when, in *Sens et non-sens* apropos two Marxist critics of Husserl, he wrote, 'So Naville and Hervé, each for his own reasons, have something other to do than master the texts of an untranslated and two-thirds unpublished Husserl? All right. But then why talk about it?' (Merleau-Ponty 1964: 135–6).

3.2 The epoché and reduction

The epoché and the reduction are crucial elements in Husserl's transcendental methodology, and a correct understanding of these concepts is consequently indispensable if one is to appraise correctly the metaphysical import of transcendental phenomenology. So let us now take a closer look at both notions.

Husserl often contrasts philosophy proper with the work done by the positive sciences. The latter are so absorbed in their investigation of the natural (or social/cultural) world that they do not pause to reflect upon their own presuppositions and conditions of possibility. They all operate on the basis of a natural (and necessary) naivety, namely the tacit belief in the existence of a mind-independent reality. This realist assumption is so fundamental and deeply rooted that it is not only accepted by the positive sciences, it also permeates our daily pre-theoretical life, for which reason Husserl calls it the 'natural attitude'. Regardless of how natural the attitude might be, simply to take it for granted is philosophically unacceptable. If philosophy is supposed to amount to a radical form of critical elucidation, it cannot simply presuppose our natural realism. Rather than continuing to live in the natural attitude, it must engage in a reflective move that will allow it to explore the epistemic and metaphysical presuppositions of the latter. To argue that the natural attitude must be philosophically investigated is not to endorse scepticism, however. That the world exists is, as Husserl writes, beyond any doubt, but it is our duty as philosophers to truly understand and clarify this indubitability (which sustains life and positive science) (Hua 5/152–3, 6/190–91).

How is such an investigation to proceed if it is to avoid prejudicing the results beforehand? Husserl's answer is deceptively simple. Positive science takes it for granted that there are objects that can be investigated, but it does not reflect upon what it means for something to be given as an object of investigation, nor how this givenness is possible in the first place. Rather than focusing on *what* the world is, we need to attend to the *how* of its givenness. To take this approach, however, is easier said than done. It calls for a number of methodological preparations. In order to avoid presupposing commonsensical naivety (as well as a number of different speculative hypotheses concerning the metaphysical status of reality), it is necessary to suspend our acceptance of the natural attitude. We keep the attitude (in order to be able to investigate it), but we bracket its validity. This procedure, which entails a suspension of our natural realist inclination, is known by the name of 'epoché'. Strictly speaking, the epoché can be seen as the first step towards what Husserl terms the 'transcendental reduction', which is his name for the systematic analysis of the correlation between subjectivity and world.

The true purpose of the epoché and the reduction is not to doubt, ignore, neglect, abandon, or exclude reality from our research; rather their aim is to suspend or neutralize a certain dogmatic *attitude* towards reality. By suspending this attitude, and by thematizing the fact that reality is always revealed and examined from some perspective or another, reality is not lost from sight, but for the first time properly understood (Hua 1/66, 6/154).

Admittedly, Husserl himself is partly to blame for some of the misinterpretations. Consider, for instance, his discussion in §52 of *Krisis*. Initially he writes that the epoché brackets all worldly interests:

Any interest in the being, actuality, or nonbeing of the world, i.e. any interest theoretically oriented toward knowledge of the world, and even any interest which is practical in the usual sense, with its dependence on the presuppositions of its situational truths, is forbidden. (Hua 6/178 [175])

But as he then explains one page later, this initial presentation is misleading:

In the reorientation of the epoché nothing is lost, none of the interests and ends of world-life, and thus also none of the ends of knowledge. But for all these things their essential subjective correlates are exhibited, and thus the full and true ontic meaning of objective being, and thus of all objective truth, is set forth. (Hua 6/179 [176])

Indeed, as he further explains, 'one of the most common misunderstandings of the transcendental epoché' is that it involves a 'turning-away' from 'all natural human life-interests' (Hua 6/180 [176]). This is a misunderstanding, for

if it were meant in this way, there would be no transcendental inquiry. How could we take perception and the perceived, memory and the remembered, the objective and every sort of verification of the objective, including art, science, and philosophy, as a transcendental theme without living through these sorts of things as examples and indeed with [their] full self-evidence? (Hua 6/180 [176])

Already in *Ideen I*, Husserl made it clear that phenomenology eventually integrates and includes everything that it had at first parenthesized for methodological reasons:

At the same time, the suspension has the character of an alteration via an operation sign that transforms the value of what follows it, and, with this alteration, what is revalued is reclassified in the phenomenological sphere. To put it more figuratively, what is bracketed is not wiped off the phenomenological board but merely bracketed and thereby provided with a marker indicating as much. With this, however, it is a major theme of research. (Hua 3/159)

The so-called exclusion of the world is actually an exclusion of a naive prejudice concerning the metaphysical status of the world:

The real actuality is not 're-interpreted' or even denied but an absurd interpretation of it set aside, absurd because the interpretation contradicts its *very* sense, which has been clarified in a patently discernible way. (Hua 3/120)

This line of thought is also to be found in the following quotes from *Zur Phänomenologie der Intersubjektivität III* and *Krisis*:

'The' world is not lost as a result of the epoché. The epoché is by no means a suspension of the being of the world and of every world-oriented judgment; rather, it is the path leading to the discovery of the correlational judgements, to the reduction of all unities of being to myself and my meaning-possessing and meaning-giving subjectivity in all its potentialities. (Hua 15/366)

What must be shown in particular and above all is that through the epoché a new way of experiencing, of thinking, of theorizing, is opened to the philosopher; here, situated *above* his own natural being and *above* the natural world, he loses nothing of their being and their objective truths [...] (Hua 6/154–5 [152])

Given statements like these, one ought to regard with some suspicion the often-repeated assertion that the Husserlian reduction involves a suspension of all existential positings. There are reasons to think that the suspension in question is merely propaedeutic and provisional. As Husserl puts it in a text dating from 1930:

If transcendental phenomenology has carried out its work, if, at least, it has encompassed the universal structure of being and world, then the significance of the method of epoché—whose import had to remain incomprehensible at the beginning—is also fully grasped. The epoché leads to that which is the primary absolute for me, i.e. to me as transcendental ego. Moreover, insofar as the epoché leads to the interpretation of this ego's concreteness in the primordiality, then to the clarification of the constitution of others as other human beings, and finally to the clarification of the constitution of myself as a human being in the world—which thereby also receives its own transcendental significance—insofar as these clarifications occur, *the abstention from the positing of the world is systematically overcome*. The transcendental presuppositions for the positing of the world, the transcendental foundations for the world are systematically revealed. They are revealed as transcendentally valid in transcendental evidence. And finally, the existing world emerges in ontological validity, in the same ontological validity it had in the naïveté, but now merely with its transcendental horizons of presupposition disclosed. (Hua 34/245, emphasis added)

In texts written between 1926 and 1935 and subsequently collected in the Husserliana volume *Zur phänomenologischen Reduktion: Texte aus dem Nachlass*, Husserl is quite explicit about the non-excluding character of the reduction, and about the fact that by adopting the phenomenological attitude and by engaging in phenomenological reflection we are by no means effectuating an inward-turn but rather continue to remain concerned with worldly objects. When the natural world is spoken of as '*ausgeschaltet*', what this means is merely that the transcendental philosopher must cease to posit the world naively (Hua 34/21). It does not imply that we cannot continue to observe, thematize, and make judgements concerning the world; but we must do so in a reflective manner that considers the world as intentional correlate (Hua 34/58). To put it differently, to perform the epoché and the reduction is to effectuate a thematic reorientation. Henceforth the world is revealed as a phenomenon, and as such it remains in the very focus of our phenomenological research (Hua 34/204, 323).

The world as 'phenomenon', as world in the epoché, is merely a modality, in which the same ego, for whom the world is pregiven, reflects on this pregivenness and on what it contains, and for that reason does not abandon the world and its validity, nor makes it disappear. (Hua 34/223; cf. Hua 34/83–4)

The reduction must consequently be appreciated as a distinct '*Reflexionssprung*' (Hua 34/219) that enlarges our understanding by enabling new insights. To effectuate the reduction is to liberate the world from a hidden abstraction, and to reveal it in its concretion as a constituted network of meaning ('*Sinngebilde*') (Hua 34/225). But of course, and importantly, Husserl is also claiming that the true significance of consciousness will be concealed as long as the existence of the world is simply taken for granted. It is only by suspending our automatic belief in the existence of the world, only by putting the world into question (which is different from doubting it), that the true contribution of consciousness can be disclosed. My ordinary natural life is according to Husserl a life lived in self-alienation ('*Selbstentfremdung*'), since it does not know of its transcendental accomplishments. The performance of the reduction removes the blinkers ('*Scheuklappen*') that normally conceal the full and concrete transcendental character of life (Hua 34/226, 233); it overcomes the self-alienation, and lifts subjectivity to a new level of transcendental self-consciousness (Hua 34/399).

3.3 Transcendental phenomenology and metaphysics

Is it true that Husserl's transcendental phenomenology has no interest in reality, and that the execution of the epoché demands abstention from ontological commitment and neutrality when it comes to all questions concerned with being and existence? As should have become clear by now, this might be a fitting description of Husserl's pre-transcendental position in *Logische Untersuchungen*, when he had not yet introduced the notions of epoché and reduction. In that early work, Husserl did in fact repeatedly claim that the *existence* of the object was phenomenologically irrelevant. But the metaphysical aim and scope of phenomenology changed the moment he took the step from a descriptive phenomenology to a transcendental phenomenology.

This is not an interpretation, however, that is shared by all Husserl scholars. In his book *The Paradox of Subjectivity* from 1999, Carr advocates the view that Husserl is not engaged in a metaphysical project at all. One key feature of Carr's interpretation is his understanding of Husserl's epoché. As Carr writes, the purpose of the epoché is to exclude from consideration the actual existence of the world (Carr 1999: 74). That is, all reference to the being of transcendent reality is excluded in order to focus instead on its sense or meaning (p. 80). Husserl's transcendental phenomenology is consequently concerned with meaning rather than with being. For the very same reason, Husserl's idealism is of a methodological kind rather than of a substantial or metaphysical kind. Its aim, according to Carr, is to make us consider the world *as if* it were nothing but sense (p. 110). Thus, transcendental phenomenology is not at all a metaphysical doctrine, but must on the contrary simply be understood as a critical reflection on the conditions of possibility for experience (p. 134). When Husserl in his investigations comes to speak of the constitutive relation between subjectivity and world, it is, according to Carr, crucial not to conflate being and meaning. The two must be kept apart, and all that transcendental subjectivity can be said to constitute is the meaning of the world rather than its being (p. 108).

Many interpreters, including Gadamer (1972: 178) and Fink (1995: 152), have claimed that Husserl's transcendental idealism transcends the traditional alternative between metaphysical idealism and metaphysical realism. Such a claim, however, can be interpreted in different ways:

- One possibility is to claim that transcendental idealism is beyond this traditional alternative because it seeks to combine elements from both positions.

- Another option is to argue that transcendental idealism transcends both positions insofar as it rejects both as misguided and misconceived theoretical enterprises.

- A third interpretation argues that transcendental idealism is beyond both positions in the sense that it is simply concerned with quite different matters altogether. It might constitute a kind of propaedeutic to a future metaphysics, but in and of itself it is not concerned with the sphere of reality.

If I read Carr correctly, he opts for the third interpretation. As he writes near the end of his book, 'both philosophers [Kant and Husserl] recognized, I think, that their transcendental procedure did not authorize the transition to metaphysical claims' (Carr 1999: 137). Such a phrasing suggests that Carr takes transcendental phenomenology to lack the resources to tackle metaphysical issues.

Some of Carr's concerns are shared by Steven Crowell, who also emphasizes the non-metaphysical direction of transcendental thought. According to Crowell, phenomenology is first and foremost a philosophy of meaning (Crowell 2001: 5). Meaning is not an empirical but a transcendental concept, and it is a concept that has priority over other philosophical starting points. In fact, if headway is to be made in contemporary metaphysics, epistemology, and philosophy of mind, it is (according to Crowell) necessary to pursue a more focused investigation of meaning, which is exactly what transcendental phenomenology is doing (pp. 18–19).

On this account, transcendental phenomenology must ultimately be viewed as a metaphilosophical or methodological endeavour rather than as a straightforwardly metaphysical doctrine about the nature and ontological status of worldly objects. Transcendental idealism must be distinguished from metaphysical idealism in that the latter, but not the former, makes first-order claims about the nature of objects (Crowell 2001: 237).[1] Husserl's epoché and reduction are methodological tools permitting us to gain a distance from the natural attitude, thereby allowing a philosophical reflection that lets us analyse something we normally take for granted, but which we rarely thematize, namely *givenness*. The task of phenomenology is not to describe the objects as precisely and meticulously as possible, nor should it concern itself with an investigation of the phenomena in all their ontic diversity. Rather— and this was also the point made earlier by Benoist—phenomenology is interested in the very dimension of givenness or appearance, and seeks to explore its essential structures and conditions of possibility. Transcendental phenomenology thematizes objects in terms of their givenness, validity, and intelligibility, and such an investigation calls for a reflective stance quite unlike the one needed in the positive sciences. In order to make this investigation possible, a new type of inquiry is called for, a type of inquiry that, to quote Husserl, '*is prior to all natural knowledge and science and is on an entirely different plane than natural science*' (Hua 24/176).

---

[1]   It should come as no surprise that Carr and Crowell both have sympathies for Allison's Kant interpretation (Carr 1999: 108–11; Crowell 2001: 238). For Allison (1983: 25), transcendental idealism must be appreciated as a metaphilosophical outlook rather than as a straightforward metaphysical doctrine. It investigates the epistemic conditions under which we have an experience of the world and does not make any first-order claims about what there is in the world. By contrast, I see a number of intriguing parallels between my own Husserl interpretation and the Kant interpretation recently proposed by Allais (2015). Just as Allais argues that we should approach Kant's transcendental idealism with a relational view as a starting point (Allais 2015: 12), I will in Chapter 4 examine whether externalism can provide a productive angle on Husserl's transcendental idealism, and just like Allais, I also think transcendental idealism should be interpreted as a position situated between strong metaphysical idealism (read 'phenomenalism') and a deflationary non-metaphysical reading (see Allais 2015: 3).

Or as Crowell puts it (2001: 182), the space of meaning cannot be approached using the resources of traditional metaphysics.

From this point of view, a metaphysical interpretation of Husserl's transcendental phenomenology entails a dramatic misunderstanding of what phenomenology is all about. It misunderstands the notion of reduction, and it overlooks the decisive difference between the natural attitude and the phenomenological attitude. Using Heideggerian terms, one could say that a metaphysical interpretation of phenomenology entails a disregard of the ontological difference. Metaphysics remains a pre-critical or naive enterprise. In its attempt to map out the building blocks of reality, it never leaves the natural attitude. It does not partake in the reflective move that is the defining moment of transcendental thought.[2]

To some extent, I agree with both Carr and Crowell, particularly when it comes to their emphasis on the reflective orientation of transcendental phenomenology. But it is one thing to make that point and something quite different to claim that phenomenology has no metaphysical

---

[2] In D. W. Smith, we find a somewhat different line of reasoning leading to a similar conclusion. Smith's key proposal is that phenomenology is only one specific part of Husserl's philosophical system—one part standing in a relation of mutual interdependence with other parts of Husserl's philosophy, including his ontology, epistemology, logic, ethics, and value theory (Smith 2013: 40). For the same reason, although Husserl's philosophy as a whole presents a unified account of our experience, the world we live in, our bodies, ourselves, our knowledge, our values, our social institutions, etc., phenomenology only encompasses 'the study of the essence of consciousness as experienced from the first-person perspective' (Smith 2013: 1) and should not be seen as the sole foundation of the edifice. Had Husserl been a straightforward idealist, phenomenology would indeed have been the centrepiece of his philosophy; but since, on Smith's reading, he is not, there is no reason to assign it that place, and no reason to ascribe phenomenology any overarching metaphysical implications. Smith's attempt to classify phenomenology as at most *primus inter pares* is not born out by Husserl's writings, however. Husserl repeatedly makes it clear that his approach to different questions, be they ontological or ethical, is a phenomenological approach, and his continuing efforts to write a comprehensive introduction to phenomenology also suggests that he thought of the latter as the cornerstone and framework for whatever other topics he was engaging with philosophically. As for textual evidence, consider as one example among many the following passage from *Ideen III*: 'Phenomenology in our sense is the science of "origins," of the "mothers" of all cognition; and it is the maternal-ground of all philosophical method: to this ground and to the work in it, everything leads back. When philosophers again and again stated, or were tacitly guided by, the fact that the natural cognition of the practical life and of the dogmatic sciences did not suffice, that it was burdened with obscurities, that the fundamental concepts of all sciences (sc. of the dogmatic ones) were in need of a "clarification," a reduction to their origins, then what is here felt as a deficiency finds everywhere its ultimate fulfillment in phenomenology' (Hua 5/80; see also 7/187–8).

implications, as if it were in principle compatible with and could live in peaceful coexistence with a variety of different metaphysical views, including eliminativism, metaphysical realism, or subjective idealism. This view, and the view that Husserl's method is not concerned with reality but only with an analysis of meaning that has no immediate bearing on metaphysical questions about 'what really exists' (Thomasson 2007: 91), cannot be correct. Had it been, Husserl would have been unable to reject both the Kantian *Ding an sich* and phenomenalism as unequivocally as he does. His phenomenological insistence on the categorical difference between the perceptual act and the perceptual object, for instance, would then have had no weight vis-à-vis claims concerning their metaphysical identity. Likewise, had his phenomenological investigations had no implication for what exists, his rich account of consciousness would have been compatible with eliminativism about experience. But even more importantly, I think this quietist interpretation runs counter to Husserl's philosophical ambitions. It is no coincidence that Husserl in *Krisis* declares that 'there is no conceivable meaningful problem in previous philosophy, and no conceivable problem of being at all, that could not be arrived at by transcendental phenomenology at some point along its way' (Hua 6/192 [188]). Indeed, eventually Husserl was quite unequivocal in his rejection of any non-metaphysical interpretation of phenomenology:

[T]ranscendental phenomenology in the sense I conceive it does in fact encompass the universal horizon of the problems of philosophy [...] including as well all so-called metaphysical questions, insofar as they have possible sense in the first place. (Hua 5/141)

Phenomenology is anti-metaphysical insofar as it rejects every metaphysics concerned with the construction of purely formal hypotheses. But like all genuine philosophical problems, all metaphysical problems return to a phenomenological base, where they find their genuine transcendental form and method, fashioned from intuition. (Hua 9/253)

Finally, lest any misunderstanding arise, I would point out that, as already stated, phenomenology indeed *excludes every naïve metaphysics* that operates with absurd things in themselves, but *does not exclude metaphysics as such*. (Hua 1/38–9)

As Husserl also wrote in a letter to Peter Wust in 1920, phenomenology was from the beginning never supposed to be anything except the path to a radically genuine 'strictly scientific metaphysics' (Hua 42/lxiv).

Statements like these strongly suggest that if one wants to counter a strong metaphysical reading of Husserl's idealism that takes it to amount to a kind of sophisticated phenomenalism, then the right approach is not to adopt a deflationary non-metaphysical interpretation of his transcendental project. This, however, is not to say that it is by any stretch straightforward to interpret Husserl's pro-metaphysical statements, since the term 'metaphysics' is notoriously ambiguous, and can be understood and defined in a variety of different ways. Consider, for instance, this list:

- Metaphysics is a speculatively constructed philosophical system dealing with the 'highest' and 'ultimate' questions concerning the existence of God, the immortality of the soul, etc.

- Metaphysics is an attempt to answer the perennial questions concerning the meaning of factual human life.

- Metaphysics is concerned with an answer to the question of *why* there is something rather than nothing.

- Metaphysics is a theoretical investigation of the fundamental building blocks, the basic 'stuff', of reality.

- Metaphysics is a fundamental reflection on and concern with the status and being of reality. Is reality mind-dependent or not, and if yes, in what manner?

What complicates matters even further is that Husserl himself used the term 'metaphysics' equivocally. In some of his later works, for instance, he also used the term to refer to a philosophical engagement with questions pertaining to the ethical-religious domain; questions concerning birth, death, fate, immortality, etc. (Hua 1/182; see also Sowa and Vongehr's extensive introduction to Husserliana 42). In the following, however, I will not primarily be concerned with this specific use of the term. Rather, when discussing the relation between phenomenology and metaphysics, when considering whether phenomenology has anything to say regarding the metaphysical status of reality, I will (unless otherwise noted) exclusively understand metaphysics as pertaining to the realism–idealism issue, i.e. to the issue of whether reality is mind-independent or not. This is the kind of metaphysics that was excluded in Husserl's pre-transcendental phenomenology, and it is also this kind of metaphysics that is typically referenced when scholars speak of Husserl's metaphysical neutrality.

As we have just seen, many interpreters have taken Husserl's methodology, his employment of the epoché and the reduction, to involve an abstention of positings, a bracketing of questions related to existence and being, and have for that very reason also denied that phenomenology has any metaphysical implications. It is, however, a misinterpretation to construe transcendental phenomenology merely as a theory about the structure of subjectivity, or as a theory about how we experience and understand the world. It would even be wrong to say that it is a theory about the world as it is for us, *if*, that is, such a theory is supposed to be complemented by a further metaphysical investigation of what the world itself is like. To construe Husserlian phenomenology in such a way would make it vulnerable to the objection that something crucial is missing from its repertoire; being and reality would be topics left for other disciplines. But this interpretation neither respects nor reflects Husserl's own assertions on the matter. As he declares in §23 of *Cartesianische Meditationen*, the topics of existence and non-existence, of being and non-being, are all-embracing themes for phenomenology, themes addressed under the broadly understood titles of reason and unreason (Hua 1/91). Indeed, as Fink points out in an article from 1939, only a fundamental misunderstanding of the aim of phenomenology would lead to the mistaken but often-repeated claim that Husserl's phenomenology is not interested in reality or the question of being, but only in subjective meaning formations in intentional consciousness (Fink 1981: 44).

As we have already seen, a standard objection to Husserl's methodological concern with the epoché and the reduction has been that, since none of his phenomenological successors made much use of either, neither can be considered essential and indispensable to phenomenological philosophizing. However, as Tugendhat points out in his classical work *Der Wahrheitsbegriff bei Husserl und Heidegger*, only a very superficial reading of Husserl's transcendental epoché and reduction would lead to the assumption that its purpose is to bracket the world. What is bracketed is the naively posited world, and it is exactly through this procedure that the world as phenomenon is discovered—a world that is essentially correlated to subjectivity, and which subjectivity is essentially related to. As Tugendhat then continues,

It is exactly through the epoché that Husserl enters the dimension of Heidegger's being-in-the-world. Heidegger does not need the epoché any more in order to gain entrance to the dimension of the modes of givenness, since he, after it was opened by Husserl, from the very start stands in it, and from now on can articulate it according to its own conditions—and not simply in exclusive orientation towards a world of objects. (Tugendhat 1970: 263)

As the passage from Tugendhat makes evident, it is a matter of contro-versy whether Heidegger's rare references to the epoché and the reduc-tion is due to the fact that he rejected both or the fact that he simply took them for granted. What is indisputable, however, is that Heidegger in some of his lecture courses from the mid-1920s actually did discuss the bracketing and the reduction. Moreover, he also provided a surprisingly accurate and precise characterization of both:

We call this basic component of phenomenological method—the leading back or re-duction of investigative vision from a naively apprehended being to being—*phenomenological reduction*. (Heidegger 1982: 21)

This bracketing of the entity takes nothing away from the entity itself, nor does it purport to assume that the entity is not. This reversal of perspective has rather the sense of making the being of the entity present. This phenomenological suspen-sion of the transcendent thesis has but the sole function of making the entity present in regard to its being. The term 'suspension' is thus always misunder-stood when it is thought that in suspending the thesis of existence and by doing so, phenomenological reflection simply has nothing more to do with the entity. Quite the contrary: in an extreme and unique way, what really is at issue now is the determination of the being of the very entity. (Heidegger 1985: 99)[3]

That Heidegger is on the right track is confirmed by some of Husserl's later reflections on methodology. As Husserl points out in the lecture *Phänomenologie und Anthropologie* that he gave in Frankfurt, Berlin, and Halle in 1931, the only thing that is excluded as a result of the epoché is a certain naivety, the naivety of simply taking the world for granted, thereby ignoring the contribution of consciousness (Hua 27/173). And as Husserl repeatedly insists in this 1931 lecture, the turn from a naive exploration of the world to a reflective exploration of the field of consciousness does not

---

[3] For a more extensive engagement with the question of Heidegger's use of epoché and reduction, see Tugendhat (1970: 262–80), Courtine (1990: 207–47), Caputo (1992), Marion (1998), Crowell (2001: 182–202), Overgaard (2004), and O'Murchadha (2008). As the latter writes, 'The fundamental elements of Husserl's phenomenology—reduction, intentionality, world—are all taken up and transformed by Heidegger. This transformation is fruitfully understood not in terms of a move from inner to outer or from epistemology to ontology or from idealism to realism, but rather as a transformation of philosophy as a questioning of the conditions of possibility of objective knowledge (*epistemé*, science) to a questioning as to its own conditions of possibility. The transformation is one in which the philosopher is no longer concerned with the grounding of logic, but rather with the grounding of philosophy itself. In this sense Heidegger (at least in *Being and Time*) radicalizes Husserl's project, but does not undermine it' (O'Murchadha 2008: 392).

entail a turning away from the world; rather, it is a turn that for the first time allows a truly radical investigation and comprehension of the world (Hua 27/178).

For Husserl, reality is not a mind-independent object, but a constituted network of validity. A proper philosophical exploration of reality does not consist in inventorying the content of the universe, but in accounting for the conditions under which something can appear as real. Rather than making reality disappear from view, the reduction is precisely what allows reality to be investigated philosophically.

Husserl occasionally compares the performance of the epoché with the transition from a two-dimensional to a three-dimensional life (Hua 6/120). It is only through such a move that we will be able to approach reality in a way that will allow a disclosure of its true sense (Hua 8/457, 465, 3/120). And to speak of the *sense* of reality in this context does not, as Husserl will eventually add, imply that the *being* of reality, i.e. the really existing world, is somehow excluded from the phenomenological sphere of research. After all, the main if not sole concern of phenomenologists is to transform 'the universal obviousness of the being of the world—for him the greatest of all enigmas—into something intelligible' (Hua 6/184 [180]). Consequently, as Husserl points out in *Erste Philosophie II*, it is better to avoid using the term '*Ausschaltung*' altogether, since the use of this term might easily lead to the mistaken view that the being of the world is no longer a phenomenological theme, whereas the truth is that transcendental research includes 'the world itself, with all its true being' (Hua 8/432).

If we want to understand the status of reality, i.e. what it means for something to exist and be real, does phenomenology—understood as a systematic investigation of the correlation between structures of intentionality and objects of experience—have anything to offer? One way to respond is to consider the spectre of global scepticism. How would Husserl respond to the 'evil demon' or the 'brain in the vat' scenario? How would he react to the suggestion that the world we live in might be nothing but a big illusion? What would he say to the proposal that our objects of experience are nothing but mind-dependent representations of something mind-independent that affects us, but about which we can have no further knowledge, i.e. to the proposal that we are forever trapped behind a veil of appearances, while the real world remains unknowable? Would he reject the hypothesis outright, or would he rather concede its possibility and admit that phenomenology (being limited to the world of appearance as it is) has no way of countering it?

As a reading of, for instance, *Ideen I* and *Erste Philosophie I* will confirm, Husserl is no defender of a two-world theory. He argues that the sceptical scenario and the possibility of global epistemic failure presupposes the possibility of a principled distinction between the world as it is understood by us and the world as it is in itself, but it is exactly this possibility and this distinction that he rejects. For him, it is the world itself that appears to us (Hua 1/32, 117, 8/441, 462). The similarity and difference to Kant (which I will return to in Chapter 4) is striking. On the one hand, Husserl is adamant in rejecting the notion of an inaccessible and ungraspable *Ding an sich* as unintelligible and nonsensical (Husserl 1/38–9, 11/19–20). Indeed, Husserl would here side with Hegel. Whereas Kant would claim that things that are in principle inaccessible to us are like 'nothing for us' (Kant 1998: A105), Hegel would, as Braver puts it, downgrade the 'nothing to us' to a 'nothing at all' (Braver 2007: 81). On the other hand, Husserl would agree with Kant that the right place to locate objectivity is in, rather than beyond, transcendentally structured experiential reality. To be more specific, Husserl is not only ruling out that there could be forms of reality that were completely off limits, i.e. in principle inaccessible to conscious subjects. He is also insisting that the world of experience can have all the required reality and objectivity. To posit a hidden world that systematically eludes experiential access and justification, and to designate that world as the really real reality, would for Husserl involve an abuse of the term 'reality':

The attempt to conceive the universe of true being as something lying outside the universe of possible consciousness, possible knowledge, possible evidence, the two being related to one another merely externally by a rigid law, is nonsensical. They belong together essentially; and, as belonging together essentially, they are also concretely one, one in the only absolute concretion: transcendental subjectivity. If transcendental subjectivity is the universe of possible sense, then an outside is precisely nonsense. (Hua 1/117)

Carried out with this systematic concreteness, phenomenology is *eo ipso 'transcendental idealism'*, though in a fundamentally and essentially new sense. It is not a psychological idealism, and most certainly not such an idealism as sensualistic psychologism proposes, an idealism that would derive a senseful world from senseless sensuous data. Nor is it a Kantian idealism, which believes it can keep open, at least as a limiting concept, the possibility of a world of things in themselves. (Hua 1/118)

As these two quotes from *Cartesianische Meditationen* suggest, and as I will argue in more detail in Chapter 4, Husserl's endorsement of transcendental idealism is tightly linked to his attempt to save the objectivity of the world of experience, and to ward off a form of global scepticism. Ruling out the possibility of a principled gap between the world that we can investigate and the real world means that global scepticism can get no purchase.

Metaphysical realism is committed to a non-epistemic account of truth, which enforces a sharp divide between truth and rational justification (Sankey 2008: 112). Not only are the truth-makers mind-independent in the sense of being 'solely determined by the existence of states of affairs which obtain independently of human thought or experience' (p. 113), but on a realist account, it is also possible for the totality of our beliefs to be ideally justified and still fail to be true (p. 113), i.e. even an ideal theory reached at the ultimate end of scientific inquiry might be false. This possibility goes hand in hand with the possibility of radical and global scepticism. Metaphysical realism is certainly not committed to the claim that there are experience-transcendent entities, or that we are in principle prevented from knowing reality as it really is. But although metaphysical realism doesn't entail these views, it cannot exclude them either.

Does Husserl also allow for a principled gap between evidence and truth? A fairly trivial outcome of our fallibility and finitude is that an object could be experienced as really existing, yet fail to exist. Likewise, an object could actually exist and yet fail to be given as existing (Hua 4/76). But would Husserl also accept that an object can be given as existing in an ideally optimal and concordant manner and still turn out not to be real, and correlatively, would he accept that an object might be real although in principle it remains beyond our epistemic reach? Hardy has argued that evidence, for Husserl, rather than being necessary and sufficient for *truth*, is only necessary and sufficient for *justification*. Evidence does not make a proposition true; it only makes us justified in believing the proposition to be true. Insisting that the relevant link is between evidence and justification, and not between evidence and truth, allows Hardy to reject the claim that truth is constituted by and dependent upon the givenness of objects for consciousness and thereby to affirm the compatibility of Husserl's theory of truth with a full-blown realism according to which truth is independent of consciousness (Hardy 2013: 83, 96). Hardy is forced to admit, however, that for Husserl there is a necessary correlation between truth and evidence; but on his view, all that Husserl is committed to is the following principle: 'p is true if and only if it is possible that the state of affairs corresponding to p be given to some possible consciousness' (p. 100). To claim that any real existing object must be experienceable is not to claim that it must necessarily be experienceable to a human being (this would be a crude form of anthropocentrism), but merely that it must be experienceable by some possible consciousness.

This interpretation is, however, deficient, since Husserl repeatedly insists that the possibility of experience must be related to the actuality of experience—or, to put it differently, that an object that isn't currently experienced but which could be experienced must belong to the horizon of an actual experience.[4] This is already clearly stated in *Ideas I*:

An object, being in itself, is never such that would not involve consciousness and ego-consciousness at all. The thing is the thing of the *environment*; so, too, is the thing not seen, also the really possible thing, the thing not experienced but capable, or perchance capable, of being experienced. *The possibility of being experienced never designates an empty logical possibility*, but instead one motiv-ated in an experiential connection. (Hua 3/101)

It is also something that Husserl is even more explicit about in texts currently gathered in the volume *Transzendentaler Idealismus*:

A nature is inconceivable without the co-existence of subjects who are able to experience it; the mere possibility of experiencing subjects is not enough. (Hua 36/156)

The actual existence of a thing, and with this the actual existence of a real world, demands more than simply the ideal possibility of an I and an I-consciousness, it demands more than the ideal possibility of experience and (ideally possible) nexuses of experience, for with all of that we do not surpass the things as ideally possible, that is, potentially sensible. It demands an I of pre-eminent and concrete content, an actually existing consciousness with actual experiences and experi-ential positings. (Hua 36/78)

An actual world belongs necessarily as intentional correlate to an actual I or to its actual stream of consciousness. A world is what it is only as over and against an

---

[4] Kant expresses a similar thought in *Kritik der reinen Vernunft*: 'That there could be inhabitants of the moon, even though no human being has ever perceived them, must of course be admitted; but this means only that in the possible progress of experience we could encounter them; for everything is actual that stands in one context with a perception in accordance with the laws of the empirical progression' (Kant 1998: A493/B521).

experiencing I. Everything it contains is either directly experienced or belongs to the determinable indeterminate horizon of the currently experienced. (Hua 36/121)

Thus, if one says a world could exist without the existence of an ego that experienced it, then this is nonsensical. For the truth 'A world can exist' is nothing without being, in principle, subject to justification. This justification, however, presupposes an actual I, that is directed thetically at the world in question. (Hua 36/119)

For Husserl, reason, being, and truth are inextricably linked. Already in *Ideen I*, he defended the view that the notions 'truly existing object' and 'rationally posited object' are equivalent (Hua 3/329):

To each object 'that truly is,' there corresponds in principle (in the a priori [sense] of an unconditioned, essential universality) the *idea of a possible consciousness* in which the object itself can be apprehended *in an originary* and thereby *perfectly adequate manner.* Conversely, if this possibility is guaranteed, then eo ipso the object truly is. (Hua 3/329)

The same idea is articulated in his lectures *Einleitung in die Philosophie* from 1922–3:

It is impossible to elude the extensive evidence that true being as well only has its meaning as the correlate of a particular intentionality of reason, i.e., as an ideal unit that is essentially inseparable from I and I-consciousness. [...] True being, and in particular the true being of nature, is not something additional to merely intentional being. This holds true, even though we have to distinguish between nature as presumptively and incompletely intended at a given time, and nature itself [...]. But nature itself, as a contrast to all the partial and incomplete modes of givenness, is not a nonsensical beyond of consciousness as such and every possible positing cognition [...] but rather a regulative idea that emerges from and is ever constituted by the ego. (Hua 35/276–7)

It is hard to reconcile such statements with metaphysical realism and a non-epistemic conception of truth. I would agree with Hardy that Husserl is interested in the question of when and under what conditions we are entitled to posit the existence of an object, and that when Husserl discusses the link between reason and reality, his discussion is situated within an evidential and justificatory context. But it would be wrong to conclude from this that Husserl is after all not interested in existence and reality, but merely in the sense of existence and reality, and that it is merely the justification with which we posit the existence of objects, rather than their reality itself, which according to Husserl is dependent upon consciousness (Hardy 2013: 192).[5] Had the latter been true, it is hard to understand why Husserl in his introduction to the English translation of *Ideen I* writes that he considers every form of philosophical realism to be in principle absurd (Hua 5/151).

Husserl wants to defend the transcendence and reality of our world of experience; he wants to reject the suggestion that this world might in the end be nothing but an immanent illusion. His way of doing so is by seeking to show the nonsensicality of declaring a world beyond the appearing world the real world, and by pronouncing the notion of an unknowable *Ding an sich* nonsensical ('*sinnlos*') (Hua 39/726).

Some might object that Husserl's rejection of scepticism is over-hasty (Crowell 2008: 349). It might be argued that scepticism is only an interesting problem for realism—can we really know something about mind-independent reality?—and that one fails to engage seriously with the problem if one opts for idealism (Stern 2000: 49–50). Indeed, some have even argued that since realism is inescapable and since it goes hand in hand with the irrefutability of scepticism, any theory that seeks to refute scepticism is itself refuted (Strawson 2008: 98).

But then again, Husserl is certainly not alone in his impatience with the sceptic. A comparable rejection of the sceptical worry can be found in Davidson and McDowell:

I set out not to 'refute' the skeptic, but to give a sketch of what I think to be a correct account of the foundations of linguistic communication and its implication for truth, belief, and knowledge. If one grants the correctness of this account, one can tell the skeptic to get lost. (Davidson 2001: 157)

The aim here is not to answer sceptical questions, but to begin to see how it might be intellectually respectable to ignore them, to treat them as unreal, in the way that common sense has always wanted to. (McDowell 1994: 113)

For now, however, the decisive issue is not whether Husserl was justified in rejecting global scepticism, but simply that he did reject the very possibility of reality being fundamentally unknowable. By rejecting inaccessible things in themselves, however, he is definitely taking a stand on the relationship between phenomena and reality, and by doing that, he is also

---

[5] That Hardy argues like this is not surprising given his own interpretation of the reduction and his acceptance of the Fregean interpretation of the noema. According to Hardy, the effectuation of the phenomenological reduction entails that reference to objects is converted into reference to the noemata by which acts achieve their reference to objects (Hardy 2013: 191). In the following chapter, I will argue against this interpretation.

making it clear that phenomenology is not restricted by a commitment to metaphysical neutrality. In its radical exploration of the structure and status of the phenomenon, transcendental phenomenology cannot permit itself to remain neutral or indifferent to the question concerning the relationship between phenomena and reality. By having to take a stand on that relationship, phenomenology by necessity has metaphysical implications.

Perhaps one could grant everything I have said so far, but still object that Husserl distinguishes metaphysics and ontology, and that we need to follow him in this. In works such as *Cartesianische Meditationen*, *Ideen III*, *Erste Philosophie II*, and *Formale und transzendentale Logik*, Husserl speaks of the ontological dimension of phenomenology and differentiates formal ontology from material (or regional) ontology. 'Formal ontology' is the name for the discipline that investigates what it means to be an object. It is considered a formal enterprise, for it abstracts from all considerations concerning content. It is not concerned with the differences between stones, trees, and violins; it is not concerned with the differences between various types of objects, but with that which holds true for any object whatsoever. Formal ontology is consequently engaged in an analysis of such categories as quality, property, relation, identity, whole, part, and so on. In contrast, material (or regional) ontology examines the essential structures belonging to a given region of objects, and seeks to determine that which holds true with necessity for any member of the region in question.[6] For instance, what is it that characterizes mathematical entities as such in contrast to social acts or mental episodes? Given this definition of ontology, ontological analyses (of both material and formal nature) are ubiquitous in Husserl's phenomenological writings, and there is no question that he would have agreed with Heidegger's statement 'There is no ontology *alongside* a phenomenology. Rather, *scientific ontology is nothing but phenomenology*' (Heidegger 1985: 72). However, and importantly, ontology does not make any claims about whether or not a certain region or object exist. It is indifferent to that very question. Could it not be argued that, although Husserl's investigations might have ontological bearing, they

---

[6] Apropos the introspectionist misreading of phenomenology discussed in Chapter 1, it should be clear that the reach and validity of these analyses are in no way restricted to the mental domain.

continue to lack metaphysical impact, since they persistently ignore and avoid questions about existence?

What this retort continues to ignore, however, is that Husserl does treat and analyse questions concerning reality and existence. Just think of his careful analysis of the different modes of givenness. I can talk *about* a slithering anaconda that I have never seen, but which I have heard about; I can see a detailed drawing *of* the anaconda; or I can perceive the anaconda myself. These different ways to intend an object are not unrelated. On the contrary, there is a strict hierarchical relation between them, in the sense that the modes can be ranked according to their ability to give us the object as directly and originally as possible. The object can be given more or less directly, that is, it can be more or less *present*. There is a manifest difference between merely thinking about an anaconda and seeing it. In the latter case, the snake isn't merely meant but given as present. Perception provides us with access to the object itself in its bodily presence. But to speak of a spatio-temporal object that is given *in propria persona*, i.e. as bodily present, is exactly to speak of an *existing* object. Of course, ultimately, mere intuitive givenness doesn't settle questions of existence and reality. We also need to consider the issue of rational coherence and intersubjective confirmation. In fact, one of Husserl's main reasons for taking the problem of intersubjectivity as seriously as he did, was precisely (as we shall see in Chapter 4) because he took reality and objectivity to be intersubjectively constituted. It is consequently decisive to realize that whereas the difference between a veridical perception and a non-veridical perception, as well as the very existence of the intentional object, was of no concern to the pre-transcendental phenomenology of *Logische Untersuchungen*, this limitation no longer holds true for Husserl's mature philosophy. This is also why for Husserl it would make no sense to suppose that an object meeting the strong condition of ultimate, intersubjective confirmation could still prove to be unreal. Seriously to entertain that possibility would, as Smith puts it, be 'to uproot our notions of reality and unreality from their experiential basis in confirmations and disconfirmations, whence these notions derive all their sense and meaning' (2003: 179).

The critic might persist, however, and claim that even if the above is correct, one could still argue that Husserl is merely dealing with the question of what it means for a given object to exist and be real, i.e. he is still merely dealing with the meaning of reality, and that any such investigation must be sharply distinguished from attempts to make metaphysical claims about the (f)actual existence of something. The latter is off-limits to phenomenology. At this point, however, it might be appropriate simply to point out that questions of fact ought to be established empirically, not through metaphysical thinking or transcendental reflection. As O'Murchadha rightly points out:

> The philosophical question for Husserl is not whether, say, this perceived tree *actually* exists, but rather what it means to say that this tree exists. If the actual existence of the tree were a philosophical question, then it would be hard to distinguish the concerns of the philosopher from the lumberjack. (O'Murchadha 2008: 381)

But whereas transcendental phenomenology has no interest in specifying the number of trees that are to be found in the municipality of Copenhagen, it is very much concerned with questions such as what it means for an object to be real and when we are justified in judging that it is. As Husserl writes, 'the "bracketing" that the experience has undergone prevents any judgment about the perceived actuality [...]. But it does not hinder any judgment about the perception being consciousness *of* an actuality' (Hua 3/209).

It is one thing to show that transcendental phenomenology has metaphysical implications—at least as far as Husserl was concerned. It is something else to spell out what exactly these implications are. We have seen that Husserl favours a form of transcendental idealism. But what exactly does this amount to? Most importantly, is it a form of idealism that can accommodate some of our realist intuitions? This will be the topic for the following chapters.

4
Internalism, externalism, and transcendental idealism

Das Delphische Wort γνῶθι σεαυτόν hat eine neue Bedeutung gewonnen. Positive Wissenschaft ist Wissenschaft in der Weltverlorenheit. Man muß erst die Welt durch ἐποχή verlieren, um sie in universaler Selbstbesinnung wiederzugewinnen. *Noli foras ire,* sagt Augustin, *in te redi, in interiore homine habitat veritas.*

Cartesianische Meditationen

Das transzendentale Ich ist weder in noch ausser der Welt, und auch die Welt ist weder in ihm noch ausser ihm.

Ms. A VI 21

Husserl is a transcendental idealist. But doesn't this fact vindicate the criticism that I have attempted to dismiss in previous chapters? Does Husserl's unapologetic endorsement of transcendental idealism not commit him to a highly controversial mixture of internalism and solipsism? As I will argue in this chapter, the right answer is 'quite to the contrary'.

4.1 Internalism and methodological solipsism

'Internalism' and 'externalism' are umbrella terms. Consequently, it makes little sense to ask in general whether somebody is an internalist or an externalist, since the answer will depend on the specific kind of internalism or externalism one has in mind. Let us for a start consider some distinctions used by Rowlands. In *Externalism: Putting Mind and World Back Together Again,* Rowlands has dubbed what he takes to be the two main components of classical (Cartesian) content internalism: the possession claim and the location claim (Rowlands 2003: 13).

(1) Possession claim: The possession of any mental phenomenon by a subject does not depend on any feature that is external to the boundaries of the subject.

(2) Location claim: Any mental phenomenon is spatially located inside the boundaries of the subject that has or undergoes it.

Externalism questions these assumptions; in fact, it is enough to reject one of the two claims in order to count as an externalist. Following Rowlands, we could call the position that merely disputes the possession claim 'reactionary externalism' and the position that rejects both claims 'radical externalism' (Rowlands 2003: 137). This distinction can then easily be linked to another distinction, the one between 'content externalism' and 'vehicle externalism'. Content externalism is the view that mental content depends upon factors that are external to the subject possessing the content. Content externalism consequently disputes the possession claim, but it remains fully compatible with the location claim, since it doesn't question the existence of ongoing internal mental processes. To put it differently, to claim that mental states are externally individuated does not exclude the possibility that they might still be internally located. This is why content externalism does not really establish the claim that has occasionally been used as a slogan for externalism, the claim that the mind 'ain't in the head'. By contrast, vehicle externalism is an externalism about the processes (be they perceptual experiences or cognitive processes) that have the content. If vehicle externalism is true, mental phenomena do not merely depend for their individuation upon what is going on in the environment; rather, they are not internal processes in the first place. They do not exist inside the subject, but only in the relationship that an experiencing organism bears toward the external world. As Neisser once put it, 'Perception and cognition are usually not just operations in the head, but transactions with the world' (Neisser 1976: 11).

How does the distinction between internalism and externalism apply to phenomenology? According to Rowlands, whereas Husserl is a traditional Cartesian internalist, Sartre is a radical externalist, since he rejects the possession as well as the location claim (Rowlands 2003: 55, 59, 74). Sartre's externalism follows directly from his interpretation of intentionality. To affirm the intentionality of consciousness is, according to Sartre, to deny the existence of any kind of mental content (including any kind of sense-data or qualia) (Sartre 2003: 15). There is nothing in consciousness. It has no content. It is completely empty. This is why Sartre can argue that the being of intentional consciousness consists in its revelation of transcendent being (p. 17). Like latter-day phenomenal externalists, Sartre consequently takes phenomenal properties to be properties of worldly objects. For the same reason, it makes no sense to say that they are located inside the head.

Rowlands is not the only one to consider Husserl an archetypical internalist. Dreyfus has for a long time defended a similar interpretation. As we have already seen, according to Dreyfus, Husserl was committed to a form of methodological solipsism, and held the view that the mind contains a number of mental representations that all have the function they have regardless of how the world is. They are all purely mental, and therefore analysable and describable without any reference to the world. Thus, on Dreyfus's reading, Husserl took mind and world to be two completely independent realms, and investigated the mental content without any regard for whether that which we are intentionally directed at does exist or not (Dreyfus 1991: 74; Dreyfus and Hall 1982: 14). However, as Dreyfus then observes, echoing Heidegger, the attempt to bridge the gap between subject and object by means of some self-contained mental content gives rise to more problems than it solves (Dreyfus 1991: 51). What is required is a rejection of the traditional view according to which our very ability to relate to objects requires 'internal representations' (Dreyfus 1988: 95).

Dreyfus's critical assessment of Husserl's phenomenology is primarily motivated by his interpretation of two of Husserl's core concepts: the reduction and the noema.

1. On the one hand, Dreyfus argues that Husserl in his search for an indubitable foundation wished to investigate consciousness from a strictly internal perspective, and that he consequently found it necessary to effectuate a procedure of purification, which would remove all external or transcendent components from consciousness. Dreyfus consequently interprets the reduction as a change of attitude that makes us turn our attention away from the objects in the world, and away from our psychological experiences of being directed at objects, in order to focus on the abstract mental representations that make intentionality possible (Dreyfus and Hall 1982: 6). This is why Dreyfus can then interpret Husserlian phenomenology as an enterprise which is exclusively interested in the mental representations that remain in consciousness after the

performance of the reduction has bracketed the world and any concern with existence (Dreyfus 1982: 108; 1991: 50). Dreyfus even argues that Husserl as a result of this move had to abandon the attempt of accounting for how objects are given or presented in order to concern himself exclusively with how they are intended (Dreyfus 1982: 108).

2. On the other hand, Dreyfus endorses Føllesdal's Fregean noema interpretation. As Dreyfus writes, it was Føllesdal who first realized what Husserl was actually up to. It was Føllesdal who pointed out that Husserl's noema is an abstract structure in virtue of which the mind is directed towards objects. It is thanks to Føllesdal's work that Husserl is now finally seen as the first to have developed a general theory of mental representation, which seeks to account for the directedness of all mental activity (Dreyfus and Hall 1982: 2).

It is not difficult to establish a fairly tight connection between Dreyfus's interpretation of the reduction and the Fregean noema interpretation. Whereas the purpose of the reduction on this (mis)interpretation is to abstract from all objects transcendent to consciousness in order to allow for a scrutiny of the very contents in virtue of which we can be directed at said objects, the noema is taken to be the semantic content that allows consciousness to be directed at its putative transcendent objects.

Like Dreyfus, Carman and McIntyre also subscribe to the Fregean noema interpretation, and consequently interpret Husserl as an internalist (McIntyre 1986: 102; Carman 2003: 31). As Carman writes, for Husserl 'it is the internal content of a mental state that makes possible an awareness of external objects' (Carman 2003: 31). Likewise, McIntyre argues that Husserl considers the problem of intentionality to be a question, not of how mental states relate to the world, but rather of how mental states come to have an internal representational character, 'which makes them *as though* actually related to extra-mental things whether they are so or not' (McIntyre 1986: 108). McIntyre insists that the very purpose of the epoché and reduction is to bracket anything extra-mental, and even goes so far as to say that Husserl's version of methodological solipsism is more radical than the one embraced by contemporary representationalists, and that it ultimately results in Husserl's transcendental version of phenomenology (McIntyre 1986: 102).

In contrast to Carman, McIntyre does admit, however, that there are elements in Husserl's account that seem to point in a somewhat different direction. Although Husserl argues that meaning determines reference, it would be a mistake to think that his theory is only geared towards handling those types of reference where the meaning-content of the act prescribes a certain object by detailing its properties descriptively. On the contrary, already early on, Husserl was aware that 'this' refers directly, rather than attributively, and even more importantly, Husserl also realized to what extent perception involves a demonstrative content of sense. When I perceive an object, I intend *this* object, and not just any object with similar properties. But as McIntyre then points out, an appeal to such external factors as the de facto relation to the environmental object of reference is not compatible with Husserl's methodological solipsism, or with his claim that intentional reference is existence-independent and determined purely by the 'phenomenological content' of an act, i.e. by its internal character (McIntyre 1982: 226, 229–31). Indeed, as McIntyre continues,

A theory of intentionality modeled on the reference of demonstratives would accordingly not be a purely phenomenological theory appealing to the meaning-content of an act alone. Rather, it would also bring into the theory, as essential to an act's intentionality, factors that philosophers of language classify as 'pragmatic' rather than 'semantic'—contextual factors concerning the subject of the act, the particular occasion on which the act takes place and the empirical situation in which it occurs. But it is precisely factors of this sort which Husserl's phenomenological conception of intentionality and his method of phenomenological reduction are designed to remove from consideration. (McIntyre 1982: 229–30)

McIntyre concedes that Husserl eventually came to expand the notion of phenomenological content to include the horizon, past experiences, etc.; but as he concludes, these modifications do not solve the basic problem facing Husserl's very conception of intentionality. No matter how much the (narrow) content includes, a theory of intentionality that confines itself to the phenomenological content of consciousness will never be able to explain our actual involvement with existing reality—which is exactly what existential phenomenologists have always emphasized (McIntyre 1982: 231).

Although Dreyfus, Carman, and McIntyre differ in their ultimate appraisal of Husserl's theory, their criticism is motivated by a shared dissatisfaction with the way in which his transcendental phenomenology conceives of the mind–world relationship.

What I intend to do now is to show that it is quite misleading to classify Husserl as a traditional internalist. My argument will proceed in several steps: I will first discuss Husserl's concept of the noema in some detail.

Dreyfus, Carman, and McIntyre all favour (a version of) Føllesdal's noema interpretation. Although Føllesdal's noema interpretation does seem to make Husserl into an internalist, there are, however, other noema interpretations available.[1] My aim is not per se to defend the exegetical accuracy of one of these alternatives—as far as I am concerned this has already been done convincingly by Drummond (1990) and Sokolowski (1984, 1987)—but to show (1) that *if* one adopts their noema interpretation it becomes far less obvious that Husserl should be an internalist, and (2) that this latter noema interpretation is far more in line with what I take to be the correct understanding of Husserl's epoché and reduction. In a further step, I will then engage directly with Husserl's idealism. I will argue that his commitment to a form of transcendental idealism is precisely what prevents his theory from being internalist in any ordinary sense of the term. I will discuss whether Husserl's transcendental idealism might actually have more in common with a certain form of externalism, but ultimately argue that Husserl's conception of the mind–world relationship cannot be captured adequately within the framework of the internalism–externalism debate. Finally, I will turn to the claim that Husserl is a methodological solipsist, and show how this interpretation fails to square with Husserl's radical account of transcendental intersubjectivity.

4.2 Intentionality and the noema

Føllesdal, Dreyfus, Miller, Smith, and McIntyre (often described as the California school, or the West Coast interpretation) have defended a Fregean interpretation of Husserl's theory of intentionality. According to them, the noema must be sharply distinguished from both act and object. It is an abstract meaning or sense that mediates the intentional relation between act and object. Thus, and very importantly, the noema is not

---

[1] The plural must be emphasized. It is a mistake to think that the only alternative to the Fregean interpretation is Gurwitsch's neo-phenomenalist noema interpretation, and to identify Gurwitsch's interpretation with the East Coast interpretation, as has occasionally been done (cf. Beyer 1997: 167–8). One decisive difference between Gurwitsch's position and the East Coast interpretation is that (briefly put) Gurwitsch conceives of the relation between the intended object and the noema as that of a whole to a part, whereas the East Coast interpretation conceives of it as that of an identity to a manifold. For an extensive discussion of this difference, see Drummond (1990).

taken to be that toward which consciousness is directed, but that by means of which it is directed, that by virtue of which we achieve a reference to the external object. The decisive feature of the Fregean approach is consequently that the intentionality of consciousness is conceived in analogy with the reference of linguistic expressions (Føllesdal 1974: 96).[2] In both cases the reference is determined by the sense, in both cases the reference is effectuated *via* the sense. As Smith and McIntyre put it, and in what follows, I will primarily focus on their elaboration of the Fregean interpretation: the noema is an abstract mediating entity that is instrumental in our intending the objects themselves.[3] As they write: 'Husserl's theory of intentionality is not an object-theory but a mediator-theory [. . .]: for Husserl, an act is directed toward an object *via* an intermediate "intentional" entity, the act's noema' (Smith and McIntyre 1982: 87), or as McIntyre puts it in later article: 'Intentionality, or representation, is again a "mediated" affair: a mental state represents an object only "via" its noema' (1986: 105).

By contrast, Sokolowski, Drummond, Hart, and Cobb-Stevens (often known as the East Coast interpretation) argue that intentionality is a fundamental feature of conscious experience, and they therefore deny what seems to follow from the mediator theory favoured by the Californians: that the intentional directedness of the act is derived from the referentiality of its content, i.e. that it is in virtue of possessing a content with particular properties that the act can be directed upon worldly objects and state of affairs. On their interpretation, the noema is to be understood neither as an ideal meaning, nor as a concept, nor as a proposition; it is not an intermediary between subject and object; it is not something that bestows intentionality on consciousness (as if consciousness prior to the introduction of the noema would be like a closed container with no bearing on the world). No, the noema is the object itself considered in the *phenomenological* reflection (and not simply in a psychological or linguistic reflection). It is the perceived object as perceived, the recollected episode as recollected, the judged state-of-affair as

---

[2] To speak of this interpretation as Fregean is not meant to imply that the interpretation would deny that Husserl's theory of intentionality contains elements that transcend a Fregean framework. The point is merely that it interprets the noema in line with the Fregean notion of sense ('*Sinn*') (Smith and McIntyre 1982: 81–2; Dreyfus 1982: 100).

[3] For a concise but illuminating discussion of the difference between Føllesdal's and Smith and McIntyre's noema interpretation, see Drummond (2012).

judged, etc. The object-as-it-is-intended is the object-that-is-intended abstractly considered (namely in abstraction from the positing that characterizes our natural attitude), and thus something capable of being given only in a phenomenological or transcendental attitude (Sokolowski 1987: 526–7). In their view, the purpose of the epoché and reduction is precisely not to reorient our focus from the worldly object to the mental representation. After the reduction, we continue to be concerned with the worldly object, but we now no longer consider it naively; rather, we focus on it precisely as it is intended and given, i.e. as a correlate of experience. To examine the object-as-it-is-intended, i.e. the object in its significance for us, is, however, as Sokolowski emphasizes, to examine the object itself (p. 527). The sense, the intentional content, on this *presentationalist* account belongs to the intended object (Drummond 2012). It is not contained in the mind, but is correlated with the mind.

On this background, the East Coast interpretation criticizes the West Coast interpretation for confusing what is an ordinary object considered abstractly in a non-ordinary (phenomenological) attitude with a non-ordinary abstract entity (Drummond 1992: 89). Insofar as an investigation of the noema is an investigation of any kind of object, aspect, dimension, or region, considered in its very manifestation, in its very significance for consciousness, the object and the noema turn out to be the same differently considered. In fact, the difference between an object and its meaning is not an empirical distinction, but rather a difference in the way one and the same object is taken, first in straightforward experience and then again in a reflective inquiry. As Crowell puts it, 'Meaning *is* the thing as it presents itself to phenomenological reflection' (2001: 89), and again 'the noema [. . .] is better seen as the object itself considered in terms of its modes of self-givenness' (2015: 252). This does not imply that there is no distinction (within the reflective stance) between the object-as-it-is-intended and the object-that-is-intended, but this distinction is exactly a structural difference, rather than an ontological difference (Drummond 1990: 108–9, 113).

One of the classical distinctions within theories of intentionality is the distinction between an object theory (also known as a dyadic theory) and a mediator theory (also known as a triadic theory). Brentano is usually considered an advocate of the first type of approach. For him, intentionality is a dyadic relation holding between an experience and an object. In itself, the intentional relation is an ordinary relation, and as an ordinary relation, it presupposes the existence of both relata. However, this apparently innocent assumption has some rather problematic consequences. When I am imagining a faun, or when I am hallucinating a pink elephant, I remain intentionally directed, but neither the faun nor the pink elephant exists in reality. The object-theoretical approach is consequently forced to claim that the faun and the pink elephant are objects with a very peculiar form of (intentional in-)existence. This is not a very comforting solution, and given the need for a unified theory of intentionality, it also causes problems for an account of veridical perceptions. When seeing a blooming apple tree, am I then in reality seeing an intentional object with a very peculiar ontological status (the same object that I would be seeing if I were merely hallucinating the apple tree), and is the only difference between hallucinating and perceiving the apple tree the (phenomenally undetectable) fact that in the latter case, the intentional object happens to correspond to an ordinary real object? On this account, we would never enjoy an immediate and direct access to reality. At best, the world itself would only be accessible via a veil of intentional objects.

Usually, Husserl has been taken to oppose the dyadic object theory proposed by Brentano. For Husserl, intentionality is not an ordinary relation to an extraordinary object, but an extraordinary relation to an ordinary object; an extraordinary 'relation' that can persist, even if the object doesn't exist. When it comes to intentions that are directed towards 'unreal' objects, they are just as much characterized by their *directedness* towards a transcendent object as are ordinary perceptions. In contrast to normal perceptions, however, the referent does not exist, neither intra-mentally nor extra-mentally. In the case of a hallucination, the pink elephant exists neither inside nor outside of consciousness, but the act of hallucination is still directed at a transcendent, extra-mental, object (Hua 19/206). This account dispenses with the need of ascribing a special kind of existence to the hallucinated object in order to preserve the intentionality of the act.

According to the Fregean West Coast interpretation, however, it is only their reconstruction of Husserl's theory of intentionality and their noema interpretation that enable Husserl to account for hallucinations in this way. Only a mediator theory, which emphasizes the ontological *difference* between the noema and the object, can account convincingly for those cases where the experience is intentional (has a noema), but where the object does not exist. Apparently, the only alternative left for the East Coast interpretation is to opt for a Brentanian solution, and this is not a particularly attractive option. To put it differently, the Fregean interpretation has typically argued that the East Coast interpretation has a hard time accounting for cases of hallucination, whereas it can easily do so itself.

If this line of argumentation sounds slightly familiar, it is no coincidence. It bears a rather striking resemblance to the 'argument from illusion' favoured by many internalists. The argument from illusion (which nowadays is actually more like an argument from hallucination) starts out by observing that hallucinations and perceptions can at times be subjectively indistinguishable. The argument then maintains that since there is no distinguishable difference between the two mental states, we must give a broadly similar account of both. This suggests that the veridical state consists of two elements, one (the common element) which obtains also in the case of the hallucination, and the other (the presence of the outer object) which obtains only if we are lucky. Generally speaking, the argument from illusion consequently argues from the indistinguishability of two states, one of which is a success and the other a failure, to what has been called the 'conjunctive thesis': what one gets in success is a conjunction of two independent elements: (1) something which success and failure have in common and (2) something only present in successful cases.

If we transfer this way of looking at the issue to the present discussion, we find a neat symmetry. The Fregean interpretation would argue that perceptions and hallucinations are intentional experiences, it would argue that both types of experiences have a noema (the common element), and finally it would argue that the object referred to is present in perception but absent in hallucination. This symmetry can be taken to confirm the earlier diagnosis: the Fregean interpretation of the noema amounts to an internalist reading of Husserl. But the symmetry also suggests a possible retort by the East Coast interpretation. The argument from illusion has typically been used as an argument for internalism and for some kind of representationalism. But the validity of the argument has been questioned by externalists and non-representationalists alike. An interesting possibility consequently presents itself. Perhaps the East Coast interpretation's ability to deal with illusions and hallucinations might profit from a closer study of externalist replies to the argument

from illusion, and more generally from ecological accounts of hallucination. To put it differently, and more bluntly, might Husserl be a
disjunctivist? This interpretation has explicitly been defended by
A. D. Smith. He has argued that a proper analysis of Husserl's theory
of intentionality shows that Husserl sees the difference between a perception and a hallucination as amounting to more than simply the
presence or absence of an extra-mental causal relation to the environment. For Husserl, hallucinations and perceptions are different in kind,
even when considered simply as experiences (Smith 2008). What is the
argument? Smith's basic move has been to highlight those passages
where Husserl not only argues that a state of consciousness must have
some object or other, but also insists that the particular object of any
conscious state belongs to the essential being of that state. As Husserl,
for instance, writes in *Cartesianische Meditationen*:

Each *cogito*, each conscious process, we may also say, '*means*' something or other
and bears in itself, in this manner peculiar to the *meant*, its peculiar *cogitatum*.
Each does this, moreover, in its own fashion. The house-perception means a
house—more precisely, as this individual house—and means it in the fashion
peculiar to perception. (Hua 1/71)

To perceive an object is consequently not simply to perceive a certain
type of object, it is to perceive *this* particular object.[4] Consider a situation,
where I am looking at a can of Heinz Tomato Soup. I then briefly close my
eyes, and when I open them again, I once again see a can of Heinz Tomato
Soup. On both occasions, I seem to see and intend the same object. In fact,
however, the can was replaced without my knowledge. Even if I happen to
believe that the two perceptions were alike, they would still, according
to Husserl, lack an identity of sense ('*Sinnesidentität*') (Hua 16/155).
In short, experiences that do not intend exactly the same object are not
identical. This also holds true for the relevant perception–hallucination
case. Even *if* a perception of an existent object were subjectively

---

[4] That this is Husserl's claim is, as already mentioned, explicitly recognized by McIntyre,
who admits that it seems to 'seriously modify our original Fregean understanding of how
meanings determine intentional relations' (1982: 228). But rather than interpreting it as
evidence that Husserl is after all not an internalist, McIntyre simply argues that it contradicts Husserl's claim that all reference depends on phenomenological content alone, which
by his definition is world-independent. McIntyre consequently claims to have revealed a
most unfortunate contradiction in Husserl's thinking (McIntyre 1982: 230–1).

indistinguishable from a hallucination of a non-existent object, they would be essentially and intrinsically different kinds of experiences (Smith 2008: 331).

Furthermore—and this could be seen as the next step of the argument—the moment we start to explore the horizon of the object, it will turn out that perceptions and hallucinations are never experientially indistinguishable (for which reason it might after all be better not to call Husserl a disjunctivist). They might initially seem so, but only when considered in isolation and abstraction from their horizonal embedding and temporal unfolding. To put it differently, how is a phenomenologist supposed to even start acknowledging the difference between a perception and hallucination, let alone analysing it? Well, certainly not by appealing to a mysterious 'viewer from nowhere' who can penetrate the 'veil of appearances' in order to determine whether the intuitively given object of experience is matched by an object that exists in itself. One might wonder whether such an approach is even halfway intelligible, but it is in any case not an approach that can be pursued *after* the effectuation of the epoché. For a phenomenologist, and this includes anybody interested in the role of the noema, the difference between a perception and hallucination has to be established intra- and inter-experientially. Whereas truly existing objects can be identified and reidentified in further actual and possible experiences (Hua 9/174), hallucinatory objects are not confirmed by further experiences and cannot be shared with others. The hallucinatory character of an experience is consequently revealed in the course of experience, which is just to say that a hallucination is indeed experientially distinguishable from a veridical perception.[5]

---

[5] Staiti has argued that it makes no sense to speak of an illusion if one is merely considering a momentary cross-section of experience, since an illusion is not an act alongside perception, phantasy, pictorial consciousness, and recollection, but rather a retrospective characterization of an earlier sequence of experiences. As he writes, 'only a *span* of experience can qualify as an illusion, and it can qualify as such only after certainty has been restored' (Staiti 2015: 132). There might be some truth to this, at least if one accepts Staiti's somewhat controversial claim that perceptual illusions like the Müller-Lyer illusion are not really to be labelled as illusions (p. 134). But we also need to distinguish illusions and hallucinations, and it is not obvious that hallucinations are only recognized as such after the fact, at least not if we are talking about real hallucinations, the ones experienced by psychiatric patients, and not about the kind of hallucinations of which philosophers usually speak.

Perhaps it could be objected that this is all fine and well, but that the East Coast interpretation remains confronted with a difficulty. How can one claim that the noema of an intentional experience is the object itself considered in the phenomenological reflection, when a hallucination, although in possession of a noema, lacks an object? One possible answer would be to insist that hallucinations, contrary to expectations, are as world-directed and world-involving as any veridical perception. As Hopp puts it:

If it [a hallucinatory experience] genuinely *fell short* of a worldly fact, it could not qualify as any sort of error about any worldly fact, since in order to nonveridically or falsely represent some object or fact, one's experience or thought must minimally be *about* it. I am not entertaining a false belief about Genghis Khan when I believe that my shoe is untied, because my belief isn't even about him. But hallucinations are errors. They don't present appearances as they are. They present the world as it is not. (Hopp 2011: 155; cf. Ali 2017)

A somewhat similar argument is made by Drummond who writes that even in those cases where a non-existent worldly thing or state of affairs is intended, we remain directed in part to the actual world, and so although reference might fail in certain respects, it doesn't fail in others. When intending something that doesn't exist, say, a mirage in the desert, I am actually apprehending something that does exist, the desert, in a manner different from how it actually exist. In such cases, as in cases where I falsely believe something about an actually existing object, the fact that I can be mistaken about the object in the specific manner in question actually reveals something about the object (Drummond 2012: 129–30). As for cases where I intend imaginary objects, like the Pegasus, Drummond argues that such imaginary presentations also draw their material and significance from the actual world (p. 131).

The East Coast interpretation would consequently argue that Husserl's theory of intentionality remains a dyadic theory, since no third element is introduced between the intentional act and the intended object (Drummond 2012: 124). The mental act is directly and in its own right, i.e. independently of any representational content, open to the world. This doesn't collapse Husserl's theory into Brentano's object theory, however, nor does it mean that there is no role for content in Husserl's theory of intentionality. The content, though, is the object itself, just as-it-is-intended. How we apprehend the object, i.e. what significance it has for us, is context-dependent. The object is always given to us as embedded within a (temporal and spatial) horizon. Our apprehension of it, the perspective we bring to bear on it, is influenced, constrained, and enabled in various ways by interests, attitudes, concerns, by previously accumulated experiences, as well as by tradition and culture (see section 4.6. for more on this). But the content in question, the meaning, remains worldly meaning. It is not contained internally in the mind, nor does it belong to some otherworldly realm; and the fact that the object presents itself to us in a specific manner, the fact that we think of it or perceive it in a particular way, doesn't mean that our access to the object is somehow indirect, somehow representationally mediated.

More could be said on these matters, but it should by now be clear that hallucinatory experiences are not as fatal to the East Coast interpretation as they are often made out to be by proponents of the West Coast interpretation.

The two competing noema interpretations have each sought to corroborate their own preferred reading by referring to specific textual passages in Husserl's oeuvre. Whereas the West Coast interpretation has typically favoured Husserl's discussion in *Ideen I* and *III*, the East Coast interpretation has often preferred the analysis offered by Husserl in *Formale und Transzendentale Logik*.

One passage taken to support the West Coast interpretation is §15 of *Ideen III*. There, Husserl writes that the domain of phenomenology is not (the eidetic character of) spatial shapes, physical things, psyches, etc. but rather transcendental consciousness. Its province is the intuition of spatial shapes, the experience of physical things, etc. Phenomenology is consequently also concerned with ontological concepts and essences, but in a quite different way from ontology. When engaged in a phenomenological investigation of the consciousness of physical things, we are not concerned with the nature of physical things, but with the character of our consciousness of physical things (Hua 5/84). As Husserl adds, however, such an investigation will include a consideration of how the thing presents and manifests itself, and also how something factually existing can legitimize itself. The investigation of consciousness consequently encompasses not only the act of consciousness but also the correlate of consciousness, where the latter is the meant-as-such, the perceived-as-such, the named-as-such, etc. (Hua 5/84). To investigate the correlate of consciousness is, as Husserl ends the paragraph, not to investigate the physical things as such: 'A "physical thing" as correlate is not a physical thing; therefore the quotation marks. The theme is therefore a totally different one, even if there are eidetic relations running back and forth' (Hua 5/85). A similar line of thinking can be found in §89 of *Ideen I*, which is entitled 'Noematic assertions and assertions of actuality: the noema in the psychological sphere':

> *The tree simply*, the thing in nature, is nothing less than this *perceived-tree as such* that belongs, as the sense of the perception, to the perception and does so inseparably. The tree itself can burn up, dissolve into its chemical elements, and so forth. The sense, however,—the sense of *this* perception, something necessarily inherent to its essence—cannot burn up; it has no chemical elements, no forces, no real properties. (Hua 3/205)

It is easy to see why such a passage has been taken to support the idea that the noema is utterly different from both act and object. Whereas the tree represented by the noema can burn, the noema of the tree cannot burn. The object perceived, the tree *simpliciter*, is in short categorically distinct from the tree as perceived, from the perceptual sense (Smith 2013: 55). Interestingly, in *Krisis*, Husserl felt the need to defend his earlier formulation:

> Thus the sentence in my *Ideas toward a Pure Phenomenology and Phenomeno-logical Philosophy* [§89], which was able to give rise to objections when it was torn from the context of the presentation there of the phenomenological epoché, was completely correct: one can say of a simple tree that it burns up, but a perceived tree 'as such' cannot burn up. (Hua 6/245 [242])

A standard reply by defenders of the East Coast interpretation has been that the point made by Husserl concerning the difference in properties ascribed to the object itself and to the noema must be maintained even if one asserts that the noema is the object just as intended (Drummond 1990: 116). The object as intended, for instance, can remain available for recollection even after the object simpliciter has been destroyed. Like-wise, when investigating the object as intended one is focusing on the experiential or cognitive availability of the object simpliciter, i.e. on the way in which the object simpliciter is given in conscious experience, and here a predicate like 'flammable' has no purchase.

Not surprisingly, defenders of the East Coast interpretation also have their own preferred quotes. Here is one from around 1922 that is less well known than the just-quoted passage from *Ideen I*:

> To claim that consciousness 'relates' itself to a transcendent object through its immanent noematic Sinn (i.e. the meaning-pole X in its noematic determinations

and its positional mode as existing) is a problematic and, to be more precise, false way of speaking. I have never meant something like this. I would be surprised if this formulation could be found in 'Ideas', but in its proper context it would then surely not have this meaning. (Ms. B III 12 IV, 82a)[6]

In *Ideen I*, Husserl writes that the noematic correlate can be called a 'sense' in a very extended use of that word (Hua 3/203). The relevant question has been: how extended? One answer is given by Fink in his 1933 article 'Die phänomenologische Philosophie Edmund Husserls in der gegenwärtigen Kritik'—an article that Husserl himself introduced with the words 'it contains no sentence which I could not completely accept as my own or openly acknowledge as my own conviction' (Fink 2000: 71). Fink criticizes *Ideen I* for not having distinguished carefully enough between phenomenology and psychology and between a psychological and a transcendental conception of the noema, and then writes:

If the psychological noema is the *meaning* of an actual intentionality which is to be distinguished from the being itself to which it is related, then by contrast the transcendental noema is this being itself. (Fink 2000: 117)

The psychological noema refers to an object which is independent of it and which announces and exhibits itself within this noema. The transcendental noema cannot refer to a being beyond and independent of the infinity involved in such endless identification; the transcendental noema is the being itself, and is so in the hitherto unknown depths of its hidden meaning of being as transcendental validity. (Fink 2000: 118, translation modified)

Fink's point is that, whereas we might distinguish between the noema and the object itself as long as we remain within a psychological stance, such a distinction is no longer appropriate when we adopt a transcendental attitude. From this perspective, there is no longer any ontological distinction between the constituted validity and significance of an object and its reality and being (a statement that incidentally also spells trouble for Carr's and Crowell's interpretation). In the same article, Fink also argues that it is only possible to understand the transcendental, i.e. truly

---

[6] 'Zu sagen, daß das Bewußtsein sich durch seinen immanenten noematischen Sinn (bzw. den Sinnespol X in seinen noematischen Bestimmungen und seinem Setzungsmodus als seiend) auf einen transzendenten Gegenstand "beziehe", ist eine bedenkliche und, genau genommen, falsche Rede. Ist so verstanden nie meine Meinung gewesen. Ich würde mich wundern, wenn diese Wendung sich in den "Ideen" fände, die im Zusammenhang dann sicher nicht diesen eigentlichen Sinn hätte' (Ms. B III 12 IV, 82a).

phenomenological concept of the noema in the light of the phenomeno-logical reduction. He dismisses the suggestion that the epoché should involve a reduction to 'the inner sphere of the psychical (together with the "representation of the world" lying within it)' (Fink 2000: 117), and writes that the difference between noema and object is in reality a difference internal to the noema, since the object that is intended is nothing but a noematic identity (pp. 117–18).

In his article 'Husserls Begriff des Noema', Rudolf Bernet has argued that Husserl's early notion of the noema is highly ambiguous, and that it is possible to distinguish no fewer than three different concepts of the noema in *Ideen I* alone: (1) the noema understood as the concrete appearance, (2) the noema understood as the ideal meaning, (3) the noema understood as the constituted object (Bernet 1990: 71). Thus, as an attempt at reconciliation, it might be claimed that Husserl's concept of the noema is so equivocal that it offers itself to several different interpretations. To a certain extent, Fink's distinction between a psycho-logical and a transcendental concept of the noema can serve as a similar argument. But, of course, the central question is then *which* concept of the noema represents Husserl's mature view. For Ströker, to mention one last interpretation, Husserl's concepts of noesis and noema are transcendental-phenomenological concepts, and on her view it is, prop-erly speaking, meaningless to suppose that the intended object should lie beyond the noematic sphere, since the claim of transcendental philoso-phy is exactly that there is no such beyond, but only a constituted transcendence. According to Ströker, however, the reason why it has nevertheless been possible to find support for the thesis that the noema is merely that by means of which we intend the transcendent object is exactly because Husserl's own presentation in *Ideen I* constantly slides between the natural and the (transcendental) phenomenological attitude (Ströker 1987: 194–200).

What is quite correctly highlighted by these various remarks is that an interpretation of Husserl's noema cannot stand on its own. It must necessarily be integrated into a more general interpretation of Husserl's transcendental philosophy. As Husserl himself points out in his intro-ductory remarks to the discussion of the relation between noesis and noema in part 3 of *Ideen I*: 'One may, of course, use the term "phenom-enology," without having apprehended the uniqueness of the transcen-dental attitude and actually made the purely phenomenological terrain one's own. In that case one uses the term, but with no hold on what it designates' (Hua 3/200). To put it differently, the noema is something that is only discovered due to the epoché and the reduction, and we have already seen how a certain (mis)interpretation of the reduction can influence one's noema interpretation.

4.3 Transcendental idealism

Given the East Coast interpretation, is Husserl then to be characterized as an internalist or as an externalist? If internalism is understood as a theory claiming that our access to the world is mediated and conditioned by (an awareness of) internal representations, Husserl is certainly not an internalist. In its dismissal of representationalism, the East Coast interpretation fully shares Dreyfus's rejection of the view that our ability to relate to objects requires the existence of internal representations in the mind (cf. Drummond 2012). But it also strongly questions the claim that Husserl's theory of intentionality ignores our involvement with existing reality, and that the noema has the function it has regardless of how the world is. After all, the noema is nothing but the worldly object-as-it-is-intended. Indeed, to the question whether the noema is in the mind or in the world, the answer would have to be that the very question is misplaced in that it offers us a false alternative. On the East Coast interpretation, Husserl does not take meaning to be contained in the mind; on the contrary, he conceives of meaning as being embedded in the world and correlated with the mind. As intentional beings, we are centres of disclosure, permitting worldly objects to appear with the meaning that is their own.

At this point, however, it might be argued that this effort to save Husserl from internalism suffers from one major drawback. It utterly fails to consider Husserl's more overarching transcendental project; and the moment this is done, the moment one takes his idealism seriously, the internalist character of his thinking will reveal itself. To see why this objection is wrong, let us move on and engage directly with the question of idealism.

The first issue that needs to be settled is whether it is correct to ascribe some kind of idealism to Husserl, and whether the idealism in question must be considered an integral part of his conception of phenomenology.

That this is so can hardly be disputed, but here are two rather unequivocal statements:

Carried out with this systematic concreteness, phenomenology is *eo ipso* 'transcendental idealism', though in a fundamentally and essentially new sense. [. . .] *The proof of this idealism is therefore phenomenology itself.* Only someone who misunderstands either the deepest sense of intentional method, or that of transcendental reduction, or perhaps both, can attempt to separate phenomenology from transcendental idealism. (Hua 1/118–19)

Strictly speaking, the route into transcendental idealism already lies delineated in the phenomenological reduction, when correctly understood, just as the whole of phenomenology is nothing other than the first rigorously scientific form of this idealism. (Hua 8/181)

It would be premature to conclude that this settles the issue, however. As Husserl writes in a late text dating from 1937:

Here at the outset I require only this one thing, that one keeps these sorts of prejudice, one's knowing in advance the meaning of those words that I have furnished with entirely new sense: phenomenology, transcendental, idealism [. . .] firmly locked away in one's breast [. . .]. Initially, one hears and sees what is being presented, one goes along and sees where it might lead and what might be accomplished with it. (Hua 6/440)

To put it differently, the issue is not whether Husserl was committed to a form of idealism. The issue is what precisely this idealism amounted to.

A few scholars have suggested that when Husserl talks of idealism, he is simply insisting on the indispensability of the ideal. In *Logische Untersuchungen*, he did indeed write that a position that defends the existence of ideal objects, or idealities, can be called idealism, and that such an idealism is a requirement for a coherent epistemology (Hua 19/112). Thus, Willard has argued that Husserl never was an idealist except insofar as he accepted universals (Willard 2011), and D. W. Smith has argued that Husserl's transcendental idealism can be interpreted as a theory about how our intentional directedness relies on ideal meaning (Smith 2013: 166). The claim that this is all that Husserl meant by idealism is hard to maintain, however. Surely, something else is at stake in the following passage:

The being-in-itself of the world might make good sense, but one thing is absolutely certain, it cannot have the sense that the world is independent of an actually existing consciousness. The world is in principle only what it is as the correlate of an experiencing consciousness that is related to it, and as correlate of a real and not merely a possible consciousness. (Hua 36/78)

To get a better grip of what Husserl might mean by idealism, let us consider some texts found in the volume *Transzendentaler Idealismus: Texte aus dem Nachlass (1908–1921)*. In text number 6, which stems from the lecture course *Ausgewählte phänomenologische Probleme* given in the summer of 1915, Husserl starts out by observing that nothing might seem more natural than to say that the objects I am aware of are outside my consciousness. When my experiences—be they perceptions or other kinds of intentional acts—present me with objects, one must ask how this could happen, and the answer seems straightforward: by means of some representational mediation. The objects of which I am conscious are outside my consciousness, but inside my consciousness, I find representations (pictures and signs) of these objects, and it is these internal objects that enable me to be conscious of the external ones. However, as Husserl then continues, such a theory is not only empirically false, it is also completely nonsensical. It conceives of consciousness as a box containing representations that resemble external objects, but it forgets to ask how the subject is supposed to know that the representations are in fact representations of external objects:

The I is not a tiny man in a box that looks at the pictures and then occasionally leaves his box in order to compare the external objects with the internal ones etc. For such a picture observing I, the picture would itself be something external; it would require its own matching internal picture, and so on *ad infinitum*. (Hua 36/106)

Husserl leaves us in no doubt regarding his contempt for such a homunculus model. As he continues, a picture or a sign is not an object, which next to its other qualities, such as form, size, and colour, also has the picture quality or sign quality. Some have argued that a picture is something that resembles what it depicts, and that it is the resemblance that imbues the picture with its pictorial or representational quality. But mere resemblances will not do. A field might contain numerous leaves of grass that resemble each other, but that does not make one leaf a picture or sign of the other. Furthermore, whereas resemblance is a reciprocal relation, representation is not. Rather, according to Husserl we should realize that a picture must be consciously apprehended *as* a picture in order to function as a representation of something else (Hua 36/106–7). It only acquires its representational quality by means of a special cognitive apprehension. More specifically, we first *perceive* the object that is to function as a sign or picture, and only subsequently do we confer its representational quality upon it. This is why the representational theory of perception must be rejected. It presupposes that which it seeks to explain.

Perception does not confront us with pictures or images of objects—except, of course, insofar as we are perceiving paintings or photographs—but with the objects themselves. In fact, this is for Husserl the defining feature of perception. Whereas we can think of objects, and thereby intend them, even in their absence, the situation is different when it comes to perceptual intentionality. Perception presents us with the object itself in its bodily presence. When we say that something *appears* perceptually, this should consequently not be understood in the sense that the perceptually given is a picture or sign of something else (Hua 36/ 107). Thus, it is clear that Husserl would dismiss the following view, which is currently defended by quite a number of neuroscientists:

> When you and I look at an object outside ourselves, we form comparable images in our respective brains. We know this well because you and I can describe the object in very similar ways, down to fine details. But that does not mean that the image we see is the copy of whatever the object outside is like. Whatever it is like, in absolute terms, we do not know. (Damasio 1999: 320)

If we are to understand the proper nature of Husserl's idealism, it is of paramount importance to be clear about his resolute rejection of the representationalist claim that our mind cannot on its own reach all the way to the objects themselves, and to understand that we therefore need to introduce some kind of representational interface between the mind and the world if we are to comprehend and explain intentionality.

Representationalism notoriously courts scepticism. Why should awareness of one thing (an inner object) enable awareness of a quite different thing (an external object), and how can we ever know that what is internally accessible actually corresponds to something external? On Husserl's anti-representationalist view, however, the fit and link between mind and world—between perception and reality—isn't merely external or coincidental: 'consciousness (experience) and real being are anything but coordinated sorts of being that peacefully live alongside one another, occasionally "relating" to one another or "linking up" with one another' (Hua 3/105). It is not as if we have two independently variable dimensions that by happenstance fit each other, as if the manifold of appearances could be given in a regulated way and the object still fail to exist, or the object exist even in the absence of the possibility of such givenness (Hua 36/30, 36/56). Rather, 'object, objective being, and consciousness belong *a priori* inseparably together' (Hua 36/73). This claim is one that resounds throughout Husserl's oeuvre. As he, years later, would write in *Cartesianische Meditationen,* it is absurd to conceive of consciousness and true being as if they were merely externally related, when the truth is that they are essentially interdependent and united (Hua 1/117).

How do they belong together? Husserl's fundamental claim is that *cogito* and *cogitatum* are bound constitutively together. As it was already phrased in *Logische Untersuchungen:*

the objects of which we are 'conscious', are not simply *in* consciousness as in a box, so that they can merely be found in it and snatched at in it; but that they are first *constituted* as being what they are for us, and as what they count as for us, in varying forms of objective intention. (Hua 19/169 [I/275])

What does this constitutive relationship that supposedly obtains between consciousness and reality amount to? Philipse and Smith both argue that it must be interpreted as a metaphysical dependence, and this is why they argue that Husserl is a metaphysical idealist.

We have already come across Philipse's interpretation. In his long essay *Transcendental Idealism,* Philipse claims that Husserl is a reductive idealist in both his early and later works. The world is ontologically dependent upon consciousness, since the former is nothing but a projection of the latter (Philipse 1995: 266).

In *Husserl and the Cartesian Meditations,* A. D. Smith makes it clear that one would misunderstand the fundamental thrust of Husserl's transcendental project if one thought it excluded questions regarding existence and reality. As Smith points out, phenomenology isn't merely concerned with the question of how consciousness is involved in the constitution of any object sense; it also addresses the question of what it means for a given type of object to exist and be real (Smith 2003: 159). To that extent, the topic of reality is crucial to Husserl's transcendental inquiry (p. 167). For Husserl, reality is a regulative ideal; it is the ideal correlate of an ultimate intersubjective confirmation. It would for Husserl make no sense to suppose that a world meeting this strong condition of ultimate, intersubjective confirmation should yet prove to be unreal. However, what follows from this, according to Smith, is that Husserl, rather than merely being a transcendental idealist like Kant, is in fact an absolute idealist. One who would claim that nothing would exist in the absence of consciousness (p. 179). More specifically, Smith proposes that Husserl's idealism amounts to the claim that physical facts and entities supervene on consciousness, they are nothing over and above experiential facts (pp. 183–5). Even if this doesn't entail that physical objects are simply mental states, or constructions out of these, the way they depend upon mental states is still such that Smith might be said to ascribe a form of sophisticated phenomenalism to Husserl.

Philipse and Smith both interpret the constitutive relation as a relation of metaphysical dependence. The very notion of metaphysical dependence is, however, also open to various interpretations. Many of these can be ruled out straight away. This goes, for instance, for the suggestion that metaphysical dependence amounts to causal dependence. Had that been the case, it would have turned the transcendental subject into some kind of prime mover, and made transcendental phenomenology a direct competitor of various astrophysical theories regarding the birth of the universe. Given that Husserl on many occasions distinguishes causality from intentionality, and explicitly warns against a countersensical conflation of psychophysical causation and intentional correlation (Hua 19/405, 17/223), I think we can safely leave aside this interpretation. Such a decision is also supported by a remark found in *Ideen I*, where Husserl makes it clear that consciousness is absolute in a totally different sense from that in which a divine being might be said to be absolute (Hua 3/125). Another possibility is to interpret the metaphysical dependence as a form of reducibility. But given that Husserl has frequently and quite explicitly distanced himself from phenomenalism, this is also not a viable option. As Husserl points out, if we carefully analyse a physical object, it will eventually dissolve not in consciousness, but in atoms and molecules (Hua 3/355, 36/28). As he also writes in texts from 1908 and 1923:

The objects of nature are obviously true objects; their being is true being, and nature is real in the true and full sense of the word. [. . .] And to say that natural science has nothing to do with nature, that the true objects it engages with are mere sensations, and that what we call things, atoms, etc., are merely symbols, abbreviations in our economy of thought, for sensations and complexes of sensations, is the pinnacle of wrongness. (Hua 36/70–71)

An idealism that so to speak beats matter to death, which explains away experienced nature as a mere illusion and which only admits truth to the being of the psyche, is nonsensical. (Hua 35/276)

Nature is real in the true and full sense of the word, and it would be misguided to measure the being of nature with a yardstick that belongs elsewhere in order somehow to discredit its status (Hua 36/70–71). Thus, Husserl would never propose that statements about botanical or geological states of affairs are henceforth to be reinterpreted as statements about mental processes. Indeed, whatever Husserl meant by idealism, it certainly didn't entail a denial of the difference between mind and world, subject and object. As he pointed out in *Ideen I*, a material thing 'is intrinsically not an experience but instead a totally different kind of being' (Hua 3/71).

A third option is to follow Smith, who as we have just seen interprets the constitutive relation as a question of supervenience (Smith 2003: 183; cf. Meixner 2010). One attractive feature of this suggestion is that one could then maintain that the object of consciousness is constitutively dependent upon the act of consciousness, without claiming that the former is identical with or definable in terms of the latter. Rather than making the metaphysical dependence reductive in kind, it would be more akin to a relation of founding. However, whereas Husserl does indeed frequently speak of relations of founding obtaining between both different types of acts as well as between different kinds of objects, he does not characterize the relation between act and object as one of founding. And with good reason, I think. If we are to clarify the constitution of an everyday object, say a loaf of bread, the constitutive analysis is not going to include references to macroscopic constituents like flour, yeast, and salt, nor will there be any reference to microscopic constituents like atoms and molecules. The constitutive analysis will rather include references to various noeses, to perceptions, to horizons, apperceptions, positings, kinesthetic sensations, etc. But the reason for their inclusion is not due to the fact that atoms and molecules supervene on conscious processes in the same way, say, as the aesthetic properties of a clay statue of Apollo supervene on the properties of the lump of clay that constitute it. To claim that the relation that obtains between the constituting subject and the constituted object is a relation of founding or supervenience would supposedly entail that a sufficiently thorough investigation of the object would eventually lead us to its supervenience base and metaphysical source, namely transcendental subjectivity. But such a proposal is misguided. If transcendental subjectivity is to be disclosed, it will be by means of a reflective move, and not by means of a meticulous investigation and dissection of the object. The proposal also erodes the distinction between transcendental idealism and metaphysical idealism, and makes it inexplicable why Husserl distinguished between the two and was happy to embrace the former while rejecting the latter.

We have, of course, already come across one alternative, deflationary interpretation of Husserl's idealism. It consists in interpreting the transcendental reduction in such a way that it involves metaphysical neutrality and a concern with the meaning and sense of reality (Carr 1999: 74). On such a reading, Husserl's idealism is taken to be of a methodological kind rather than of a substantial or metaphysical kind, and all that transcendental subjectivity can be said to be constituting is the meaning of the world and not its being (Carr 1999).

As should be clear by now, however, I think this is the wrong way to counter the interpretations of Philipse and Smith. I do not think it is correct to interpret transcendental phenomenology as if it is metaphysically neutral and in principle compatible with a variety of different metaphysical views, such as objectivism, eliminativism, or subjective idealism. Husserl's idealism is not transcendental rather than metaphysical, because it lacks metaphysical impact. Husserl's idealism is not transcendental rather than metaphysical, because Husserl retained the notion of the *Ding an sich* and like Kant believed that 'we cannot have knowledge of the intrinsic nature of reality' (Allais 2015: 232). No, Husserl's idealism is transcendental rather than metaphysical, because of the way in which he interprets the dependency relation. For a comparison, consider the (once widespread) claim that reality is language-dependent. It would be rather odd to interpret such a claim as if it were meant to suggest that, say, a physical object is either reducible to or supervenes on language. It is equally odd—indeed, a category mistake— to interpret transcendental idealism as amounting to the claim that the mind-dependence of reality is due to the fact that worldly objects can be reduced to or supervene on the 'stuff' that mental states are made of. Transcendental idealism is not participating in or contributing to the debate between monists and dualists. Its adversary is not materialism, but objectivism. Its aim is to understand the status of reality and the nature of objectivity, and its claim is that the following correlational principle holds true:

No object is thinkable as actual without the actual subjectivity that is capable of realizing this object in actual cognition. One can very well say, no object without a subject, and no subject without an object, where object should be taken in the broadest possible sense. (Hua 35/277–8)

Such phrasing might suggest straightforward equality, but, of course, although Husserl might be denying the existence of a mindless world, he is (in)famous for not having ruled out the existence of a worldless mind. As Husserl writes in the notorious §49 of *Ideen I*, pure consciousness can be considered an independent realm of being; even though consciousness would be modified if the world of objects were annihilated, it would not be affected in its own existence (Hua 3/104–5). This is not to be dismissed as an isolated blunder. We can find various other statements from the period 1913–15 in which Husserl repeats what he said in *Ideen I* and claims that the existence of consciousness does not require an actually existing world (Hua 36/78–9). Whereas the existence of consciousness is absolute and necessary, the existence of the world is merely accidental and relative (Hua 36/111). This is also why consciousness, according to Husserl, must be considered the root (*'Wurzel'*) or source (*'Quelle'*) of every other form of being (Hua 36/70).

Can one really reconcile such statements with the claim that Husserl is neither an internalist nor a metaphysical idealist? Let us take a closer look.

To start with, it is important to make it clear that Husserl's imagined annihilation of the world should not be seen as an endorsement of some kind of global scepticism. Husserl is not trying to drive a wedge between the world that is given to us and the real world, as if the world could appear as it does while nevertheless not really existing. In short, if the required regularities of experience obtain and if 'nothing was lacking that would be requisite for the appearance of a uniform world' (Hua 3/105), would it then still be '*conceivable* and not rather absurd for the corresponding, transcendent world *not* to be' (Hua 3/105)? If anybody should be uncertain about the rhetorical character of that question, Husserl's is even clearer in later texts. There again, he asks whether the presence of a system of coherently ordered and rationally motivated intentional experiences might be compatible with the world not existing (or being utterly different). His reply is that such a proposal, which he identifies with both Cartesian dualism and traditional realism, is completely non-sensical ('*vollkommener Widersinn*') (Hua 34/402, 39/248). So again, rather than reading §49 as testifying to either an unprecedented strong form of internalism or some kind of crude phenomenalism, I think it testifies to Husserl's insistence on the world-involving character of *intentional experience*. In the case of perception, for instance, a perceptual act is an act that involves the presence to consciousness of the object perceived, which is why the former cannot occur in the absence of the latter. At the same time, however, Husserl also wants to insist on the possibility of non-intentional consciousness. Thus, contrary to a widespread misinterpretation, Husserl is not saying that consciousness is essentially characterized by intentionality, and he is not saying that the existence or non-existence of the world makes no difference to intentional consciousness. The world-annihilation is not supposed to show that every type of experience is compatible with the absence of the world or that every type of experience would remain the same even if the world didn't exist. The point is quite different: that some form of consciousness could exist and persist even when not being world-disclosing, i.e. even in cases where there is not yet (say, in infantile experience) or no longer (say, in psychosis) a harmonious and coherently regulated set of experiences that allow for the constitution of worldly objects. Thus, when Husserl writes that '*no real being*, none of the sort that would display and identify itself through appearances in conformity with consciousness, *is necessary for the being of consciousness itself* (in the widest sense of the stream of experience)' (Hua 3/104), he is affirming the possibility of non-intentional experiences.

Before proceeding, let me emphasize that I am not disputing that Husserl's account in section 2, chapter 3 of *Ideen I* (§§47–55) is problematic. First of all—and this was something that attracted criticism early on—it is by no means obvious that the possibility of a breakdown or disintegration of one's object-experience also entails the possibility of a breakdown in one's world-experience. To make this move is to ignore the difference between an object and the world. This was, however, later on recognized by Husserl, who, for instance, in a text from 1937 states that the very possibility of doubt and non-being presupposes the being of the world (Hua 39/254), and that the possibility of doubting every single object does not entail that the totality of the world is also doubtful (Hua 39/256). Fallibility regarding worldly objects cannot without further ado be transferred to the world itself.

Another problematic feature of Husserl's discussion in *Ideen I* is his repeated reference to transcendental subjectivity as an independent 'region' of being (Hua 3/108, 3/159). Such a phrasing suggests that the investigation of transcendental subjectivity is a regional-ontological investigation comparable to the investigation of, say, the region of ideal objects or physical objects. But this approach arguably misses what is unique and distinctive about the transcendental inquiry. I earlier referenced Ströker's claim that Husserl's presentation in *Ideen I* is marred by the fact that he tends to slide between the natural and the transcendental attitudes. I think this verdict also holds true of his account in §§49ff., and can explain why he occasionally expresses himself inadequately. Consider, for example, Husserl's statements that 'consciousness considered in its *"purity"* must be held to be a *self-contained complex of being* into which nothing can penetrate and out of which nothing can slip' (Hua 3/105) and that the experiential region 'is in itself rigidly closed off' (Hua 3/108). When read in isolation, both statements appear overly Cartesian and seem to confirm the suspicion that Husserl is advocating the view that the mind is an isolated substance. When considered more carefully, however, it becomes clear that Husserl, despite the awkward phrasings, is actually seeking to articulate a quite different idea. Whereas the first quote continues 'to which nothing is spatiotemporally external and which cannot be within any spatiotemporal complex' (Hua 3/105), the continuation of the second quote reads 'and yet without borders that could separate it from other regions' (Hua 3/108). In both cases—and this is an interpretation I will return to and defend in more detail in section 4.5— Husserl is rejecting the idea that the relation between consciousness and what is other than consciousness, i.e. between transcendental being and transcendent being, can be adequately characterized with the help of the spatial metaphors of 'inner' and 'outer'. Transcendental subjectivity is not one region of being next to (or perhaps more fundamental than) other regions, but a dative of manifestation that constitutively grounds any kind of inter- or intraregional (inter)dependency relation. To conceive of the constitutive relation and of the intentional correlation in terms of supervenience is precisely to overlook this point.

Let me finally also acknowledge that the transcendental idealism we find espoused in these paragraphs of *Ideen I*, by focusing exclusively on the contribution of the solitary subject, fails to properly address the problem of intersubjectivity. It is important to realize, though, that this limitation was partially self-chosen, rather than expressive of Husserl's conviction at the time. Already by 1913, Husserl was aware of the transcendental significance of intersubjectivity, and as he explains in a preface written especially for the English translation of *Ideen I* (1931), the reason why his original presentation did not account for transcendental intersubjectivity, and thereby omitted a crucial aspect of a comprehensive analysis of the foundation of idealism, was because this account was supposed to have been supplied by *Ideen II*, which had been drafted at the same time as *Ideen I*, and which Husserl had expected to see published shortly after the latter work (Hua 5/150). As it turned out, *Ideen II* was only published posthumously, with almost forty years' delay, in 1952. And as Husserl remarks with regret in the preface from 1931, much of the scandal caused by his idealism and its alleged solipsism might have been avoided if the account offered in *Ideen I* had not been incomplete (Hua 5/150–51). As we shall see in section 4.6, rather than being committed to a form of solipsism, Husserl's idealism assigns a crucial transcendental role to the intersubjective community of embodied subjects. For now, however, let us return to §49.

In that paragraph, Husserl is not only talking about the possibility of non-intentional experiences; he is also claiming that whereas objects possess relative being, the subject possesses absolute being (Hua 3/105). Does such a claim not support those who argue that Husserl is a metaphysical or even absolute idealist? In order to decide the matter, it is crucial to get clear on what exactly Husserl means by 'absolute' and 'absolute being'. It is here decisive not to forget the phenomenological context. Husserl often speaks about 'absolute givenness' (Hua 3/92, 97, 105). One suggestion might consequently be that all that Husserl means by calling consciousness 'absolute' is that consciousness in contrast to spatial objects does not appear perspectivally or adumbrationally. This answer falls short, though. A more adequate answer can be found in Husserl's discussion of inner time-consciousness, since that is where we find his most frequent references to the absolute (see, e.g. Hua 10/73, 75, 83, 112). As he writes in *Ideen I*, only an analysis of inner time-consciousness will disclose the truly absolute dimension (Hua 3/182).

Let us recall Husserl's reason for investigating time-consciousness in the first place. His analysis was supposed to serve a double purpose. It was meant to explain not only how we can be aware of objects with temporal extension, but also how we can be aware of our own stream of experiences. The reason why he speaks of a phenomenological absolute and, more generally, of the analysis of temporality as constituting the bedrock of phenomenology is precisely because it is much more than an investigation of the temporal givenness of objects. It is also an account of the temporal *self-givenness* of consciousness itself.

In a manner not unlike Sartre, Husserl was committed to the idea that the experiential dimension is as such characterized by a pre-reflective givenness (see Zahavi 1999; 2003a; 2004; 2005). On his account, reflective self-consciousness is founded. When we reflect, the experience that we reflect upon is not simply given as existing here and now, but also as having already been given prior to reflection. That is, it is in the nature of reflection to grasp something that was already given prior to and independently of the grasping. The reason an intentional act can become the object of a reflection is precisely because it was already conscious. Indeed, ultimately Husserl would argue that the experiential dimension as such is inherently self-manifesting:

When I say 'I,' I grasp myself in a simple reflection. But this self-experience [*Selbsterfahrung*] is like every experience [*Erfahrung*], and in particular every perception, a mere directing myself towards something that was already there for me, that was already conscious, but not thematically experienced, not noticed. (Hua 15/492–3)

We can reflect on each act and in so doing turn it into an object of an act of immanent 'perception.' Prior to this perception (to which belongs the form of the cogito), we have the 'inner consciousness' which lacks this form. (Hua 4/118)

The flow of the consciousness that constitutes immanent time not only *exists* but is so remarkably and yet intelligibly fashioned that a self-appearance of the flow necessarily exists in it, and therefore the flow itself must necessarily be apprehensible in the flowing. The self-appearance of the flow does not require a second flow; on the contrary, it constitutes itself as a phenomenon in itself. (Hua 10/83)

That the notion of the absolute is intimately linked to the issue of self-consciousness, self-presencing, or self-manifestation is explicitly affirmed by Husserl on numerous occasions:

An absolute existent is existent in the form, an intentional life—which, no matter what else it may be intrinsically conscious of, is, at the same time, consciousness of itself. (Hua 17/279)

Thus only the subject has an abidingly actualised and actually independent being; or as we can also say, an absolute being, understood precisely as being in being-for-itself. (Hua 35/278)

Or, as it is rephrased a couple of pages later: the reality of the I is the reality of 'An absolute being, a being that is self-experiencing and self-constituting' (Hua 35/282; see also 15/371–2). In short, subjectivity is for-itself, it is self-manifesting or self-constituting, whereas this determination, for Husserl, is something that all objects by definition lack (Hua 35/278). Objects are constituted by subjects; their manifestation is always a manifestation *for* somebody. This is why subjectivity is absolute, and objects relative and dependent.

It is easy to demonstrate that Husserl was not the only phenomenologist to employ the notion of the absolute in this way. Consider the following statement by Sartre in his introductions to *L'être et le néant*:

Consciousness has nothing substantial, it is pure 'appearance' in the sense that it exists only to the degree to which it appears. But it is precisely because consciousness is pure appearance, because it is total emptiness (since the entire world is outside it)—it is because of this identity of appearance and existence within it that it can be considered as the absolute. (Sartre 2003: 12; see also Merleau-Ponty 2012: lxxii)

An even clearer articulation of this conception of the absolute can be found in the work of Henry. As Henry points out, phenomenology is quite unlike positive sciences such as physics, chemistry, biology, history, and law. Rather than studying particular objects and phenomena, phenomenology is a distinct transcendental enterprise the task of which is to disclose and analyse the condition of possibility for manifestation. In the course of his own investigation, Henry dwells upon what he considers the radical and decisive difference between the phenomenality of constituted objects and the phenomenality of constituting subjectivity, i.e. the radical difference between object-manifestation and self-manifestation (Henry 1973: 40–1), and argues that whereas object-manifestation presupposes self-manifestation, the reverse dependency doesn't hold. It is only because we are already given to ourselves that we can be affected by the world (Henry 1973: 467, 479, 490), or, as Henry writes, '*Self-manifestation is the essence of manifestation*' (Henry 1973: 143). One of his further claims is that self-manifestation is an immediate, non-objectifying and passive occurrence, and therefore best described as a purely interior 'self-affection' (Henry 1973: 234–6, 243), and it is in this context that he comes to talk of the absolute. In his view, subjectivity is absolute in the sense of being irrelative and completely self-sufficient in its radical interiority:

Affectivity reveals the absolute in its totality because it is nothing other than its perfect adherence to self, nothing other than its coincidence with self, because it is the auto-affection of Being in the absolute unity of its radical immanence. (Henry 1973: 682)

When Henry talks of the absolute, he is talking about the self-sufficiency of self-manifestation. When Husserl talked of the absolute, he was making a similar claim. As we shall see in a moment, however, there are reasons to think that Husserl later came to modify this claim in an important way.

4.4 Facticity and constitution

For Husserl reality is constituted by consciousness. To that extent, Smith is right in saying that for Husserl nothing would exist—nothing would be real, nothing would be objective and mind-independent—in the absence of consciousness. But is this really an 'extreme' idealist claim (Smith 2003: 179)? After all, there is quite a difference between the claim that consciousness is a necessary condition and the far more radical claim that consciousness is a sufficient condition, which is how Philipse (1995: 311) reads Husserl. Compare Boehm, who in an article originally published in 1959 wrote:

> [N]othing could be if there were no absolute consciousness. This does *not* mean, however, that everything which is exists *by means of* absolute consciousness. [...] *[T]here is nothing without absolute consciousness, although there is also nothing with absolute consciousness alone.* Namely, consciousness is a transcendental absolute insofar as it is the 'absolutely' necessary foundation for all other (real) being. But by no means does—or can—all other being exist if there is simply absolute consciousness. [...] Transcendental consciousness is not an absolute being such that it is able to create all other (real) being from the being that is its own. (Boehm 2000: 184)

It is no coincidence, I think, that Husserl frequently spoke of how an object 'constitutes itself' ('*konstituiert sich*') in consciousness (e.g. Hua 1/102, 1/120, 1/137, 3/117, 3/275, 4/23, 15/19). To understand properly the character of the constitutive accomplishment, we need to keep the correlation in mind. An appearance is an appearance *of* something *for* somebody. There is not only a dative of manifestation, but also a genitive of manifestation, and as Levinas once observed in a contribution fittingly entitled 'The ruin of representation' which he wrote for a commemorative volume on Husserl:

> Intentionality means that all consciousness is consciousness of something, but above all that *every object calls forth and as it were gives rise to the consciousness through which its being shines and, in doing so, appears.* (Levinas 1998: 119)

In his own writings, Husserl often made it clear that the concrete ego cannot be thought of independently of its relation to that which is foreign to it (Hua 14/14). This was already spelled out in his theory of intentionality:

It actually belongs to the essence of the intentional relation (which is precisely the relation between consciousness and the object of consciousness), that consciousness, i.e. the respective *cogitatio*, is conscious of something that is not itself. (Hua 13/170)

The I is not conceivable without a non-I that it is intentionally related to. (Hua 14/244)

The I is not something for itself, just as what is foreign to the I is not something separate from it, and between the two there is no space in which to turn; rather the I and what is foreign to it are inseparable. (Hua Mat 8/351–2)

Husserl's reference to sense-bestowal ('*Sinngebung*') (e.g. Hua 3/192–4) does evoke the picture of an active subject that freely imposes structure and meaning, thereby resulting in the kind of 'frictionless spinning in a void' that McDowell has warned against (McDowell 1994: 11). But as the following quotes show, Husserl did fully realize the importance of passivity:

[E]goic activity presupposes passivity—egoic passivity—and both presuppose association and preconsciousness in the form of the ultimate hyletic substratum. (Hua Mat 8/53)

We would then have to say that the concrete I has, throughout its life as conscious life, a core of hyle, of what is not I but essentially belongs to the I. Without a realm of pregivenness, a realm of constituted unities, constituted as non-I, no I is possible. (Hua 14/379)

In early works such as *Logische Untersuchungen* and *Ideen I*, Husserl argued that sensory experiences only become intentional after being animated by an objectifying interpretation (Hua 3/192). It has often been claimed that his reliance on the notion of a non-intentional sensory experience reveals his indebtedness to the sensualism of British empiricism, rather than being the outcome of a proper phenomenological analysis. Not only is it difficult to identify and recognize these (supposedly) meaningless sensory experiences in ordinary life, where we always are already faced with meaningful experiences, but the suggestion that our sensory experiences are per se meaningless also makes it incomprehensible how they could ever guide and constrain our interpretation. As has been documented in the scholarly literature, however, Husserl eventually came to abandon the strict division between sensations and intentions (Sokolowski 1970: 142–3) and came to view the former as intrinsically meaningful (Sokolowski 1970: 210–11; Holenstein 1972: 86–117). It is no coincidence that in *Cartesianische Meditationen* he was keen to distinguish his own form of idealism from the idealism of 'sensualistic psychologism' which attempts to 'derive a senseful world from senseless sensuous data' (Hua 1/118). On Husserl's later view, our sensory experience is not self-enclosed, but is rather seen as an openness towards the world, even if it is not yet a world of fully constituted objects. As sensed, the passively pre-given hyletic datum is already the manifested worldly being: 'Hyle in the extended sense as the impressional or perceptual worldly appearing as such' (Hua Mat 8/ 70). Nevertheless, a distinction remains in place. The sensed remains underdetermined and inchoate; it is only by apprehending and interpreting it as something that a full-fledged object is constituted. We can still distinguish between hearing an increasing loudness and hearing an approaching car, or feeling a localized pain and feeling the prick of a needle.

Whatever one holds of Husserl's reference to the hyle, one thing ought to be clear. His account of constitution does not commit him to the view that the content of experience can somehow be deduced from formal egoic structures. His recurrent reference to the role of facticity is precisely meant to rule this out.

> The word 'impression' is appropriate only to original sensations; the word expresses well what is 'there' of itself, and indeed originally: namely, what is pregiven to the Ego, presenting itself to the Ego in the manner of something affecting it as foreign [*ichfremd*]. (Hua 4/336)

> Consciousness is nothing without impression. When something endures, then a passes into xa', xa' into yx'a", and so on. But the production for which consciousness is responsible only reaches from a to a', from xa' to x'a"; the a, x, y, on the other hand, is nothing produced by consciousness. It is what is primally produced—the 'new,' that which has come into being alien to consciousness, that which has been received, as opposed to what has been produced through consciousness's own spontaneity. The peculiarity of this spontaneity of consciousness, however, is that it creates nothing 'new' but only brings what has been primally generated to growth, to development. (Hua 10/100)

The hyle is a domain of facticity which escapes my control and which is passively pre-given without any active participation or contribution by the ego (Hua 13/427, 11/386). And, as Husserl argues in manuscripts from 1931, far from being an independent and sole principle of constitution, the constituting ego is dependent upon its relation to the non-ego and relies upon the primordial fact of the hyle, without which no world and no intersubjectivity would be possible. We are here, as Husserl writes, dealing with the ultimate facts or primordial facts (Hua 15/385). Thus, it might even be argued that constitution has two primal sources, the primal ego and the primal non-ego. Both are inseparably one, and thus abstract if regarded on their own (Hua Mat 8/199). Both are irreducible structural moments in the process of constitution, the process of bringing to appearance. Since Husserl occasionally identifies the non-ego with the world (Hua 15/131, 15/287)—thereby operating with a more fundamental notion of the world than the concept of an objective reality which he attempted to annihilate in §49 of *Ideen I*—and even speaks of the world as the 'transcendental non-ego' (Hua Mat 8/120)—it seems natural to conclude that, although he certainly took subjectivity to be a condition of possibility for manifestation, he did not consider it the only one. That is, although it is a necessary condition, it is not a sufficient one. Ultimately, the process of constitution must be conceived as a process involving several intertwined transcendental constituents. Subjectivity and world are both necessary, and cannot be understood in separation from each other. To ask what one is without the other is like asking what a background is in itself, independently of the foreground. Husserl's position consequently seems rather close to the one Merleau-Ponty is articulating in the following passage:

The world is inseparable from the subject, but from a subject who is nothing but a project of the world; and the subject is inseparable from the world, but from a world that it itself projects. The subject is being-in-the-world and the world remains 'subjective,' since its texture and its articulations are sketched out by the subject's movement of transcendence. (Merleau-Ponty 2012: 454)

So far, I have argued that Husserl did not claim that transcendental subjectivity qua dative of manifestation is a sufficient constitutive principle. One might, however, wonder whether his analyses did not eventually also lead him to a position where consciousness is considered indispensable rather than absolute, i.e. where the self-sufficiency of its self-manifestation is put into question.

We have already seen how Husserl characterized the investigation of inner time-consciousness as an investigation of the truly absolute dimension (Hua 3/182). In *Analysen zur passiven Synthesis*, however, he also explicitly states that inner time-consciousness taken on its own is a pure but *abstract* form:

> If, now, time-consciousness is the primordial place of the constitution of the unity of identity or of an objectlike formation, [. . .], then we are still only talking about that consciousness which produces a general form. Mere form is admittedly an abstraction, and thus from the very beginning the analysis of the intentionality of time-consciousness and its accomplishment is an analysis that works on <the level of> abstractions. (Hua 11/128)

The analysis of time-consciousness is abstract in the sense that it only addresses certain formal structures of intentional consciousness (Hua 11/163–4, 174). The tripartite structure of inner time-consciousness (protention-primal impression-retention) must be appreciated as an account of the (micro)structure of self-manifestation, but there can be no primal impression without a content, and the most basic content is provided by our sensuous affectivity (Hua 5/11). This is why Husserl can write, 'We regard sensing as the original consciousness of time' (Hua 10/107), and why he eventually insists that the phenomenology of inner time-consciousness must be complemented by a phenomenology of *association* dealing with the fundamental laws and forms governing the syntheses pertaining to the *content* (Hua 11/118, 11/128, 1/28). Against this background, one might then wonder whether the self-manifestation of consciousness is as self-reliant and self-sufficient as Husserl made it out to be in works like *Ideen I*, or whether self-manifestation does not always go hand in hand with hetero-manifestation. In Straus's memorable words, 'In sensory experience I always experience myself *and* the world at the same time, not myself directly and the *Other* by inference, not myself before the *Other*, not myself without the *Other*, nor the *Other* without myself' (Straus 1958: 148).[7]

I have rejected the claim that Husserl is conceiving of a worldless ego as the sole and supreme ground of constitution. But his reference to facticity, his appeal to the world as a transcendental non-ego, i.e. as a contributing factor, and the fact that 'constituted by' does not mean

---

[7] For a more comprehensive discussion of this topic, see Zahavi (1999).

'being composed of' or 'supervening on' or 'being causally dependent upon', do not entail—contrary to what both Sebold and Hardy have recently proposed (Sebold 2014: 230; Hardy 2013: 101)—that Husserl's transcendental idealism is ultimately compatible with metaphysical realism. Husserl's account of the constitution of objectivity is not simply an account of how we as epistemic agents come to gain access to an already independently existing objective reality. As Sartre wrote in an early text on Husserl's theory of intentionality:

> Against the digestive philosophy of empirico-criticism, of neo-Kantianism, against all 'psychologism,' Husserl persistently affirmed that one cannot dissolve things in consciousness. You see this tree, to be sure. But you see it just where it is: at the side of the road, in the midst of the dust, alone and writhing in the heat, eight miles from the Mediterranean coast. It could not enter into your consciousness, for it is not of the same nature as consciousness. [. . .] But Husserl is not a realist: this tree on its bit of parched earth is not an absolute that would subsequently enter into communication with me. Consciousness and the world are given at one stroke: essentially external to consciousness, the world is nevertheless essentially relative to consciousness. (Sartre 1970: 4)

In her recent work on Kant, Allais has contrasted essentially manifest properties with manifest properties. Whereas the latter are properties of objects that can be presented to us in experience, the former are properties whose existence is not independent of the possibility of being presented to us in experience (Allais 2015: 101). Much of what Allais says about the essentially manifest in Kant (Allais 2015: ch. 5) can also be used to clarify Husserl's position.

For Husserl, the lesson of intentionality is that there is something transcendent to consciousness, something transcendent that is available and accessible to and correlated with consciousness. The mind is essentially open and reality is essentially manifest. Everything that is real must in principle be something we can become acquainted with, something that can be presented to us in experience. To speak of an object being presented for consciousness is necessarily to speak of a relation between two interdependent factors, an object and a conscious subject. The qualities, features, and properties of the former cannot be divorced from their relation to the latter. To that extent, they are mind-dependent, but this does not mean that they literally exist in the mind or that they are intramental modifications or constructions. Nor does it mean that they only exist when actually experienced. Objects have their essentially manifest properties even when not being experienced, and can also truth-fully possess them before the emergence of conscious creatures and after their eventual extinction. They exist in public space and are inter-subjectively accessible and are to that extent given as transcendent; but as essentially manifestable, they do not have a nature that transcends what can be given in experience.

For Husserl, the study of intentionality doesn't merely tell us some-thing about the workings of the mind, it also gives us insight into the status of reality. It does so since mind and world are bound together. Husserl is a correlationist—to use a term that I will later have reason to return to—and by being that he is well beyond both metaphysical neutrality and metaphysical realism. As Beck wrote in 1928:

'Correlationism' can here serve as the term for a position developed by Husserl and Dilthey, according to which the old alternatives between idealism or realism, subjectivism or objectivism, philosophy of immanence and phenomenalism or philosophy of the real, must be overcome in favour of the following claim: Neither does a world in itself exist independently of consciousness, nor does only consciousness or a conscious subject exist and the world merely as a mode (experience, function, content) of consciousness or the subject. And neither do we know the world as it is in itself, i.e. independently of our consciousness, nor do we merely know an illusory world, behind which the real, true world exists in itself. The positive counter-thesis of correlationism is the following: Conscious-ness and world, subject and object, I and world stand in a correlative, i.e. mutually dependent context of being, such that the disjunctions mentioned above are meaningless. (Beck 1928: 611)

Where does this take us vis-à-vis an understanding of Husserl's tran-scendental idealism and the constitutive (inter)dependence between mind and reality? Husserl is not a metaphysical idealist if that entails that everything is either reducible to or supervenes on the mental. He is a transcendental idealist insofar as he advocates the view that worldly objects are constitutively dependent upon transcendental subjectivity. Transcendental subjectivity, however, does not create the objects it constitutes. Nor is it their source, in the sense that they can somehow be deduced from or explained by its operations. It is not as if the fact that water is composed of hydrogen and oxygen, rather than helium and xenon, is somehow to be explained with reference to consciousness. To speak of constituting transcendental subjectivity is not to speak of a mind that shapes the world in its own image; rather, the constitutive process must be understood as a process that permits that which is constituted to appear, unfold, manifest, and present itself as what it is (Hua 15/434, 14/47). As Heidegger once remarked: '"*Constituting*" does not mean producing in the sense of making and fabricating; it means *letting the entity be seen in its objectivity*' (Heidegger 1985: 71). When Husserl speaks of an object's being-sense ('*Seinssinn*') and existential validity ('*Seinsgeltung*') and provides a detailed description of their constitution, he is however not simply engaged in an investigation of the meaning of the object, which can then be supplemented by a subsequent (non-phenomenological) investigation of its being. After the adoption of the transcendental attitude, after the effectuation of the epoché and the reduction, it is (as already mentioned) no longer permissible to separate the validity and significance of an object from its reality and being (cf. Fink 2000: 117). As Sokolowski once put it, in an effort to explain Husserl's particular version of idealism:

when we examine things philosophically, when we examine how they appear or manifest themselves, we are also examining their being. Their appearance is not something to be distinguished from the way they exist; part of their existence is to be presentable to consciousness. In medieval terminology, truth is a transcendental, a characteristic of being as such. Presentability or knowability belongs to things insofar as they are beings, not insofar as they are spatial or colored or large or small. We would do an incomplete job as philosophers of being were we to neglect discussing being in its presentability. Now the presentability of being requires a dative of manifestation, so it is true that in order to exercise its capacity of being truthful, a thing must be examined in relation to consciousness. Hence from the philosophical viewpoint, from the viewpoint in which we examine the presentability of things, things must be seen as relative to a dative of manifestation. But if consciousness is a condition for the appearance of things, consciousness does not create them. (Sokolowski 1977: 179)

4.5 Beyond internalism and externalism

Where should one place phenomenology on the internalism–externalism scale? One reply is that no univocal answer can be given. Whereas Husserl remains a Cartesian, a methodological solipsist, and a representationalist, Heidegger and Merleau-Ponty break with Cartesianism, are methodological socialists, and dispense with representations in favour of a direct opening onto the world. According to this kind of reading, Husserl's transcendental methodology commits him to internalism, whereas the existential phenomenologies of Heidegger and Merleau-Ponty are committed to a form of externalism, since they fully endorse the view that the mind is essentially determined by its intentional relationship to the world (cf. McClamrock 1995; Keller 1999; Carman 2003).

As should be clear by now, this interpretation is far too simplistic. It ignores plenty of evidence showing that Husserl is no traditional internalist. At the same time, however, one might also question the attempt to depict, say, Heidegger as a traditional externalist. Heidegger's notion of being-in-the-world is frequently taken to epitomize the embedded and world-involving character of the mind. But Heidegger occasionally expresses views that sound remarkably internalist. Lafont, for instance, has argued that Heidegger's claim that there can be no access to entities without a prior understanding of their being expresses his commitment to the internalist view that meaning determines reference (Lafont 2005: 523–5). In *Prolegomena zur Geschichte des Zeitbegriffs* from 1925, Heidegger denies that a perception only becomes intentional if its object somehow enters into a relation with it, as if it would lose its intentionality if the object did not exist. As a perception, it is, as Heidegger writes, 'intrinsically intentional' regardless of whether or not the perceived is in reality at hand (Heidegger 1985: 31). In *Die Grundprobleme der Phänomenologie* from 1927, Heidegger repeats this characterization, and adds that it is a decisive error to interpret intentionality as a relation between a psychical subject and a physical object. The truth of the matter is that the subject is intentionally structured within itself. Intentionality does not first arise through the actual presence of objects, but lies in the perceiving itself, whether veridical or illusory (Heidegger 1982: 59–61). These statements—and quite similar can also be found in Husserl (Hua 19/451)—might at first sight look rather internalist, and they also match well with another recurrent idea of the early Heidegger—the idea namely that life is characterized by a self-sufficiency (*Selbstgenügsamkeit*), in the sense that the intentional and world-directed character of life is a feature of life itself, and not something that is added from outside (Heidegger 1993: 261).

If externalism denies that intentionality is determined by meaning and conditioned by subjectivity, but rather holds that it is reducible to some kind of causal co-variation, none of the phenomenologists would count as externalists. But this is not the only way to define externalism. Just like internalism, externalism can hold that meaning determines reference as long as the meaning in question is externally embedded or world-involving. McDowell has explicitly argued that an externalist account of meaning should be complemented by an externalist account of the mind. Putnam is famous for having argued that meaning 'just ain't in the *head*' (Putnam 1975: 227), but as McDowell adds, neither is the mind (McDowell 1992: 36). The moment both mind and meaning are taken to be world-embedded, there is no reason to deny that meaning is related to the working of the mind, and that meaning determines and fixes reference. On occasion, McDowell has been quite explicit in affirming his sympathy for post-Kantian (transcendental) idealism (McDowell 2002: 271), and he sees no conflict between doing so and at the same time endorsing an externalist view on the mind. As McDowell argues, the direct perceptual realism that he recommends on transcendental grounds is one that lets experience be an openness to how things are, i.e. one that denies that we as cognizing beings are somehow cut off from the world as it exists 'in itself' (McDowell 2002: 291). Thus, he might be seen as someone whose intention is to domesticate the rhetoric of absolute idealism so that it stands revealed as a kind of direct realism aimed at protecting a commonsense respect for the independence of the ordinary world (McDowell 1994: 44; cf. Friedman 2002: 33).

In his book *Expressing the World,* Anthony Rudd introduced a helpful distinction between 'realist externalism' and 'Kantian externalism' (Rudd 2003: 44). Both forms of externalism take intentionality seriously. Both deny the self-contained nature of the mind and argue that it is tied to the world. But Kantian externalism then adds a twist by arguing that the reverse also holds true. In his refutation of idealism, Kant argued that I can only be aware of myself when I am aware of the world around me. But the world to which the mind is bound is the phenomenal world, which is equally bound to the mind. This move allowed Kant to reject the scepticism that sought to drive a wedge between mind and world; but since Kant—at least according to one influential interpretation—went on to distinguish the phenomenal world and the noumenal reality of the things in themselves, he might be said to have simply relocated the sceptical problem (Rudd 2003: 5). A more radical move was effectuated by the phenomenologists, who rejected the notion of the *Ding an sich* as unintelligible and nonsensical (cf. Hua 1/38–9). In their view, mind and world are not distinct entities; rather, they are bound constitutively together. To put it differently, phenomenologists would typically argue that the relation between mind and world is an internal relation, a relation constitutive of its relata, and not an external one of causality (cf. Rudd 2003: 53, 60). So what should we conclude? That phenomenologists, rather than being internalists, are pursuing a form of idealist externalism, a kind of phenomenological externalism?

A natural way to present the choice between internalism and externalism is by asking the following question: is intentionality determined by factors *internal* to the mind or by factors *external* to the mind? However, this apparently straightforward way of presenting the available options is on closer inspection quite inadequate, for whereas internalism typically postulates a gap between mind and world, externalism argues precisely that the world is *not* external to the mind. But the moment externalism is seen as arguing that mind and world are inseparable, it could also quite easily be defined as a position that takes intentionality to be determined by factors *internal* to this whole. Thus defined, however, externalism is difficult to distinguish from the kind of internalism which insists that intentionality is determined by factors internal to the mind, but which conceives of the mind in sufficiently broad terms. Consider the following famous passage from *Sein und Zeit*:

In directing itself toward [. . .] and in grasping something, Dasein does not first go outside of the inner sphere in which it is initially encapsulated, but, rather, in its primary kind of being, it is always already 'outside' together with some being encountered in the world already discovered. Nor is any inner sphere abandoned when Dasein dwells together with a being to be known and determines its character. Rather, even in this 'being outside' together with its object, Dasein is 'inside' correctly understood; that is, it itself exists as the being-in-the-world which knows. Again, the perception of what is known does not take place as a return with one's booty to the 'cabinet' of consciousness after one has gone out and grasped it. Rather, in perceiving, preserving, and retaining, the Dasein that knows *remains outside as Dasein*. (Heidegger 1996: 58, translation modified)

As Heidegger makes abundantly clear, the relation between Dasein and world cannot be characterized adequately with the help of the concepts 'inner' and 'outer'. Since Dasein is always already dwelling among things, it has no outside, which is also why it is nonsensical to talk of it as having an inside (Heidegger 1982: 66).

The very alternative between internalism and externalism remains bound to a Cartesian inner/outer division, but this division is precisely one with which phenomenology plays havoc. As Merleau-Ponty puts it, 'The interior and the exterior are inseparable. The world is entirely on the inside, and I am entirely outside of myself' (Merleau-Ponty 2012: 430).

Importantly, this was not a late insight of Heidegger and Merleau-Ponty. Already in *Logische Untersuchungen*, Husserl argued that the facile divide between inside and outside had its origin in a naive commonsensical metaphysics and was quite inappropriate for a proper understanding of the nature of intentionality (Hua 19/673, 708). Husserl's dismissal of the commonsensical divide between mind and world is even more pronounced after his transcendental turn. As Husserl writes in a text from 1921: 'The transcendental ego has no exterior; the very suggestion is quite nonsensical' (Hua 36/179). Or, as it is stated even more clearly in the manuscript A VI 21: 'The transcendental ego is neither in the world nor outside it, and the world, in turn, is neither in it nor outside of it.'[8]

For Husserl, it is as misleading to regard the world as somehow outside or external to us as it is to conceive of consciousness as somehow located inside an interior sphere. To argue that consciousness has no exterior is consequently not to insist that everything that is, is internal to consciousness. It is as wrong to claim that consciousness absorbs the world in knowing it as it is to say that consciousness must literally get outside itself in order to reach the world. All of these proposals are equally absurd, and all fail to realize that consciousness is neither a container nor a special place, but rather to be defined in terms of its openness.

Considering how Husserl conceives of intentionality, of the mind–world relationship, I consequently find it doubtful whether it really makes sense to situate his thoughts within the framework of the internalism/externalism debate—contrary to what interpreters like Rowlands, Carman, Dreyfus, and McIntyre have done. Avoiding the two terms will not solve all the problems, but might at least permit us to avoid letting our investigation be guided by misleading metaphors.

Given the transcendental framework of Husserl's thinking, the internalism/externalism divide loses its relevance. Indeed, one might say that the main lesson of the reduction is the rejection of the dualism between a self-enclosed mind and a mindless world. Ultimately, we should appreciate that the phenomenological investigations of the structure of phenomenality are antecedent to any divide between psychical interiority and physical exteriority, since they are investigations of the

---

[8] Ms. A VI 21, 25a: 'Das transzendentale Ich ist weder in noch ausser der Welt, und auch die Welt ist weder in ihm noch ausser ihm.'

very dimension in which any object—be it external or internal—manifests itself (cf. Heidegger 1996: 385; Waldenfels 2000: 217).

4.6 Intersubjectivity and the transcendental

At this point, the critics might however launch a final counterattack. Even if it should turn out that Husserl's theory of intentionality does not commit him to an inward-looking internalism, his deep-seated internalism is manifest elsewhere, namely in his unflinching commitment to a form of methodological (if not metaphysical) solipsism.

The claim that solipsism might constitute the fatal weakness of Husserlian phenomenology is not new. As I will argue in what follows, however, not only is Husserl not a solipsist, but most of Husserl's critics have failed to grasp the radicality of his thinking on this topic. For Husserl, intersubjectivity is not an isolated problem that transcendental phenomenology has to address. Rather, we can only really understand the genuine sense of transcendental idealism the moment intersubjectivity is taken into consideration. Or as Husserl himself puts it, it was his reflections on intersubjectivity that for the first time made the 'full and proper sense' of transcendental phenomenology understandable (Hua 1/176).[9]

Let me approach this issue through a brief examination of Husserl's relationship to Kant. In 1925, Husserl wrote a letter to Ernst Cassirer where he described the development of his own appreciation of Kant in some detail (Hua Dok 3-V/4). Initially, Husserl had been strongly influenced by Brentano's negative appraisal of Kant, but subsequent studies had made Husserl realize the affinity between his own project and that of Kant.

My own development—which originally was hostile towards Kant but admittedly also insensitive to the proper sense of the Kantian philosophy—linked up with Descartes and the pre-Kantian philosophy of the eighteenth century, and I was of

---

[9] It should not come as a surprise that Philipse, in his treatment of Husserl's transcendental idealism, simply writes that Husserl because of his commitment to phenomenalism was forced to confront the problem of solipsism, and that this was a problem he was unable to solve (1995: 281). An alternative approach would have been to engage seriously with Husserl's extensive discussion of intersubjectivity, and with his claim that spatial objects are public, and on that basis conclude that Husserl could not possibly have been a phenomenalist.

course also influenced by important impulses from Brentano, Lotze and Bolzano. But as I, continually reflecting on the possibility of a presuppositionless ascertainment and absolute accountability, was driven from the foundational problems belonging to the theory of science (which were the questions that were most familiar to me as a mathematician) towards a method of eidetic analysis of consciousness, and as the domain of the origins of all knowledge was disclosed to me through the phenomenological reduction, I had to acknowledge that the science that became closer to me, although with quite different methods, embraced Kant's entire complex of problems (which only now acquired a profound and clear meaning), and that it confirmed and justified Kant's main results in a strictly scientific grounding and delimitation. (Hua Dok 3-V/4)

There is, of course, one place where Kant's influence on Husserl is particularly visible. As Husserl admits in *Erste Philosophie I*, when he decided to designate his own phenomenology as 'transcendental', he was making use of a Kantian concept (Hua 7/230). He goes on:

His [Kant's] eternal significance lies in the much discussed but little understood 'Copernican' turn to a fundamentally new and, what is more, strictly scientific interpretation of the sense of the world; but at the same time it lies in the first establishment of a corresponding, and 'entirely new,' science—the science of the transcendental. (Hua 7/240)

When it comes to an appraisal of Husserl's phenomenology, a reference to Kant is quite appropriate, in particular when confronted with the repeated claim that Husserlian phenomenology is merely a form of introspective psychology. Having said this, however, one should also be careful not to overlook some significant differences between Kant and Husserl. In short, it would be a mistake to think that transcendental philosophy is all one thing, and to overlook the difference between a Kantian (and neo-Kantian) transcendental philosophy and the form of transcendental philosophy we find in phenomenology.

Husserl's own account in *Krisis* is in this context both interesting and revealing. His teleological approach to the history of philosophy comes to the fore when he describes phenomenology as the final gestalt ('*Endform*') of transcendental philosophy (Hua 6/71 [70]). When accounting for the history of transcendental philosophy, however, Husserl insists that he is operating with a broader conception of transcendental philosophy than Kant did, namely as referring to a fundamental reflective inquiry into the first-personal basis of all knowledge formations (Hua 6/100). A couple of pages later, he adds that transcendental philosophy is characterized by its criticism of objectivism and by its elucidation of subjectivity as the locus of all objective formations of sense and validity (Hua 6/102). It is on the basis of such a general definition that Husserl, somewhat surprisingly perhaps, counts not only Kant but also Descartes, Berkeley, and Hume as transcendental philosophers (Hua 6/272). Indeed, Descartes's insistence on the importance of first-person reflection is what makes Husserl consider Descartes the true innovator, the first to intro-duce the transcendental motive into modern philosophy (Hua 6/100).

If we look closer at some of Husserl's scattered remarks about Kant, already in *Logische Untersuchungen* we find Husserl criticizing Kant for not having managed to stay clear of a metaphysically contaminated epistemology (Hua 19/732). Later on, we find Husserl faulting Kant for not having a proper concept of the a priori, for operating with too strong a distinction between sensation and understanding, for being too oriented towards the natural sciences, for confusing noetic and noematic analyses, and for lacking methodological rigour (Hua 7/198–9, 235, 282, 6/420–21, 5/128, 3/246, 1/48). When it comes to the difference in method, a telling statement can be found in a manuscript from 1920, where Husserl writes as follows: 'Kant's deduction is a masterpiece of top-down transcendental reasoning. It remains far removed from all phenomenological analyses.' And as he then adds, such a deduction can only be met with disapproval ('*Kopfschütteln*') by phenomenologists (quoted in Kern 1964: 104). Some years later, Husserl expands on this remark, and writes that a transcendental deduction of the a priori structures of the world can take two paths. There is the direct way from below, which takes its point of departure in the concrete pre-predicative experience of the world, and then there is the way from above, which takes its point of departure in logic. The first way is the phenomeno-logical way, the second the Kantian way (Hua 32/103, 112). Due to his fear of psychologizing the transcendental, Kant renounced the attempt to base his investigation on experiential evidence and instead resorted to a regressive procedure that, according to Husserl, remained too dependent on construction and left the transcendental concepts fundamentally unclear (Hua 6/104, 117). Husserl consequently distances himself from any sort of regressive transcendental argumentation, and criticizes Kant's deductive method for being regressive-constructive. It lacks an intuitive basis, and is unable to provide us with a proper account of consciousness. By contrast, a phenomenological transcendental philosophy is committed to the idea that the structures of transcendental, constituting consciousness must be brought to intuitive givenness, i.e. they must be experientially accessible. Mohanty once pointed to the difference between what he called a *'prinzipien-theoretisch'* and an *'evidenz-theoretisch'* type of transcendental philosophy (Mohanty 1985: 215). In contrast to Kantian transcendental philosophy, which remains critical (*'prinzipien-theoretisch'*), phenomenology has insisted upon grounding its investigation in a theory of intentionality, since only such a theory could provide the clarification of evidence and first-personal givenness that is needed if dogmatism is to be avoided (Crowell 2001: 54, 58).

In one of his longest texts on Kant, *Kant und die Idee der Transzendentalphilosophie*, written for and presented in commemoration of Kant's bicentennial in 1924, Husserl writes that transcendental philosophy should be based upon a systematic description and analysis of consciousness in all of its modalities (Hua 7/234–5). For Husserl, transcendental consciousness is not merely a formal principle of constitution, however. It is not 'a dead pole of identity' (Hua 9/208), which is why phenomenology must insist upon an in-depth investigation of consciousness. It is this demand which eventually necessitates an *extension* of Kant's concept of the transcendental, since it proves necessary to include the humanities and the manifold of human sociality and culture in the transcendental analysis (Hua 7/282). This line of thinking is further elaborated some years later, when Husserl writes that:

as long as one interprets transcendental subjectivity as an isolated ego and—like the Kantian tradition—ignores the whole task of establishing the legitimacy of the transcendental community of subjects, any prospect of a transcendental knowledge of self and world is lost. (Hua 29/120)

It is consequently no coincidence that Husserl at times describes his own project as a *sociological* transcendental philosophy (Hua 9/539), and even declares that the development of phenomenology necessarily implied the move from an '"egological" [. . .] phenomenology into a transcendental sociological phenomenology having reference to a manifest multiplicity of conscious subjects communicating with one another' (Husserl 1981: 68).

On many occasions, Husserl states that the reduction to transcendental subjectivity simultaneously means reduction to the transcendental intersubjectivity made accessible within it (Hua 15/73–5, 403). And as he makes clear in *Zur Phänomenologie der Intersubjektivität III*, the introduction of intersubjectivity does not mean some external expansion of transcendental subjectivity; rather, it simply expresses a better understanding of what subjectivity amounts to in the first place (Hua 15/17). Similar ideas can be found elsewhere in Husserl's oeuvre. In *Erste Philosophie II*, for instance, Husserl writes that transcendental subjectivity in its full universality is exactly *inter*-subjectivity (Hua 8/480); in a research manuscript from 1927, which has been published in *Zur Phänomenologie der Intersubjektivität I*, Husserl writes that the absolute reveals itself as the intersubjective relation between subjects (Hua 13/480); and as he eventually puts it in a famous quote from *Krisis* that Merleau-Ponty was later to discuss in detail: 'subjectivity is what it is—an ego functioning constitutively—only within intersubjectivity' (Hua 6/175 [172]).

The link between transcendental philosophy and intersubjectivity is confirmed on many occasions by Husserl. He frequently writes that his phenomenological treatment of intersubjectivity has the goal of bringing his constitutive analyses to completion—a completion that is achieved the moment it is realized that transcendental intersubjective sociality is the basis in which all truth and all true being have their intentional source (cf. Hua 1/35, 182, 8/449, 9/295, 344, 474). As we have already seen, phenomenology is transcendental precisely because it deals with the problem of how transcendence is to be understood constitutively. And this clarification is (as Husserl repeatedly states) only possible by way of an analysis of intersubjectivity (Hua 8/465, 17/259, 1/10). As he writes in two late texts:

The transcendence with which the world is constituted consists therein, that it constitutes itself by means of others, by means of the *generatively constituted co-subjectivity*. It is through them that it acquires its being-sense [*Seinssinn*] as an infinite world. (Hua Mat 8/393)

Here we have the only transcendence that is genuinely worthy of the name—and everything else that is still called transcendence, such as the objective world, rests on the transcendence of foreign subjectivity. (Hua 8/495)

Husserl also describes the other as '*the intrinsically first other*' (Hua 1/137; cf. 17/248) and argues that only constitutive phenomenology has recognized the true sense and true scope of the problem of other minds, namely, by recognizing how 'the otherness of "someone else" becomes extended to the whole world, as its "Objectivity", giving it this sense in the first place' (Hua 1/173).[10]

Husserl's deliberations do not merely occur at this very high level of abstraction. He also offers analyses of the specific self–other relations that are required if objectivity is to be constituted. It is through the encounter with another that I come to realize that I am only one among many, and that my own perspective on the world is only one among several (Hua 17/245, 15/645, 1/157). It is by experiencing that others experience the same objects as I do that I come to experience objects as being more than merely objects-for-me. When I realize that the intentional object of my apprehension can also be experienced by others, I come to understand that the same object can appear for different subjects (Hua 13/9), and that there is a difference between the object-as-such and the way it appears to me, which is a decisive step towards the constitution of proper objectivity. In his description of the different ways in which I relate to others, Husserl further highlights the importance of a special kind of other-experience, namely the one where I experience the other as experiencing myself. My experience of being an object-for-another, i.e. my other-mediated self-apprehension, is, on his view, of decisive importance for the constitution of objectivity. When I realize that I can be an *alter ego* for the other, just as she can be it for me, when I realize that the other conceives of me as an other, just as I conceive of her as a self, the

difference between oneself and the foreign I vanishes; the other apprehends me as foreign, just as I grasp him as foreign for me, and he himself is a 'self,' etc. Parity thus ensues: a multiplicity of feeling, willing I's that are alike in kind and each independent in the same sense. (Hua 13/243–4; cf. Hua 15/635)

A central idea of Husserl's is consequently that a transcendental clarification of objectivity understood as 'valid for everybody' requires an analysis of intersubjectivity (Hua 17/243). This is so not only because my apprehension of objects as real and objective is mediated by and depends upon my encounter with other world-related subjects, but also because Husserl considers objectivity in the sense of an ultimately valid true world the correlate of an ideal intersubjective concordance (Hua 8/47–8). There is no other meaningful true reality than the one we agree

---

[10] For a book-length discussion of this aspect of Husserl's thinking, see Zahavi (2001).

upon at the end of the road of inquiry. Husserl's view is here somewhat akin to Peirce's:

The real, then, is that which, sooner or later, information and reasoning would finally result in, and which is therefore independent of the vagaries of me and you. Thus, the very origin of the conception of reality shows that this conception essentially involves the notion of a COMMUNITY, without definite limits, and capable of a definite increase of knowledge. (Peirce 1955: 247)

Although ideas like these are articulated most forcefully in Husserl's later work, they are by no means exclusive to that period of his thinking. Already in texts written around the time of *Ideen I*, Husserl's analysis of the link between intersubjectivity and objectivity had ramifications for his conception of transcendental subjectivity. In a text from around 1914–15, for instance, he considers the proposal that actual being, or the being of actual reality, rather than simply entailing a relation to a formal cognizing subject, must be related to an embodied and embedded subject. What is the argument? The objective world is intersubjectively constituted, but intersubjectivity is only possible between embodied and embedded subjects. To put it differently, already at this relatively early stage of his thinking, Husserl is considering the idea that the subject in order to constitute the world must necessarily be bodily embedded in the very world that it is seeking to constitute (Hua 36/133–5, 5/128). In later works, such as *Cartesianische Meditationen*, he would be more unequivocal, and insist that the constitution of the world implies a mundanization of the constituting subject (Hua 1/130)—that is, in order to constitute an objective world, transcendental subjectivity must necessarily apprehend itself as a worldly being.

Such ideas fit rather uneasily with the assumption that Husserl is a methodological solipsist, an archetypical internalist, and that he should consider the mind some kind of self-sufficient constitutive principle. Husserl's formulations and terminology are not always transparently clear, but I think the view he eventually came to adopt amounts to something like the following. He consistently maintained the view that reality is always a reality for someone; it is always correlated to a constituting subjectivity. But eventually he came to realize that the subject does not remain untouched by its constitutive performance, just as constitution is not simply a relation involving a single subject and the world, but rather something that must be considered an intersubjective process. The problem he then faced was to clarify the exact interrelation between self, world, and others. This is made most explicit in his last writings, where the three are increasingly intertwined and interdependent (cf. Hua 8/505, 14/373), and where Husserl seems to be converging on ideas also pursued in different ways by Heidegger and Merleau-Ponty. As an example, consider a text from 1931, written during Husserl's attempt to revise and improve the exposition he had offered in *Cartesianische Meditationen* (see Hua 15/li–lviii). In this text, he speaks of how I cannot be who I am without the others who are for me, and vice versa (Hua 15/370), and of how the intentional being-for-one-another, this intertwining of the absolute, is a 'metaphysical' primordial fact (*Urtatsache*) (Hua 15/366). Indeed, no absolute can withdraw from this transcendental co-existence: 'Not only am I not *solus ipse*, but no conceivable absolute is *solus ipse*' (Hua 15/371). In addition, however, he writes that it is nonsensical to posit a nature that is absolutely self-subsisting. Nature is only thinkable as a surrounding world of embodied humans, as correlated to and constituted by a transcendental intersubjectivity. Ultimately, he then suggests that the co-existence of self, others, and nature (world) amounts to an irreducible facticity, which it is nonsensical to seek to overcome (or ground) (Hua 15/371).

One worry that this conclusion might occasion is that it seems to return us to where we started. We have gone full circle. In our pre-philosophical naivety, we took it for granted that we live in a world with others. Phenomenological reflection was supposed to exemplify a break with this naivety. Rather than simply presupposing the existence of objectivity and intersubjectivity, the purpose of the transcendental reduction was precisely to allow for an elucidation of their constitution. But now, it seems, rather than offering a constitutive analysis, we have instead simply elevated the world and others to co-constituting factors. Isn't the end result that no real analysis has been offered and no real increase in understanding has been gained? In reply, it might be argued that the criticism is misguided. The fact that we find ourselves back where we started could be considered a sign of success, rather than of failure. As also Wittgenstein and Heidegger have argued, the task of philosophy is not to discover new facts, but to call attention to and elucidate those aspects of existence that are so familiar to us, so taken for granted, that we often fail to realize their true significance. Furthermore, even if we end up having to recognize the interdependency of self, world, others, we have gained an understanding of their intertwining that is quite different from the one we started out with. To show that self and world are constitutively equiprimordial is, for instance, very different from arguing, let alone simply assuming, that we as subjects always find ourselves in an already independently existing reality. Likewise, to show how intersubjectivity is involved in the constitution of objectivity, and how our comprehension of something as objective is dependent upon our interaction with others, is quite different from simply observing that we as biological creatures are born from others, and to that extent together with others from the very start. Finally, to argue that self, world, and others are all involved in the constitutive process is not to say that they are all involved in the same way or all involved on all levels. Indeed, part of the challenge (and part of Husserl's analytic contribution) has precisely been to disentangle different constitutive levels and processes (temporal, bodily, pre-linguistic, communal, scientific, etc.) in order to determine whether and how self, world, and others are involved.

Be that as it may, it should in any case be clear by now that the development of Husserl's thinking eventually made him move quite far away from the position articulated in §49 of *Ideen I*. But how should this affect our appraisal of Husserl's notion of the transcendental? In a recent publication, De Palma has insisted that Husserl's phenomenology is not a type of transcendental philosophy at all, and that Husserl's own assertions to the contrary merely reveal that he did not understand the nature of transcendental philosophy (De Palma 2015: 13–14). How does De Palma reach such a surprising conclusion? According to him, transcendental philosophy is concerned with a principled investigation of the very conditions of possibility of experience and by necessity must go beyond experience in pursuing this endeavour, since the conditions in question can only be unearthed regressively. If one abandons the regressive method, as Husserl did, one also abandons transcendental philosophy (De Palma 2015: 21). A further argument against the purported transcendental character of Husserl's phenomenology is that Husserl considers consciousness a mere formal condition of possibility for objectual experience. Rather than attempting to deduce the content of experience from consciousness, rather than letting consciousness be the source of the difference between lemons and swans, rather than attempting to ground regional ontological differences in the structure of consciousness, Husserl insisted on the importance of passivity and facticity. On Husserl's view, consciousness is merely a necessary and not a sufficient constitutive condition, since the constitution of an objective world also depends upon the presence and contribution of specific factual conditions (De Palma 2015: 29–32).[11] According to De Palma, this shows that Husserl rather than being a transcendental philosopher is in truth an (eidetic) empiricist (p. 43).

Is this a convincing conclusion? De Palma's insistence on Husserl not being a transcendental philosopher is certainly warranted, given his own definition of transcendental philosophy. The question, though, is why one should accept this overly narrow definition. Rather than concluding that the differences between Husserl and Kant entail that Husserl is not a transcendental philosopher, a more reasonable conclusion would be that Husserl is not a Kantian transcendental philosopher. As Merleau-Ponty wrote in the preface to *Phénoménologie de la perception*: 'Husserl's transcendental is not Kant's' (Merleau-Ponty 2012: lxxvii). To insist that Kant's definition of transcendental philosophy is the only permissible one is a stipulatory move that is philosophically rather uninteresting, and which simply disregards and derides all the different ways in which transcendental philosophy has developed and been transformed by post-Kantian philosophy, starting with Fichte and continuing up through the twentieth century. As Mohanty writes, 'Transcendental philosophies are not all of the same sort' (Mohanty 1985: 213; but see also, e.g. Malpas 2002; Braver 2007; Heinämaa, Hartimo, and Miettinen 2014; Gardner and Grist 2015). A far more plausible interpretation than De Palma's is offered by Heinämaa, Hartimo, and Miettinen in their editorial introduction to the volume *Phenomenology and the Transcendental*:

Husserl's relation to the very content of transcendental philosophy can be viewed as a radicalization, a rearticulation, and a distention of the Kantian concept of the transcendental. It was a radicalization insofar as Husserl extended the transcendental critique also to logic that Kant had taken for granted. It was a rearticulation insofar as Husserl, by emphasizing the idea of givenness rather than

---

[11] De Palma (2015: 29) claims that this last point has been almost entirely overlooked by previous interpreters. This claim is hard to reconcile with the kind of discussions found in the existing research literature, however. The proposal that consciousness is merely a necessary and not a sufficient condition already figured centrally in Sokolowski's classical *The Formation of Husserl's Concept of Constitution* (Sokolowski 1970: 159), and was also highlighted in my own *Husserl's Phenomenology* (Zahavi 2003c).

deduction, located the domain of transcendental within the individual ego, thus making the transcendental ego inextricably *personal* and *singular*. But it was also a distention, as Husserl significantly broadened the scope of transcendental investigation to include the temporal development of the ego, its bodily existence, and intersubjective relations. (Heinämaa et al. 2014: 8)

One salient example of this latter broadening can be found in Husserl's work on normality. Husserl was already from early on interested in how we in daily life operate within an unquestioned normality, how we simply take certain matters for granted. The moment he became interested in intersubjectivity, his concern with normality changed to also include more focused discussions of abnormality. If my constitution of objectivity is dependent upon my assurance that others experience or can experience the same as I, it will be a problem if they claim to be experiencing something different—although the fact that we can agree upon there being a disagreement already indicates a common ground (Hua 15/47). As Husserl points out, however, it is only disagreement with those with whom one expects to agree that has this effect. It is only the (dis)agreement with the *normal* members of the community that is of relevance. When it is said that real being has to be experientially accessible to everybody, we are dealing with a certain averageness and idealization (Hua 15/141, 231, 629). *Everybody* is the person who belongs to a normality of subjects, and who is exactly normal in and through the community (Hua 15/142). Only with her do we fight over the truth and falsity, the being and non–being, of our common lifeworld. Only the normal is apprehended as being co-constitutive (Hua 15/162, 166, 9/497), whereas my disagreement with an abnormal is (at first) considered inconsequential: 'The animals, the "savages," the infants, and the insane did not count in the world-constitution. They do not co-constitute and have not co-constituted the world that is pregiven to me as existing' (Hua 39/486).

As Husserl continues his investigation, however, it becomes clear to him that we have to distinguish different kinds of normality. We might speak of normality when we are dealing with a mature, healthy, and rational person. Here the abnormal will be the infant, the blind, or the schizophrenic. But we also speak of normality, when it concerns our own homeworld, whereas abnormality is attributed to the foreigner or alien, who can be apprehended as a member of a foreign normality, an alien world.

The encounter with the alien world has important constitutive implications. It transforms our notion of objectivity. What we have hitherto simply apprehended as the world now reveals itself as the correlate of a particular system of normality; it is merely a homeworld. At the same time, the experience of discrepancy between subjects that belong to different normalities can urge us to aim for a truth that is valid for us all, can motivate the constitution of *scientific* objectivity (Hua 6/324). That is to say, 'if we set up the goal of a truth about the objects which is unconditionally valid for all subjects, beginning with that on which normal Europeans, normal Hindus, Chinese, etc., agree in spite of all relativity', we are on the way to an objective science (Hua 6/142). In short, it turns out to be necessary to differentiate between (1) normal objectivity, which is correlated with a limited intersubjectivity (a community of normal subjects) and (2) rigorous objectivity, which is correlated with the unlimited totality of all rational subjects (Hua 14/111). Husserl consequently believed a correlation to exist between different levels of normality and different levels of objectivity (Hua 15/155). Science possesses a different kind of objectivity from that of ordinary experience. It is privileged by and excels in being valid for all subjects whatsoever and not merely for a limited intersubjective community. But even absolute objective being and truth are correlated with a subject-dependent normality: the normality of rational subjects (Hua 15/35–6).

In rejecting objectivism and in exploring the constitutive correlation between mind and world, Husserl is undoubtedly a transcendental philosopher. But the kind of transcendental philosophy he is advocating is one that is quite aware of the finitude of the transcendental subject. This is clear not only from Husserl's appeal to a plurality of transcendental subjects, but also from his accentuation of the diachronic or generative dimension of intersubjectivity. I learn what counts as normal from others, and I thereby partake in a common tradition. Indeed, the accomplishments of previous generations are operative in our individual experiences:

That which I have constituted originally (primally instituted [*urstiftend*]) is mine. But I am a 'child of the times'; I am a member of a we-community in the broadest sense—a community that has its tradition and that, for its part, is connected in a novel manner with the generative subjects, the closest and the most distant ancestors. And they have 'influenced' me: I am what I am as an heir. What is really and originally my own? To what extent am I really primally instituting? I am it on the basis of the 'tradition'; everything of my own is founded, in part through the tradition of my ancestors, in part through the tradition of my contemporaries. (Hua 14/223)

Husserl also refers to 'normal life' as 'generative life', and argues that every (normal) human being is 'historical' by virtue of being constituted as a member of a historically enduring community (Hua 15/138–9, 431). In the volume *Zur Phänomenologie der Intersubjektivität III*, he claims that the constitution of objectivity must be understood as the culmination of the development of transcendental intersubjectivity, which is to be conceived as an ongoing process of cultivating ever-newer systems of norms at ever higher levels (Hua 15/421). Ever new generations cooperate in transcendentally building up the structures of validity pertaining to the objective world, which is precisely a world handed down in tradition (Hua 15/463). There is, as Husserl writes, no 'fixed world'; rather, it is what it is for us only in the relativity of normalities and abnormalities (Hua 15/212, 381, Hua 6/270).

That Husserl tried to add a historical dimension to transcendental philosophy can also be illustrated in a different way. In a passage quoted earlier, he writes that the transcendence of the world is constituted through others and through the generatively constituted co-subjectivity. Exactly this concept of 'generative intersubjectivity' (Hua 15/199) indicates that Husserl no longer regarded the birth and death of the subject as mere contingent facts, but as transcendental conditions of possibility for the constitution of the world (Hua 15/171). As he would write in *Krisis*, being embedded in 'the unitary flow of a historical development'— in a generative nexus of birth and death—belongs as indissolubly to the I as does its temporal form (Hua 6/256 [253]). Ultimately, he would consider the subject's birth into a living tradition to have constitutive implications. It is not merely the case that I live in a world which as a correlate of normality is permeated by references to others, and which others have already furnished with meaning, or that I understand the world (and myself) through a traditional, handed-down linguistic conventionality. The very meaning that the world has for me is such that it has its origin outside me, in a historical past. For the very same reason, creatures who are unaware that they are born and will die, i.e. unaware of their own participation in a transgenerational chain, will be unable to fully share the constitutive accomplishment of generative intersubjectivity (Heinämaa 2014: 139), and therefore also lack the capacity to constitute a truly objective world.

In *Les mots et les choses*, Foucault argued that phenomenology exemplifies a type of modern discourse that in its investigation of experience

TRANSCENDENTAL IDEALISM   133

seeks both to separate and to integrate the empirical and the transcendental. It is an investigation of experience that in the face of positivism has tried to restore the lost dimension of the transcendental, but which at the same time has made experience concrete enough to include both body and culture. To Foucault it is quite clear that this modern type of transcendental reflection differs from the Kantian type by taking its point of departure in the paradox of human existence rather than in the existence of natural science. Although Husserl had apparently succeeded in unifying the Cartesian theme of the *cogito* with the transcendental motif of Kant, the truth is that Husserl was only able to accomplish this union insofar as he changed the very nature of transcendental analysis. When transcendental subjectivity is placed in the more fundamental dimension of time, the strict division between the transcendental and the empirical is compromised. The questions of validity and of genesis become entangled. It is this transformation that in Foucault's view has resulted in phenomenology's simultaneously promising and threatening proximity to empirical analyses of man (Foucault 2002: 351–5).

I think Foucault's diagnosis is correct; and as I will show in Chapter 5, the fact that phenomenology conceives of transcendental subjectivity as both embodied and socially embedded is something than makes it more open to inputs and challenges from empirical science that one might initially assume. I see no reason, however, to accept Foucault's claim that Husserl's transcendental phenomenology as a result must eventually 'topple over' into anthropology (Foucault 2002: 270).

Foucault is known for presenting his own account as a distinct alternative to the phenomenological approach 'which gives absolute priority to the observing subject, which attributes a constituent role to an act, which places its own point of view at the origin of all historicity—which, in short, leads to a transcendental consciousness' (Foucault 2002: xv). As various Foucault scholars have recently argued, however, rather than simply reading Foucault as a critic of phenomenology, one might also see his thinking as an attempt to radicalize some of the ideas found in Husserl's later philosophy, in particular the latter's notion of the 'historical a priori' (Oksala 2011; Thompson 2016).

As Husserl makes clear in the introduction to *Krisis*, the plan of the book was to motivate the transcendental-phenomenological enterprise through a teleological-historical reflection upon the origins of our critical scientific and philosophical situation (Hua 6/xiv). One of the central aims was to show how ideal entities and theories have a historical origin, and how part of the transcendental task is to engage in a kind of archaeology in which hidden layers of sense formations and sedimentations are excavated in order to lay bare the intentional achievements that current science is based upon. Among the most decisive presuppositions for the constitution of scientific objectivity, Husserl lists the invention of language, particularly written language. As he writes in the appendix *Ursprung der Geometrie,*

One is conscious of civilization from the start as an immediate and mediate linguistic community. Clearly it is only through language and its far-reaching documentations, as possible communications, that the horizon of civilization can be an open and endless one, as it always is for men. (Hua 6/369 [358])

The important function of written, documenting linguistic expression is that it makes communications possible without immediate or mediate personal address; it is, so to speak, communication become virtual. Through this, the communalization of man is lifted to a new level. (Hua 6/371 [360–61])

As written down, meaning can be handed down to later generations and thereby become incorporated into a body of knowledge, which generations of scientists can draw on and add to. Language enables a '*sharing over time*' (Taipale 2014: 104). Indeed, were it not for the capacity of written language to function as a kind of reservoir of knowledge and collective memory, comprehensive and complex theories, which are developed through centuries, would not have been possible (Hua 6/369–74, 17/38, 349, 15/224). Rather than attempting to unearth a fixed and static set of a priori categories, Husserl's transcendental phenomenology is consequently characterized by its willingness to acknowledge the open-ended and dynamically changing character of the process of constitution.

Foucault too aimed to write a history of the transcendental, a history of the varying conditions of possibility of knowledge in different periods (Oksala 2011). But one significant difference between the two is, of course, that Foucault, in contrast to Husserl, subscribes to what Braver calls the doctrine of 'Impersonal Conceptual Schemes' (Braver 2007: 360). For Foucault, the transcendental conditions are divorced from consciousness. They are non-subjective and anonymous, and cannot be revealed by any kind of first-person reflection or analysis. Furthermore, rather than being a constitutive source, the subject is itself through and through historically constituted. Indeed, Foucault's solution to the paradox of man as an empirico-transcendental double is to reject the very notion of a transcendental subject. By contrast, Husserl's aim, as we shall see in more detail in Chapter 5, is to make the co-existence between the transcendental and the empirical perspective less paradoxical. Rather than conceiving of the two as mutually incompatible, they are seen as intertwined and complementary perspectives. Indeed, as Mohanty observes, 'We do not need the myth of two worlds. The transcendental *is* the mundane, only freed from that self-forgetfulness, that naïvety and that self-interpretation which constitutes mundaneity' (Mohanty 1985: 222). Another important difference between Foucault and Husserl is that the latter, despite his recognition of the importance of historical change and context, also conceived of this development as evolving according to a certain teleology. Husserl remained a universalist and rationalist (cf. Hua 6/373), and would, as Moran observes, have been 'dissatisfied with Foucault's account of epistemes as discontinuous, subject to rupture and irruption' (Moran 2016: 25).

The fact that Husserl's phenomenology operates with an enlarged notion of the transcendental, the fact that it includes topics such as embodiment, intersubjectivity, and historicity in its transcendental analysis, gives it a different scope and character from that of a more traditional Kantian type of transcendental philosophy. Needless to say, such a transformation also generates new challenges of its own. But although the merits of Husserl's idealism might remain contentious, I hope to have made it clear that it would be a mistake to dismiss it offhandedly with the argument that it exemplifies an outdated form of solipsism, internalism, and representationalism. Rather than amounting to an unprecedentedly strong version of internalism—a version that emphasizes the self-sufficiency of the mind to such an extent that it basically eliminates the world from the picture—Husserl's transcendental idealism is (1) motivated by an attempt to save the objectivity and transcendence of the world of experience, (2) characterized by its anti-representationalist criticism of metaphysical realism, and (3) committed to the essential interdependence of mind and world. In addition, Husserl also (4) holds the view that the world is correlated with an intersubjective community of embodied subjects. These features happen to make his transcendental idealism far less marginal than one might initially have expected. By endorsing the view that the only justification obtainable and the only justification required is one that is internal to the world of experience and to its intersubjective practices, Husserl offers a view on the transcendental that points forward in time rather than backwards to Kant. In that sense, and to that extent, Husserl's conception of the transcendental is distinctly modern, and might even be said to have quite a presence in twentieth-century continental and analytic philosophy.

5

The Naturalist challenge

Wenn wirklich die Naturwissenschaft spricht, hören wir gerne und als Jünger. Aber nicht immer spricht die Naturwissenschaft, wenn die Naturforscher sprechen; und sicherlich nicht, wenn sie über 'Naturphilosophie' und 'naturwissenschaftliche Erkenntnistheorie' sprechen.

Ideen I

It is always risky to make sweeping statements about the development of philosophy, but if one were nevertheless asked to characterize twentieth-century philosophy in broad strokes, one noteworthy feature might be the following. Whereas important thinkers at the beginning of the century, including Frege and Husserl, were very explicit in their rejection of naturalism (in particular the attempt to naturalize the laws of logic), the situation has changed considerably. Today many philosophers—not least within analytic philosophy—would consider naturalism the default metaphysical position. If you do not subscribe to naturalism, you must be subscribing to some form of Cartesian substance dualism. Thus, whereas one around 1980 might have been inclined to characterize the development of twentieth-century philosophy in terms of a linguistic turn, from a philosophy of subjectivity to a philosophy of language, it might today be more apt to describe the development in terms of a turn from anti-naturalism to naturalism.

According to some readings, a commitment to naturalism simply amounts to taking one's departure in what is natural (rather than supernatural or spooky), but generally speaking, the use of the term in the current discourse is far more narrow, and indicates an alignment with the natural sciences. As Sellars famously put it, 'in the dimension of describing and explaining the world, science is the measure of all things, of what is that it is and of what is not that it is not' (Sellars 1963: 173). More specifically, naturalism is typically distinguished by *methodological* as well as *ontological* commitments. The methodological commitment amounts to the idea that the correct procedures and the right types of justification are those found in and employed by the natural sciences. All genuine questions are natural scientific questions, and all genuine knowledge is objective knowledge gained by natural scientific means. Given that the resolutely third-person methods of natural science are considered to provide the sole means of epistemic access to the world, any appeal to first-person methods should be avoided. The ontological commitment amounts to the monistic view that reality consists only of those entities, properties, and structures that are (or could be) accepted by natural science. Jointly, the two commitments amount to the view that everything which exists (including everything pertaining to human life, such as consciousness, intentionality, meaning, rationality, normativity, values, culture, or history) has to be studied by the methods of natural science, and is ultimately explanatorily and ontologically reducible to natural scientific facts (cf. Papineau 2015).

What are the implications of this naturalistic turn? It has some decisive metaphilosophical implications. It has implications for the way we view the relation between philosophy and science. A vivid illustration of this can be found in the field of consciousness studies. As Francis Crick insists, 'it is hopeless to try to solve the problems of consciousness by general philosophical arguments; what is needed are suggestions for new experiments that might throw light on these problems' (Crick 1995: 19). Indeed, on Crick's view, 'the study of consciousness is a scientific problem. [. . .] There is no justification for the view that only philosophers can deal with it' (pp. 257–8). Quite on the contrary, in fact: since philosophers 'have had such a poor record over the last two thousand years that they would do better to show a certain modesty rather than the lofty superiority that they usually display' (p. 258). This is not to say that philosophers cannot make some kind of contribution; but they must 'learn how to abandon their pet theories when the scientific evidence goes against them or they will only expose themselves to ridicule' (p. 258). In short, philosophers are welcome to join the common enterprise, but only as junior partners. Indeed, one suspects that philosophy (of mind) on Crick's view will ultimately turn out to be dispensable. Whatever contribution it can make is propaedeutic and will eventually be replaced by a proper scientific account.

It is doubtful whether all philosophers committed to naturalism would accept this line of thought, but there is no question that naturalism does

THE NATURALIST CHALLENGE 139

pose a challenge to philosophy. Insofar as naturalists would consider the scientific account of reality authoritative, a commitment to naturalism is bound to put pressure on the idea that philosophy (including phenom-enology) can make a distinctive contribution to the study of reality.

Given this situation, it should not come as a surprise that the question of how to understand and respond to naturalism has been of concern to phenomenology ever since its commencement. It figured centrally in Husserl's discussion of psychologism in *Logische Untersuchungen*, in his programmatic manifesto *Philosophie als strenge Wissenschaft*, in his 1927 lectures *Natur und Geist*, and in his last work, *Die Krisis der europäischen Wissenschaften und die transzendentale Phänomenologie*, to mention just a few relevant texts. Given this background, it might appear surprising that quite a few have recently advocated a naturalization of phenomen-ology. What should one make of such a proposal? Is a naturalized phenomenology a desideratum or a category mistake? The answer to this question very much depends on what one takes the question to be, and (as will become clear in the following) we need to distinguish a number of different readings of what both phenomenology and natur-alization amount to. As will also become clear, Husserl's own response is less straightforward than one might assume, and is directly linked to the conception of transcendental philosophy he ended up defending.

5.1 Naturalizing phenomenology

Is it possible to bridge the gap between phenomenological analyses and naturalistic models of consciousness? Although the question has been discussed since the beginning of the twentieth century, there is no doubt that Francisco Varela's work has been decisive in rekindling interest in the issue. Back in 1991, Varela, Thompson, and Rosch pub-lished *The Embodied Mind: Cognitive Science and Human Experience*. The book was an important milestone. It criticized mainstream computation-alist and cognitivist tendencies in cognitive science by arguing persuasively that the scientific study of the mind could not continue to ignore the experiential and embodied dimensions of human cognition. In outlining an alternative, it drew on various sources, including Buddhism, phenom-enology, and Varela and Maturana's earlier work on autopoiesis. Phenom-enology was by and large defined through the work of Merleau-Ponty, who was heralded as somebody who had 'argued for the mutual illumination among a phenomenology of direct lived experience, psychology, and neurophysiology' (Varela et al. 1991: 15). *The Embodied Mind* proved immensely influential, and what back then might have appeared visionary has these days become far more mainstream. It is today commonplace to characterize cognition in terms of '4Es': embodied, embedded, enactive and extended. In such discussions, *The Embodied Mind* is almost invariably listed as one of the core references.

In subsequent work, Varela appropriated and redefined the term 'neurophenomenology' to designate a novel approach in cognitive science, one that considered the data from phenomenologically disciplined analyses of lived experience and the experimentally based accounts found in cognitive neuroscience to have equal status and to be linked by mutual constraints. For Varela, if cognitive science was to accomplish its goal, namely to provide a truly scientific theory of consciousness, it could not ignore the phenomenological dimension. To put it differently, if our aim is to have a comprehensive understanding of the mind, focusing narrowly on the nature of the sub-personal events that underlie experience without considering the qualities and structures of experience itself will just not take us very far. More specifically, Varela sought to incorporate phenomenological forms of investigation into the experimental protocols of neuroscientific research on consciousness (Varela 1996, 1997; Lutz et al. 2002; Lutz 2002; Lutz and Thompson 2003). Varela's initial publications in the area generated intense debate about the relation between phenomenology and cognitive science, and more generally about whether phenomenology could and ought to be naturalized.

Another milestone in the debate was the volume *Naturalizing Phenomenology* (Petitot et al. 1999), in which Varela and his three co-editors argued that it was crucial for the future development of cognitive science that cognitive scientists learned to use some of the methodological tools that were developed by Husserl and Merleau-Ponty. Cognitive science has been heralded as the first truly scientific theory of consciousness, but as Roy, Petitot, Pachoud, and Varela point out in their joint introduction to the volume, although one cannot deny the many results obtained by cognitive science, it is also characterized by a glaring omission. Cognitive science has persistently ignored what might be called the phenomenological dimension, arguing that this dimension is either irrelevant or inherently unreliable. However, by disregarding this dimension, by disregarding subjectivity and the first-person perspective, cognitive science is also disregarding a crucial aspect of the mental phenomena. Currently, cognitive science is, as the editors put it, 'a theory of the mind without being a theory of consciousness. It is a theory of what goes on in our minds when they are cognizing without being a theory of what it is like to be a cognizing mind' (Roy et al. 1999: 7). Cognitive science does represent a big improvement compared to classical behaviourism. In contrast to behaviourism, cognitive science has not held back from trying to explain what is happening *inside* the black box. To explain what is happening inside the black box, however, is not yet to explain what is happening *for* the black box (Roy et al. 1999: 12). And that is precisely what is needed.

One way to characterize the situation is by saying that cognitive science is confronted by what Joseph Levine called 'the explanatory gap' (Levine 1983). Briefly put, the problem is that we seem unable to bridge the gap between the neurophysiological processes that we can describe and analyse scientifically from a third-person perspective and the experiences that we are all familiar with from a first-person perspective. There seems to be an unbridgeable gap between the neurophysiological level and the experiential level. This situation is theoretically unsatisfactory and has to be remedied, but what options do we have? The surprising suggestion put forth by Roy et al. was the following. Given some of the recent developments in cognitive science, particularly the turn towards more embodied, embedded, and enactive accounts, it would be counterproductive to ignore the refined accounts of consciousness found in Husserlian phenomenology. The fact that subjectivity was always of central concern to Husserl, and that he devoted much time to a scrutiny of the first-person perspective, the structures of experience, time-consciousness, body-awareness, self-consciousness, intentionality, and so forth, makes him an obvious interlocutor. In fact, given its impressive past achievements in describing and analysing the dimension of phenomenality and the surprising frequency with which its results have been found to resonate with the results obtained by cognitive science, perhaps Husserlian phenomenology would allow for a closure of the explanatory gap.

However, if phenomenology were to play this role, if it really were to provide us with a better understanding of the relation between the cognitive processes and their phenomenal manifestation, it would first, according to the proposal, have to be 'naturalized', i.e.—to use the definition the editors themselves provide—it would have to be integrated into an explanatory framework where every kind of ontological dualism is avoided, and where every posited property is made continuous with the properties admitted by natural science (Roy et al. 1999: 1–2, 19).

The appeal to phenomenology is not unique. During the past 25 years, quite a number of figures have called on phenomenology to do its part of the job. A prominent example is Flanagan, who in his book *Consciousness Reconsidered* from 1992 argues for what he calls the 'natural method': if we wish to undertake a serious investigation of consciousness we cannot make do with neuroscientific or psychological (that is, functional) analyses alone, we also need to take the phenomenological aspect seriously (Flanagan 1992: 11). The disciplines of neuroscience, psychology, and phenomenology must be understood as mutually constraining approaches to the cognitive phenomena. Apart from Flanagan, others to defend similar ideas include John Searle, David Chalmers, Galen Strawson, Uriah Kriegel, and many others as well.

What was distinctive about the proposal currently under discussion is that Roy et al. were prepared to go much further. First, when talking of phenomenology, they didn't merely refer to some kind of introspective account of 'what it is like' to undergo certain experience, which (for instance) is how Flanagan was using the term. Rather, they were specifically referring to philosophical phenomenology. To that extent, they were in strong disagreement with those, like Metzinger, who claimed that empirical science didn't need phenomenology, and that it should just go ahead with its own work without wasting any time on a discredited research programme that had been intellectually bankrupt for many decades.[1] Second, they explicitly argued that the goal was to take Husserlian phenomenology seriously again—something that for instance clearly distinguished their proposal from the approach chosen by Dreyfus(ians). Thirdly, they claimed that phenomenology itself needed to be naturalized if the explanatory gap were to be bridged. This would on the one hand provide us with a more adequate theory of mind, i.e. a theory that didn't simply ignore the subjective dimension and on the other hand allow us to avoid any residue of mysterianism—the view that the true nature of consciousness is cognitively closed off to us given our limited human cognitive capacities—since the stated aim was precisely to

---

[1]   Cf. the editorial in *Journal of Consciousness Studies* (1997: 385).

offer a *natural* explanation of consciousness (Roy et al. 1999: 8). In short, the ambition was to show how experiences we are all familiar with from the first-person perspective are ultimately amenable to a natural scientific investigation and explanation.

The opinions were divided about this proposal. Some rejected it outright, others were much more excited about it. But even people who were kindly disposed towards it—and I am here in particular thinking of phenomenologists who cherished the idea of being indispensable to cognitive science—knew the proposal confronted some obvious obstacles.

It is one thing to counter the objection that the phenomenological dimension is beyond any scientific account with the retort that it is altogether possible to come up with systematic descriptions of consciousness that can be intersubjectively validated. But what about the objection that the phenomenological dimension is beyond any naturalized science? What about the fact that Husserl himself is known as a staunch anti-naturalist?

Our four editors were not unaware of this, of course, and they confronted it head on (Roy et al. 1999: 38). But the way they did so was somewhat surprising. To start with, they pointed out that Husserl distinguished two types of eidetic sciences, an axiomatic type and a descriptive type. The descriptive type deals with non-exact, vague, or morphological essences, whereas the axiomatic type deals with exact essences. When it comes to subjectivity and the investigation of experiential structures, Husserl was emphatic about the fact that lived experiences belong to the domain of vague essences. And according to Roy et al. (1999), Husserl's anti-naturalism was closely linked to his rejection of the possibility of developing a mathematical description or reconstruction of the vague, morphological, essences. Despite his own background in mathematics, Husserl had been convinced that mathematics was only of limited usefulness for phenomenology. As he wrote at the very beginning of *Ideen* I: 'In philosophy one cannot define as in mathematics; in this respect imitation of the mathematical procedure is invariably not only fruitless but perverse and leads to the most harmful consequences' (Hua 3/9). According to Roy et al., however, the opposition that Husserl introduces between mathematics and phenomenology was

the result of having mistaken certain contingent limitations of the mathematical and material sciences of his time for absolute ones. In our opinion it is indeed arguable that scientific progress has made Husserl's position on this point largely obsolete and that this *factum rationis* puts into question the properly scientific foundations of his anti-naturalism. (Roy et al. 1999: 42–3)

To put it differently, in their view, most of Husserl's scientific reasons for opposing naturalism had been invalidated by the progress of science (p. 54). Vague morphological essences (including those pertaining to the experiential dimension) are in fact amenable to a mathematical account provided only that one uses *morphodynamical* models. Given that a genuine mathematical description of experiential consciousness is possible, one of the big impediments to the naturalization of phenomenology has consequently been removed (pp. 55–6), since 'phenomenological descriptions of any kind can only be naturalized, in the sense of being integrated into the general framework of natural sciences, if they can be mathematized' (p. 42). The force of mathematical formalism is precisely that it is valid regardless of whether we are working on the neurobiological or the phenomenological level (pp. 51, 68). The moment we are in possession of a mathematical reconstruction of the phenomenological descriptions, the only remaining problem is then to articulate those reconstructions with the tools of the relevant lower-level natural sciences, in particular the tools of neurobiology (pp. 48, 63).

5.2 Husserl's anti-naturalism

I find this line of argumentation puzzling. Husserl's opposition to naturalism is not primarily based on his so-called scientific motives, i.e. on his rejection of the attempt to mathematically formalize the morphological structures of experience. Rather, it is mainly based on a number of philosophical reasons, or to be more exact, on a number of transcendental philosophical arguments, which are only mentioned in passing by the editors (Roy et al. 1999: 39).

In the long essay *Philosophie als strenge Wissenschaft* from 1911, for instance, Husserl called naturalism a fundamentally flawed philosophy (Hua 25/41) and argued that it has typically had two different aims: the naturalization of ideality and normativity, and the naturalization of consciousness (Hua 25/9). In his view, however, both attempts fail and both are misguided. The naturalistic attempt to reduce the ideal truths and laws of logic to empirical truths, its conflation of logical and real necessity, of normative and causal regulation, leads to scepticism (Hua

25/7, 24/47–8). This, in fact, was one of Husserl's main arguments in his fight against psychologism in the *Logische Untersuchungen*. As he argued, this and any other attempt by naturalized epistemology to justify scientific knowledge is self-refuting and amounts to a form of 'cognitive suicide', to use Hanna's apt phrase (2014: 757).

Why did Husserl oppose the attempt to implement a thorough naturalistic account of consciousness? Because naturalism in his view is incapable of doing full justice to consciousness. Not only has it—in the shape of experimental psychology—tended to lose sight of (subjective) consciousness (Hua 25/104), but even more importantly, naturalism treats consciousness as an object in the world, on a par with—though possibly more complex than—volcanoes, waterfalls, ice crystals, gold nuggets, rhododendrons, or black holes. But on Husserl's view this is precisely what is unacceptable, since consciousness, rather than merely being an *object in the world*, is also *a subject for the world*, i.e. a necessary condition of possibility for any entity to appear as an object in the way it does and with the meaning it has. To put it differently, according to Husserl, the decisive limitation of naturalism is that it has failed to recognize the *transcendental* dimension of consciousness. As he occasionally puts it, the 'naturalization of the psychic' and more generally, the rise of 'physicalistically oriented naturalism' (Hua 6/64 [63]) is due to a 'blindness to the transcendental' (Hua 6/269 [265]).

When Husserl denies that consciousness is an objective occurrence existing side by side with the object of which it is conscious, he is not denying the possibility of a reductive account of qualia and urging us to adopt some kind of non-reductive or even dualist account. Husserl is not concerned with the question of what kind of stuff consciousness is made of, and to read him in this way is to misunderstand his philosophical project. Husserl's criticism is instead directed at the very attempt of finding room for consciousness within an already well-established naturalistic framework. To engage in such an attempt is to assume that consciousness is simply an object in the world; but it is precisely this assumption which according to Husserl prevents one from disclosing, let alone clarifying, some of the most interesting aspects of consciousness, including the true epistemic and ontological significance of the first-person perspective. In his view, it is, for instance, not acceptable to address the problem of whether and how we can obtain knowledge about the world by appealing to a model that conceives of the epistemic agent as a worldly object that is causally related to other parts of the world, since such an approach simply begs the question. Indeed, as Husserl argues in *Die Idee der Phänomenologie*, such an approach merely reveals that one has failed to grasp the proper radicality of the epistemological query (Hua 2/6).

For Husserl, the problem of consciousness should not be addressed against the background of an unquestioned objectivism, but in connection with overarching transcendental considerations. Frequently, the assumption has been that a better understanding of the physical world will allow us to understand consciousness better, and rarely that a better understanding of consciousness might allow for a better understanding of what it means for something to be real. However, one of the reasons why the theory of intentionality occupies centre stage in Husserl's thinking is precisely because he considers a study of the world-directedness of consciousness to provide us with insights into not only the structure of subjectivity but also the nature of objectivity—that something like a conscious appropriation of the world is possible does not merely tell us something about consciousness, but also about the world. But, of course, this way of discussing consciousness, as the constitutive dimension that makes any worldly manifestation possible, as the 'place in which' the world can reveal and articulate itself is quite different from any attempt to treat it naturalistically as merely yet another (psychical or physical) object in the world.

When confronted with the question of the relation between the phenomenological account of how subjectivity constitutes objectivity and the naturalistic account of how subjectivity emerges in an objective world, the naturalist might be tempted to respond as follows. Even if the two enterprises are different and to that extent might also be compatible, we should not fool ourselves into thinking that we are dealing with equal partners. There is no question that causality is more fundamental than intentionality, and that physics and biology always trump phenomenology. However, when asking what is most fundamental, one always has to ask: most fundamental in respect to what? Otherwise one will end up comparing apples and oranges.

For Husserl, the positive sciences take their subject matter, nature, for granted. Reality is assumed to be out there, waiting to be discovered and investigated. And the aim of natural science is to acquire a strict and objectively valid knowledge about this given realm. But this attitude must be contrasted with the properly philosophical attitude, which critically questions the very foundation of experience and scientific thought (Hua 25/13–14). Philosophy is a discipline which does not simply contribute to or augment the scope of our positive knowledge, but instead investigates the basis of this knowledge and asks how it is possible. Some naturalists have denied the existence of a particular philosophical method, and have claimed that philosophy (be it epistemology, metaphysics, etc.) should adopt and employ the methods of the natural sciences. For Husserl, however, this line of reasoning merely shows that one has failed to understand what philosophy is all about. Philosophy has its own aims and methodological requirements—requirements that for Husserl are epitomized in the notion of 'phenomenological reduction' (Hua 24/238–9). For Husserl, the reduction is meant to make us maintain the radical difference between philosophical reflection and all other modes of thought. As he wrote in 1907: 'The "phenomenological reduction" accordingly signifies nothing other than the requirement to remain constantly within the meaning of one's own investigation and not confuse theory of knowledge with natural scientific (objective) investigation' (Hua 24/410). Every positive science rests upon a field of givenness that is presupposed but not investigated by the sciences themselves. Every object-oriented investigation presupposes the availability of a framework of intelligibility that permits objects to appear in such a manner that they can be targets of further exploration and explanation. In order to examine the structures that allow and enable such object manifestation, a new type of inquiry is called for, a type of reflective inquiry that 'is prior to all natural knowledge and science and is on an entirely different plane than natural science' (Hua 24/176). This, of course, is one reason why the phenomenological attitude has frequently been described as an unnatural direction of thought (cf. Hua 19/14). To describe phenomenology as unnatural is also to deny any straightforward continuity between philosophy and natural science.

For Husserl, science is not simply a collection of systematically interrelated justified propositions. Science is performed by somebody; it is a specific theoretical stance towards the world. This stance is not a view from nowhere—it did not fall from the sky, nor did it emerge fully formed like Athena from Zeus' forehead. Rather, it has its own presuppositions and origin. Science is performed by embodied and embedded subjects, and if we wish to comprehend the performance and limits of science, we have to investigate the forms of intentionality employed by the cognizing subjects. As Merleau-Ponty wrote in *Phénoménologie de la perception*, the one-sided focus of science on what is available from a third-person perspective is both naïve and dishonest, since the scientific practice constantly presupposes the scientist's first-personal and pre-scientific experience of the world (Merleau-Ponty 2012: lxxii). The standardizations of procedures and the development of instruments that provide precise measurements have facilitated the generation and accumulation of data and the establishment of intersubjective consensus. But without conscious subjects to interpret and discuss them, meter settings, computer printouts, x-ray pictures, and the like remain meaningless (Velmans 2000: 179). Thus, according to this view, rather than being a hindrance or obstacle, consciousness turns out to be a far more important requisite for objectivity and the pursuit of scientific knowledge than, say, microscopes and scanners. This is also why the usual opposition of first-person vs third-person accounts is misleading. It makes us forget that so-called third-person objective accounts are accomplished and generated by a community of conscious subjects. There is no pure third-person perspective, just as there is no view from nowhere. To believe in the existence of a pure third-person perspective is to succumb to an objectivist illusion. This is not, of course, to say that there is no third-person perspective, but merely that such a perspective is, precisely, a perspective from somewhere. It is a view that we can adopt on the world. Objectivity is certainly something to strive for, but scientific knowledge depends on the observations and experiences of individuals; it is knowledge that is shared by a community of experiencing subjects, and presupposes a triangulation of points of view or perspectives.

In the light of such considerations, it is again not surprising that phenomenology's response to naturalism has been unequivocal. Contrary to some proposals, it is not naturalism's endorsement of some form of physicalism that constitutes the main obstacle to a reconciliation. It is not as if matters would improve if naturalism opted for some version of emergentism or property dualism. The real problem has to do with naturalism's inherent objectivism and its ensuing transcendental naïvety (Hua 6/196). The naturalistic insistence that only those entities and facts that are (or can be) known by natural science are objectively real not only typically fails to properly engage with and address the philosophical question of what precisely reality and objectivity amount to. It is also a self-undermining enterprise in that it fails to adequately account for those experiential and cognitive achievements that make naturalism—as a specific attitude to and perspective on the world—possible in the first place.

Husserl's central claim is that phenomenology can provide a clarification of naturalism's tacit presuppositions, and that this philosophical clarification is more fundamental than anything naturalism itself can offer. This is also why Husserl considered the rejection of (an all-encompassing) naturalism crucial. As he explained in a letter to the neo-Kantian Rickert:

> Thus, for the last decade, I feel tightly bound to the main figures of the German idealist schools: we are allies in the battle against the naturalism of our era, our common adversary. We serve, each of us in his own way, the same gods, and since this is something serious and holy to us, something to which we committed our entire life, each of these ways harbours in itself its own necessities and is bound to be indispensable for the advancement of philosophy. (Hua Dok 3-V/178)

Given this outlook, it is no surprise that transcendental phenomenology has traditionally been seen as an autonomous discipline whose investigation of the condition of possibility for knowledge and experience must take place in a sphere entirely separate from that of the sciences. A concise articulation of this view can be found in the following quote from Murray:

> [P]henomenological descriptions and neurobiological explanations can not be viewed as a set of mutually enriching methodological options which, together, will allow us to build up a picture of cognition, aspect by aspect, as it were, because the two kinds of accounts have an entirely different status. For in seeking to lay bare the fundamental structures of experience, phenomenology is also seeking to establish the foundations of any possible knowledge. Consequently, phenomenological accounts cannot simply be conjoined to neurobiological ones, because the ultimate purpose of the former is to ascertain the validity of the latter. In other words, to suppose that naturalizing phenomenology is simply a matter of overcoming some traditional ontological divide is to fail to see that the difference between phenomenology and neurobiology is not just a difference with respect to the objects of their investigations, but a fundamental difference in their theoretical orientation—a difference which is taken to be typical of philosophical and scientific investigations in general. For while the neuroscientist allegedly takes for granted the possibility of understanding the world, the philosopher believes there is a need for some kind of preliminary investigation into how such an understanding might arise. Consequently, a phenomenologist who embraced naturalisation might be seen as having, in effect, ceased to be a philosopher. (Murray 2002: 30–31)

Where does this leave us? Is the entire attempt to naturalize phenomenology doomed from the very start due to its misunderstanding of what phenomenology is all about? It might look that way, but in the rest of this chapter I will argue that the situation is somewhat more complex.

5.3 Transcendental phenomenology and phenomenological psychology

Were one to embrace and implement the strategy found in the introduction to *Naturalizing Phenomenology* (Roy et al. 1999), were one to ease the way for a naturalization of phenomenology by abandoning its transcendental aspirations, one would by the same token abandon much of what is philosophically distinctive about phenomenology. Thus, it is certainly no coincidence that Roy et al. at one point urge us to consider 'the possibility of dissociating the specific philosophical interpretation he [Husserl] hoped to confer upon his descriptions from what one is tempted to call their scientific content' (Roy et al. 1999: 52). Faced with such a proposal, Lawlor is right when he writes that naturalism is incapable of solving the transcendental problem that was of concern to Husserl, and that the project of naturalization in general and especially the project of naturalizing phenomenology only makes the crisis addressed by Husserl in his late work *Die Krisis der europäischen Wissenschaften und die transzendentale Phänomenologie* even worse (Lawlor 2009: 4). But (and there is a but) there are more ways of understanding what a naturalization of phenomenology amounts to than the one just outlined.

In this and the following section, let me sketch two alternative takes on what a naturalized phenomenology might amount to. I want to suggest that our appraisal of the desirability of a naturalized phenomenology ought to be more positive, if we opt for one or both of the following proposals.

One very different way of approaching the issue—a way that has both classical roots, but which has also received a dramatic revival in recent years—is to hold that a naturalization of phenomenology, rather than amounting to an abandonment of its transcendental aspirations, simply entails letting phenomenology engage in a fruitful exchange and collaboration with empirical science.

What form might this take? In an article from 2000 entitled 'Bridging Embodied Cognition and Brain Function: The Role of Phenomenology', Borrett, Kelly, and Kwan argued as follows:

[T]he right relation between phenomenology and brain science is that of data to model: brain science is ultimately concerned with explaining the way the physical processes of the brain conspire to produce the phenomena of human experience; insofar as phenomenology devotes itself to the accurate description of these phenomena, it provides the most complete and accurate presentation of the data that ultimately must be accounted for by models of brain function [. . .]. Thus, the phenomenological account of a given aspect of human behavior is meant to provide a description of the characteristics of that behavior which any physical explanation of it must be able to reproduce. (Borrett et al. 2000: 214)

This suggestion is far too modest. Phenomenology might indeed offer detailed analyses of perception, imagination, body-awareness, recollection, social cognition, self-experience, temporality, etc.; but in providing such analyses, phenomenology can do more than simply offer more refined descriptions of an already fixed explanandum, or merely provide more data to existing models. Phenomenology is not merely in the descriptive business. It also offers theoretical accounts of its own that can challenge existing models and background assumptions, and which might occasionally lead to the discovery of quite different explananda. Furthermore, on the proposal currently under consideration, to naturalize phenomenology is not simply to stress the usefulness of phenomenological analyses and distinctions for empirical science. If we are to have a fruitful exchange, the influence must also go the other way and make it appropriate to speak of 'mutual enlightenment' (Gallagher 1997).[2] Phenomenology studies phenomena that are also open to empirical investigation, and insofar as phenomenology concerns itself with such phenomena, it might be argued that it ought to be informed by the best available scientific knowledge, and that empirical findings can help us improve and refine the classical phenomenological analyses. The phenomenological credo 'To the things themselves' calls for us to let our experience guide our theories. We should pay attention to the way in which reality is experientially manifest. Empirical researchers might not pay much attention to deep philosophical questions, but as empirical researchers they do in fact pay quite a lot of attention to concrete phenomena, and might consequently be less apt than the average armchair philosopher to underestimate the richness, complexity, and variety of the phenomena.

---

[2] Contrary to what Ramstead has recently suggested (2015: 938), however, the notion of mutual enlightenment does not automatically entail a commitment to a form of methodological naturalism.

Such a proposal is confronted with some immediate and rather obvious objections. Let me discuss them in turn.

1. Is the idea really that a phenomenological account of, say, perception or action should be informed and constrained by, say, investigations of the neuronal mechanisms and processes involved in action and perception? More generally speaking, how can analyses pertaining to various sub-personal processes and mechanisms possibly influence and enrich phenomenological accounts that attempt to do justice to the first-person perspective and seek to understand the experience in terms of the meaning it has for the subject?

Two things can be said in response. First, in some cases, neuroscientific explorations may in fact turn out to have relevance for phenomenological analysis. For instance, assume that our initial phenomenological description presents us with what appears to be a simple and unified perceptual phenomenon. When studying the neural correlates of this phenomenon, however, we discover that not only areas correlated with perception but also areas correlated with episodic memory are activated. This discovery might motivate us to return to our initial phenomenological description in order to see whether the phenomenon in question is indeed as simple as we thought. Assuming that phenomenologists are not infallible and that their first attempts are not always perfect, it is possible that a more careful phenomenological analysis will reveal that the experience harbours a concealed complexity. It is important, however, to emphasize that the discovery of a significant complexity on the sub-personal level—to stick to this simple example—by itself cannot force us to refine or revise our phenomenological description. It can only serve as motivation for further inquiry. There is no straightforward isomorphism between the sub-personal and personal level, and ultimately the only way to justify a claim concerning a complexity on the phenomenological level is by cashing it out in experiential terms.

Second, and more importantly, when talking of a productive cross-fertilization between phenomenology and the sciences, the primary example that comes to mind is not how research into neurons, axons, and dendrites might change phenomenology. We should instead look at disciplines such as psychopathology, neuropathology, developmental psychology, cognitive psychology, anthropology, and social psychology, and consider to what extent they can provide person-level *descriptions* that might be of phenomenological relevance. Many examples could be mentioned, but here are a few:

- Neuropsychological descriptions of various disorders of body-awareness. Consider, for example, Jonathan Cole's (1995) careful analysis of Ian Waterman, who at the age of 19, due to illness, lost all sense of touch and proprioception from the neck down. One might relate and compare Cole's analysis of how dramatic and disabling this impairment is to the classical phenomenological investigation of the lived body that we find in Husserl and Merleau-Ponty.

- Psychopathological descriptions of schizophrenic disturbances of self-experience and intentionality. Psychiatrists and clinical psychologists, such as Minkowski, Blankenburg, Parnas, and Sass, have all provided careful analyses of the disturbed self- and world-experience we find in schizophrenic patients. One can productively compare such accounts to phenomenological explorations of the relation between our world-immersed life and different forms of self-consciousness (see Parnas et al. 2005).

- Developmental descriptions of social interactions in early childhood. Developmental psychologists like Rochat, Reddy, Hobson, and Carpenter have provided careful accounts of fundamental but primitive forms of social understanding found in infants and young children. One might relate such accounts to the work on empathy, pairing, and intercorporeity that we find in Scheler, Stein, Husserl, and Merleau-Ponty.

Empirical science can present phenomenology with concrete findings that it cannot simply ignore, but must be able to accommodate—evidence that might force it to refine or revise its own analyses. At the same time, phenomenology might not only contribute with its own careful descriptions of the explanandum, but might also question and elucidate basic theoretical assumptions made by empirical science, just as insights developed in phenomenological analyses might aid in the development of new experimental paradigms and inform the way experiments are set up. Gallagher has described such a procedure as 'front-loading phenomenology' (Gallagher 2003; Gallagher and Zahavi 2012).

To exemplify further, consider first the case of self-consciousness. Within developmental psychology, the so-called mirror-recognition task has occasionally been heralded as the decisive test for self-consciousness. From around 18 months of age, children will engage in self-directed behaviour when confronted with their mirror-image, and it has been argued that self-consciousness is only present from the moment the child is capable of recognizing itself in the mirror (cf. Lewis 2003). Needless to say, this line of reasoning makes use of a very specific notion of self-consciousness. Rather than simply letting phenomenological insights guide our interpretation of the results obtained through the testing of mirror-recognition, one possibility would be to let the phenomenological notion and analysis of pre-reflective self-consciousness guide our design of the experimental paradigm. It would no longer involve the testing of mirror-recognition—which phenomenologists would typically consider evidence for the presence of a rather sophisticated form of self-consciousness (cf. Rochat and Zahavi 2011)—but rather aim at detecting the presence of more primitive forms of self-consciousness, including, for instance, proprioceptive body-awareness. To front-load phenomenology, however, would not imply that one simply presupposes well-rehearsed phenomenological results. Rather, it involves testing those results; more generally, it incorporates a dialectical movement between previous insights gained in phenomenology and preliminary trials that will specify or extend these insights for purposes of the particular experiment or empirical investigation (Gallagher 2003).

Consider next recent work on mirror neurons. Several mirror-neuron theorists have emphasized the similarity between their account of embodied simulation and work done in the phenomenological tradition on empathy and 'intercorporeity'. Gallese has referred favourably to the analyses found in Stein, Husserl, and Merleau-Ponty (Gallese 2001: 43–4), and Iacoboni has claimed that discovery of the mirror neurons has provided a plausible neurophysiological explanation of complex forms of social cognition and interaction (Iacoboni 2009: 5). Iacoboni has even argued that the existence of mirror neurons can explain why 'existential phenomenologists were correct all along' (Iacoboni 2009: 262). As a closer study of the phenomenological work on empathy will reveal, however, marked differences remain between this corpus of work and the model proposed by the embodied simulationists. For one, Husserl has on occasion distanced himself explicitly from the idea that the best way to conceive of the relation between self and other is in terms of mirroring. On his view, that notion doesn't capture the dynamic and dialectical intertwinement between self and other. Furthermore, any comparison of the phenomenological account of empathy with the attempt to explain empathy in terms of mirror-resonance mechanisms should not forget that we are dealing with accounts targeting a personal and a subpersonal level, respectively. As long as one is not so naïve as to believe in straightforward isomorphism between the two levels, it is not at all clear that the accounts can be compared in any direct fashion. If nothing else, such differences can motivate a renewed scrutiny of some of the conceptual assumptions at play in the mirror-neuron literature (for an extended discussion, see Zahavi 2014). It might be best to avoid the claim that the discovery of the mirror neurons has confirmed the phenomenological account or that the latter supports the mirror-neuron hypothesis. A more prudent and more cautious claim would be that work on mirror neurons as well as other neuroscientific findings can complement the phenomenological description by clarifying the empathic relation described and showing how it 'need not be something mysterious or even impossible' (Ratcliffe 2006: 336).

2. At this point, a further objection might be raised. Is there not an obvious mismatch between the eidetic a priori analyses pursued by phenomenology and the empirical a posteriori results obtained by cognitive science? I think it is easy to dismiss this worry, as long as we are operating within a Husserlian framework. For Husserl, we can obtain insights into essential a priori structures through eidetic variation. However, such insights always possess a certain provisionality, a certain presumptiveness, and necessarily remain open for future modifications in the light of new evidence. As Husserl writes in *Formal and Transcendental Logic*:

The *possibility of deception* is inherent in the evidence of experience [. . .]. This too holds for *every* evidence, for every 'experience' in the amplified sense. Even an ostensibly apodictic evidence can become disclosed as deception and, in that event, presupposes a similar evidence by which it is 'shattered'. (Hua 17/164)

Our a priori knowledge is, in short, fallible; if we come across putative empirical counterexamples to our alleged eidetic insights, they need to be taken seriously and cannot simply be dismissed as irrelevant. In fact, if we want to test and probe the validity of our eidetic claims, considering a range of more or less exceptional cases might be quite illuminating. One way to do so is by engaging in various thought experiments. As Wilkes has pointed out, however, if thought experiments are to be of value, they must be performed with as much attention to detail and as many stringent constraints as real experiments conducted in the laboratory. Otherwise, we might easily end in a situation where we believe that we have succeeded in imagining a possible state of affairs yet, in reality, have done nothing of the sort, as we will realize when we acquire more information and are able to think the scenario through more carefully. The more ignorant we are, the easier it will seem to imagine something since 'the obstructive facts are not there to obtrude' (Wilkes 1988: 31). An alternative is to abandon fiction altogether and instead pay more attention to the startling facts found in the actual world. Real-life deviations can serve the same function as thought experiments. They can also probe and test our concepts and intuitions. If we are looking for phenomena that can shake our ingrained assumptions and force us to refine, revise, or even abandon our habitual way of thinking, all we have to do is to turn to psychopathology, neurology, developmental psychology, anthropology, etc.; all of these disciplines present us with rich sources of challenging material. In other words, if we wish to test our phenomenological analysis of the unity of mind, the nature of agency, or the role of emotions, much can be learned from a closer examination of phenomena such as depersonalization, thought-insertion, dissociative identity disorder, apraxia, or anhedonia.

3. Let us move on and consider a further objection. On the current reading of what a naturalized phenomenology amounts to, there is no attempt at making phenomenology part of or continuous with natural science. As already mentioned, the idea is merely to let phenomenology and empirical science engage in a collaboration that is beneficial for both parties. The contribution of phenomenology amounts to more than simply describing the explanandum (and has little to do with introspective data gathering), since phenomenology is taken to have a genuine theoretical impact. Furthermore, insisting on the fact that phenomenology can learn from empirical science is not meant to jeopardize or challenge the eidetic character of the former. The problem, however, is this: so far there has been no reference to the distinctive transcendental character of phenomenology. But does that not simply demonstrate the futility of the project? Let us not forget what Husserl said in an earlier quoted passage from his 1917 lecture 'Phänomenologie und

Psychologie': to engage in an eidetic and a priori analysis of experiential consciousness is to do psychology—and not yet phenomenology proper (Hua 25/104–5).

In order to deal with this objection, we need to take another look at Husserl's view on the relation between psychology and phenomenology.

As I have already pointed out, in the first edition of the *Logische Untersuchungen* Husserl still designated phenomenology as a form of descriptive psychology (Hua 19/24). This was a characterization he quickly came to regret and reject (Hua 22/206–8), and with good reasons. Nevertheless, as this initial blunder illustrates, the distinction between phenomenology and psychology can at times be hard to draw. Although phenomenology and psychology differ, this does not make them unrelated, and it is no coincidence that their relationship remained of interest to Husserl until the very end. Husserl occasionally characterizes phenomenology (a phenomenology not misled by naturalistic prejudices, as he adds) as the foundation and presupposition for a truly scientific psychology (Hua 24/383–4, 25/39). In later writings, Husserl distinguishes two different phenomenological approaches to consciousness. On the one hand, we have transcendental phenomenology, and on the other, we have what he calls 'phenomenological psychology' (Hua 9/35). What is the difference between these two approaches? Both of them deal with consciousness, but they do so with rather different agendas in mind. For Husserl, the task of phenomenological psychology is to investigate intentional consciousness in a non-reductive manner, that is, in a manner that respects its peculiarity and distinctive features. Phenomenological psychology is a form of philosophical psychology which takes the first-person perspective seriously, but which—in contrast to transcendental phenomenology—remains within the natural attitude. The difference between the two is consequently that phenomenological psychology might be described as a regional-ontological analysis that investigates consciousness for its own sake. In contrast, transcendental phenomenology is a more ambitious enterprise. It is interested in the constitutive dimension of subjectivity, i.e. it is interested in an investigation of consciousness insofar as consciousness is taken to be a condition of possibility for meaning, truth, validity, and manifestation.

What is the relevance of this distinction? Although Husserl was primarily interested in the development of transcendental phenomenology, he was not blind to the fact that his analyses might have ramifications for and be of pertinence to the psychological study of consciousness *and conversely*. After all, the relation between the transcendental subject and the empirical subject is for Husserl not a relation between two different subjects, but between two different self-apprehensions. The transcendental subject and the empirical subject is but one subject, though viewed from different perspectives. The transcendental subject is the subject in its primary constitutive function. The empirical subject is the same subject, but now apprehended and interpreted as an object in the world. As Husserl writes in the *Encyclopedia Britannica* article:

My transcendental ego is thus evidently 'different' from the natural ego, but by no means as a second, as one separated from it in the natural sense of the word, just as on the contrary it is by no means bound up with it or intertwined with it, in the usual sense of these words. It is just the field of transcendental self-experience (conceived in full concreteness) which can in every case, through mere alteration of attitude, be changed into psychological self-experience. In this transition, an identity of the I is necessarily brought about; in transcendental reflection on this transition the psychological Objectivation becomes visible as self-objectivation of the transcendental ego, and so it is as if in every moment of the natural attitude the I finds itself with an apperception imposed upon it. (Hua 9/294)

Given this account, there would for Husserl ideally speaking only be one way to accurately analyse, say, perceptual intentionality descriptively, although the analysis offered could then be subjected to both a transcendental and an objectifying interpretation (Hua 6/210). At times, Husserl even emphasizes the propaedeutic advantages of approaching transcendental phenomenology through phenomenological psychology. As he puts it, one might start out with no interest whatsoever in transcendental philosophy, and merely be concerned with the establishing of a strictly scientific psychology. If this task is pursued in a radical manner, and if the structures of consciousness are investigated with sufficient precision and care, it will eventually be necessary to take the full step, to effect a transcendental turn, and thereby reach transcendental phenomenology (Hua 9/347).

On occasions, Husserl speaks of a parallelism between phenomenological psychology and transcendental phenomenology and claims that it is possible to step from one to the other through an attitudinal change. As he writes:

every analysis or theory of transcendental phenomenology—including [. . .] the theory of the transcendental constitution of an objective world—can be carried out in the natural realm, when we give up the transcendental attitude. Thus transposed to the realm of transcendental naïveté, it becomes a theory pertaining to internal psychology. Eidetically and empirically, a *pure* psychology—a psychology that merely explicates what belongs to the psyche, to a concrete human Ego, as its own intentional essence—corresponds to a *transcendental phenomenology*, and vice versa. (Hua 1/159, trans. modified)

In late works such as *Cartesian Meditations* and *Krisis*, Husserl even argues that it is pointless to treat transcendental phenomenology and psychology separately. At first he suggests that the former should pave the way, and that the latter could then take over some of the results (without having to bother with the transcendental considerations); but as he eventually goes on to say, in its core psychology qua the study of consciousness contains a transcendental dimension and is ultimately part of transcendental philosophy, though this will remain concealed until psychology is relieved of its naivety (Hua 1/174):

Thus we understand that in fact an indissoluble inner alliance obtains between psychology and transcendental philosophy. But from this perspective we can also foresee that there must be a way whereby a concretely executed psychology could lead to a transcendental philosophy. (Hua 6/210 [206])

By arguing in this fashion, Husserl seems to allow for the possibility that the positive sciences can unearth matters that transcendental phenomenology will have to take into account.[3] Though, of course, he is admittedly primarily thinking of an exchange between disciplines that all take their point of departure from the first-person perspective. More specifically, I see no reason why Husserl should rule out the possibility that findings in the domain of psychopathology or developmental psychology (if based on a meticulous analysis of the phenomena and if subjected to the requisite modifications) might be taken up by, and consequently influence or

---

[3] The interest in positive science and in its significance for phenomenology is, of course, also prominent in many of Merleau-Ponty's works. His use of neuropathology, in particular Gelb and Goldstein's famous Schneider Case, is well known. It is revealing that Merleau-Ponty apparently shared Husserl's view regarding the incipient transcendental character of psychology. As Merleau-Ponty writes in *Phénoménologie de la perception*: 'To concern oneself with psychology is necessarily to encounter, beneath the objective thought that moves among ready-made things, a primary opening onto things without which there could be no objective knowledge. The psychologist cannot fail to rediscover himself as an experience, that is, as an immediate presence to the past, the world, the body, and others, at the very moment he wanted to see himself as just one object among others' (Merleau-Ponty 2012: 99).

constrain, an analysis of transcendental subjectivity. Let us not forget how Husserl emphasized the contrast between Kant's top-down and his own bottom-up approach, and the extent to which, in pursuing the latter, he also found it relevant to consider the social, historical, cultural, and linguistic domains.

In order to clarify the distinctive character of this approach to the relation between philosophy and empirical science, let me briefly contrast it with the position advocated by Bennett and Hacker in their book *Philosophical Foundations of Neuroscience*. According to their outlook, a philosophical investigation of consciousness differs in principle from an empirical one, for which reason it is meaningless to suggest that the latter can challenge or even replace the former. Philosophy is not concerned with matters of fact, but with matters of meaning. The business of philosophy is with logical possibilities, not with empirical actualities. Its province is not the domain of empirical truth or falsehood, but the domain of sense and nonsense. To put it differently, philosophy clarifies what does and does not make sense. It investigates and describes the bounds of sense: that is, the limits of what can coherently be thought and said. The boundary between what does and what does not make sense, between what is meaningful and what transgresses the bounds of sense, is determined by the concepts we use, and the way philosophy can contribute to an investigation of the nature of the mind is consequently by clarifying our concept of mind and the way this concept is linked to related concepts (Bennett and Hacker 2003: 399, 402). The primary method of dissolving conceptual puzzlement is by carefully examining and describing the use of words—i.e. we should investigate what competent speakers, using words correctly, do and do not say. Rather than engaging in first-order claims about the nature of things (which can be left to various scientific disciplines), philosophy should consequently concern itself with the conceptual preconditions for any such empirical inquiries. Conceptual questions antecede matters of truth and falsehood. They are presupposed by any scientific investigation, and any lack of clarity regarding the relevant concepts will be reflected in a corresponding lack of clarity in the questions posed, and hence in the design of the experiments intended to answer them (Bennett and Hacker 2003: 2). To put it more directly, empirical research that proceeds from conceptually flawed premises is likely to yield incoherent empirical questions and answers. Bennett and Hacker then proceed by arguing that the relationship between conceptual and empirical issues is unidirectional, and that philosophy is of much greater importance to science than vice versa. For while philosophers can clarify the concepts used in science and thereby offer an immense service to science, it is a mistake to think that science could have much of an impact on philosophy. In fact, Bennett and Hacker even consider ridiculous the supposition that scientific evidence may contravene a philosophical analysis (Bennett and Hacker 2003: 404). In their view, we should not commit the mistake of confusing metaphysical or epistemological theories with empirical claims which can be corroborated by some *experimentum crucis*. Thus, the relation between philosophy and empirical science is a one-way enterprise. It is an application of ready-made concepts. There is no reciprocity, and there is no feedback. The application does not lead to a modification of the original analysis.[4]

This is certainly one type of response to the challenge posed to philosophy by the revival of naturalism. But as I have just suggested, I don't think this is the way phenomenology ought to respond. After all, on the proposal currently under consideration, the idea is not simply to let empirical science be constrained by phenomenological demarcations and analyses. Rather, the argument is that influence goes both ways, and that phenomenology might also profit from and be challenged by empirical findings. Furthermore, to let an examination of ordinary language use be our primary, if not exclusive, guide to a philosophical

[4] Although I have reservations regarding Bennett and Hacker's depiction of the relation between philosophy of mind and empirical science, I find their criticism of certain grandiose tendencies in contemporary cognitive neuroscience quite to the point. The first two generations of modern neuroscientists, including scientists such as Eccles and Penfield, were neo-Cartesians. The third generation repudiated the dualism of their teachers and explicitly endorsed a form of physicalism. But as Bennett and Hacker point out, neuroscience has continued to remain bedevilled by a crypto-Cartesian and empiricist legacy. It might have replaced the immaterial Cartesian mind with the material brain, but it has maintained the dualism between brain and body, and thereby the logical structure of dualist psychology. Indeed, most of the neuroscientists who have castigated philosophy for its alleged failings—for not having accomplished anything scientifically worthwhile in its 2,500-year history—are unaware of the extent to which much of their own framework of thought has a philosophical heritage. It is a simple fact that the 17th-century philosophical conception of reality, of what is objective and what is subjective, of the nature of perception and its objects, has profoundly affected the ways in which brain scientists currently conceive of their own investigations (Bennett and Hacker 2003: 134). And as they then polemically ask, is what 21st-century neuroscience can offer to philosophy simply a rehash of 17th-century epistemology and metaphysics (Bennett and Hacker 2003: 407)?

investigation of the mind seems far too restrictive, and underestimates the degree to which ordinary language reflects commonsense metaphysics. Adhering to this method would block the way for concrete phenomenological analyses that might reveal aspects and dimensions of the mind that are not simply available to any reflection on common sense (consider e.g. Husserl's investigations of the structures of time-consciousness or pictorial consciousness). It is perhaps not entirely without reason that the style of analytic philosophy defended by Bennett and Hacker has been accused of promoting a kind of semantic inertia and conceptual conservatism (Dennett 2007: 89).

5.4 Phenomenological naturalism

So far, I have distinguished two different understandings of what a naturalized phenomenology might amount to:

- The initial proposal claimed that phenomenology has to become a part of, or at least an extension of, natural science. I consider this proposal misguided. It denies the legitimacy of methods and questions that are unique to philosophy, and wants to replace the transcendental clarification that phenomenology offers with an explanatory account. Were one to pursue this strategy, and treat consciousness as an object in the world, one would abandon by the same stroke a good deal of what is philosophically interesting about phenomenology.

- The first alternative to this proposal argues that phenomenology can and ought to be naturalized, but only in the sense that it should engage in a meaningful and productive exchange with empirical science. Phenomenology can question and elucidate basic theoretical assumptions made by empirical science, just as it might aid in the development of new experimental paradigms. Empirical science can present phenomenology with concrete findings that it cannot simply ignore, but must be able to accommodate. Such evidence might force it to refine or revise its own analyses of, say, the role of embodiment, the relation between perception and imagination, the link between time-consciousness and memory, or the nature of social cognition. It is important to remember, though, that empirical findings are open to interpretation, and that their interpretation will typically depend upon the framework within which one is operating. Thus, the theoretical impact of an empirical case is not necessarily something that can be easily determined. Even if phenomenology ought to pay attention to empirical findings, this does not entail that it should also simply accept the (metaphysical and epistemological) interpretation that science gives of these findings. The possibility of a fruitful exchange between phenomenology and empirical science is consequently not meant to make us deny their difference. I see no incoherence in claiming that phenomenology should be informed by the best available scientific knowledge, while at the same time insisting that the ultimate concern of phenomenology is transcendental philosophical, and that transcendental philosophy differs from empirical science.

An important limitation of this more modest proposal is the following. Although empirical findings might supplement or challenge the phenomenological descriptions, and although such revisions due to the 'indissoluble inner alliance [. . .] between psychology and transcendental philosophy' (Hua 6/210 [206]) can be taken up by and have an impact on transcendental phenomenology, the very conceptions of naturalism and transcendental analysis remain unaffected. There is nothing in the more modest proposal that entails or necessitates the need for a more fundamental rethinking of the relation between the constituting and the constituted, between the transcendental and the natural. Phrasing it like this, however, suggests that there might be another alternative proposal worth exploring.

The volume *Naturalizing Phenomenology* had four editors. The programmatic introduction to the volume had four authors, and there are some indications in the text that they might not all have been perfectly in agreement. Next to the view I presented earlier, we also find places in the introduction where the editors explicitly describe their own project as entailing a re-examination of 'the usual concept of naturalization in order to lay bare its possible limitations and insufficiencies' (Roy et al. 1999: 46). They also speak in favour of recasting the very idea of nature, and of the need to modify our modern conception of objectivity, subjectivity, and knowledge (Roy et al. 1999: 54). They explicitly reject the claim that scientific objectivity presupposes a belief in an observer-independent reality, and, referring to quantum mechanics and to Heisenberg's uncertainty principle, they argue that physical knowledge is about physical *phenomena* which are then treated in an intersubject-ively valid manner (Roy et al. 1999: 16–17). They also suggestively write that Husserl's and Merleau-Ponty's investigations of the lived body focus on a locus where 'a *transcendental analysis and a natural account are intrinsically joined*' (Roy et al. 1999: 61). Most revealing of all, however, is perhaps a reply given by Varela to a question that I posed to him at a meeting in Paris in 2000. The volume *Naturalizing Phenomenology* was only intended as the first part of a larger project. The second, complementary volume, which unfortunately was never realized due to Varela's untimely death, was planned to carry the title *Phenomenologizing Natural Science*.

The currently most comprehensive attempt to subsequently realize this project can be found in Thompson's 2007 book *Mind in Life: Biology, Phenomenology, and the Sciences of Mind*. In his introduction, Thompson starts out by outlining and discussing some of the prevailing options in cognitive science, including cognitivism, connectionism and what he labels 'embodied dynamicism'. Whereas classical cognitivism viewed the mind as a digital computer and located it inside the skull, and connectionism saw it as a neural network, embodied dynamicism, the most recent proposal, sees the mind as an embodied dynamic system in the world, and explicitly criticizes the disembodied approach to cogni-tion favoured by the two other options (Thompson 2007: 4). Whereas the more orthodox approaches in cognitive science have persistently ignored the subjective and experiential dimension of consciousness, Thompson's ambition is to show that a special trend within embodied dynamicism, labelled 'the enactive approach', can make real progress when it comes to bridging the apparent gap between our first-personal experiential life and the neurophysiological processes that we can describe and analyse scientifically from a third-person perspective.

On Thompson's view, it is not only possible but also necessary to pursue phenomenology and experimental science as mutually constrain-ing and enlightening projects. If our aim is to have a comprehensive understanding of the mind, then focusing narrowly on the nature of the sub-personal events that underlie experience without considering the qualities of the experience itself will not take us very far (Thompson 2007: 273). In that sense, a careful description of the explanandum is an important prerequisite. More radically, however, Thompson also claims that a naturalization of phenomenology will lead to a renewed understanding of the nature of both life and mind (Thompson 2007: 14). Indeed, on his view, phenomenology provides a way of observing and describing natural phenomena that brings out features that would otherwise remain invisible to science—features such as selfhood, normativity, subjectivity, intentionality, and temporality. One of the decisive ambitions of *Mind in Life* is precisely to show how phenomenology might enable us to appreciate the inner life of biological systems (Thompson 2007: 358).

For an initial idea of what Thompson has in mind, a useful point of comparison is Merleau-Ponty's discussion in *La structure du comportement*. In that early work, Merleau-Ponty directly engaged with various scientists of his time, including Pavlov, Freud, Koffka, Piaget, Watson, and Wallon. The last section of the book carries the heading 'Is there not a truth in naturalism?' It contains a criticism of Kantian transcendental philosophy, and on the very final page of the book Merleau-Ponty called for a redefinition of transcendental philosophy that made it pay heed to the real world (Merleau-Ponty 1963: 224). Thus, rather than making us choose between an external scientific explanation or an internal phenomenological reflection—a choice that would rip asunder the living relation between consciousness and nature—Merleau-Ponty asked us to reconsider the opposition itself, and to search for a dimension that is beyond both objectivism and subjectivism. This is a view that Thompson shares, though Thompson's account—and that is indeed one of the fascinating features of *Mind in Life*—is informed by much more recent advances in science.

A core concept at work in Thompson's account is the concept of self-organization or autopoiesis. Thompson argues that living organisms have a different, emergent form of individuality and unity from those of physical being. Already at the metabolic level, living organisms preserve their identity through material changes, and in that sense one might speak of their self-identity in terms of an invariant dynamic pattern (Thompson 2007: 75). As Thompson puts it, to exist as an individual means not only to be numerically distinct from other things but to be a self-pole in a dynamic relationship with that which is other (p. 153). Even at the minimal cellular level, living organisms maintain their own identities by differentiating themselves from their surroundings. Thompson emphasizes that this differentiation between self and world, this boundary between inside and outside, should not be conflated with independence or separation. The identity and individuality of the organism is established in constant exchange with, assimilation of, and accommodation to the world (Thompson 2007: 149–50).

Although Thompson concedes that there are distinctive differences between human and animal cognition, he nevertheless defines cognition broadly in terms of the meaning that stimuli have for the organism, a meaning that emerges from its dynamically self-organizing sensorimotor activity. As he also writes, 'Cognition is behavior or conduct in relation to meaning and norms that the system itself enacts or brings forth on the basis of its autonomy' (Thompson 2007: 159). Insofar as an organism is self-organizing, things will have significance or valence *for it*, and this means that it, qua living being, embodies a kind of interiority. This interiority of life is a precursor to the interiority of consciousness. On Thompson's account, life and mind consequently share a set of basic organizational properties. The properties distinctive of mind are an enriched version of those fundamental to life. Mind is life-like and life is mind-like (Thompson 2007: 128). Thus, Thompson's general idea is that by articulating a biologically based conception of cognition that gives a natural place to the significance things have for an organism, one might join biology to subjectivity and phenomenology, where other theories are left with an explanatory gap. In his view, Chalmers' hard problem of consciousness presupposes a radical discontinuity between life and consciousness, and is consequently ill-posed and ultimately unsolvable (Thompson 2007: 223–225). Thompson's own suggestion is that we have to redefine both sides if we are to unite mind and nature.

In many ways, *Mind in Life* can be seen as a follow-up to *The Embodied Mind*. Whereas the latter work quickly dismissed Husserl as a Cartesian, a representationalist and methodological solipsist who ignored the embodied and consensual aspect of experience (Varela et al. 1991: 16–17, 68), *Mind in Life* presents a far more nuanced and well-informed interpretation, one that relies not only on Thompson's careful reading of Husserl's own writings but also on his increasing familiarity with more recent Husserl scholarship. Indeed, although Merleau-Ponty continues to play an important role, Husserl has gained a central position. This is readily visible in Thompson's extensive discussion of, and reliance on, such notions as static, genetic, and generative phenomenology, epoché, phenomenological reduction, constitution, intentionality, and life-world. The change in question is so noticeable that Thompson finds reason to offer an explanation himself. As he points out in a brief appendix entitled 'Husserl and Cognitive Science', he simply does not subscribe to the earlier Husserl interpretation any longer. He has come to realize that Husserlian phenomenology contains far more resources for a productive cross-fertilization with cognitive science than he initially thought. As he explains, when he co-authored *The Embodied Mind* not only did he have limited knowledge of Husserl's own writings and of the relevant secondary literature; his interpretation was also influenced by Heidegger's uncharitable reading of Husserl, as well as by the quite influential criticism that Dreyfus gave voice to in the volume *Husserl, Intentionality and Cognitive Science*. And as Thompson concludes, although Dreyfus should be credited for having brought Husserl into the purview of cognitive science, it is now urgent 'to go beyond his interpretation and to reevaluate Husserl's relationship to cognitive science on the basis of a thorough assessment of his life's work' (Thompson 2007: 416).

How does Thompson deal with Husserl's critical stance towards naturalism? He attempts to tackle it in different ways. To start with, he points out that one of Husserl's reasons for opposing naturalism was that he considered its reductionism incompatible with the essential difference between the mental and physical. In response, Thompson emphasizes that the naturalism he favours is of a non-reductive kind; indeed one of his points is precisely that phenomenology and biology are on equal footing. He also argues that our best contemporary scientific understanding of (physical and biological) nature differs rather markedly from the view that Husserl was criticizing—nature is no longer seen simply as an assemblage of externally juxtaposed objects—and that part of Husserl's motive for embracing anti-naturalism has for this reason simply been superseded by more recent developments in science (Thompson 2007: 357). Most significantly, however, Thompson shares Husserl's opposition to objectivism, and sees his own project as one that fully respects the transcendental status of consciousness and conceives of it as a condition of possibility for the disclosure of any object (p. 86). For Husserl, objectivity is not something pre-existing, but something constituted, and Thompson explicitly argues that this fundamental insight is one that the enactive approach shares (p. 154).

We are now in a position to articulate what the second alternative proposal amounts to. To naturalize phenomenology would be to reconsider our usual understanding of what is natural and what is transcendental. It would involve not only a renewed reflection on what transcendental philosophy is (rather than simply abandoning the transcendental project), but also a rethinking of the concept of nature, about which Hume once declared that 'there is none more ambiguous and equivocal' (Hume 2007: 304)—a rethinking that might ultimately lead to a transformation of natural science.

Regardless of how theoretically fascinating such a proposal might seem, it should be clear that the task is daunting and that there is still a long way to go. It would, however, not be a completely unprecedented proposal. In 1922, Moritz Schlick argued that the general theory of relativity had disconfirmed transcendental philosophy and vindicated empiricist philosophy. As Ryckman has shown, Schlick's verdict is quite incorrect. The outstanding mathematician and theoretical physicist Hermann Weyl, who was one of Einstein's colleagues in Zürich, and who contributed decisively to the development of both the general theory of relativity and the field of quantum mechanics, not only drew quite extensively on Husserl's criticism of naturalism but was also deeply influenced by Husserl's transcendental idealism (Ryckman 2005: 6, 110). Ultimately, one might wonder whether the decisive developments in theoretical physics at the beginning of the twentieth century really left untouched our standard scientific conception of subjectivity, objectivity, and knowledge. This is something Merleau-Ponty, for one, would dispute:

The physics of relativity confirms that absolute and final objectivity is a mere dream by showing how each particular observation is strictly linked to the location of the observer and cannot be abstracted from this particular situation; it also rejects the notion of an absolute observer. We can no longer flatter ourselves with the idea that, in science, the exercise of a pure and unsituated intellect can allow us to gain access to an object free of all human traces. (Merleau-Ponty 2004: 44–5)

But what about Husserl? To what extent would he have welcomed a naturalization of phenomenology where this didn't merely consist in promoting a fruitful exchange between phenomenology and empirical science, but rather involved a fundamental rethinking of the relation between the transcendental and the natural? As Husserl writes in the lecture course *Natur und Geist* from 1927: 'Nature is not conceivable without spirit [*Geist*], spirit not without nature' (Hua 32/16). One possibility would now have been to explore some of Husserl's somewhat speculative reflections on panpsychism, natural teleology, and transcendental instincts (cf. Hua 42 and Lee 1993). I want to end this chapter, however, by simply reminding the reader of another possible route.

As I showed in Chapter 4, one of the distinctive features of Husserl's interest in the transcendental significance of embodiment and intersubjectivity was that it led him to an exploration of the social, historical, cultural, and linguistic domains and made him engage philosophically with issues such as generativity, historicity, and normality. As we also saw, this was precisely what made Foucault refer to phenomenology's simultaneously promising and threatening proximity to empirical analyses of man (Foucault 2002: 355).

Given the extent to which phenomenological thought has attempted to reconceive the relation between the transcendental and the empirical, one might consequently wonder whether the standard argument against a naturalization of phenomenology (which was succinctly summed up by Murray)—namely that it fails to respect the strict division between the empirical and the transcendental—is not motivated by a too Kantian conception of transcendental philosophy. Is it not ignoring what is distinctive about phenomenological transcendental philosophy?

The two alternative takes on what a naturalized phenomenology might amount to that I have presented in this chapter should not be seen as incompatible alternatives between which we have to choose. Although they differ in their radicality, they might be pursued simultaneously. However, they both contrast with the more traditional conception of naturalism that classical phenomenologists opposed. So, to repeat what I wrote at the beginning of this chapter, if we want to assess whether or not a naturalized phenomenology is a desideratum or a category mistake, we need to be quite clear about what kind of phenomenology and what type of naturalization we are discussing.

6

Real realism

Kein gewöhnlicher 'Realist' ist je so realistisch and so concret
gewesen als ich, der phänomenologische 'idealist' (ein Wort, das ich
übrigens nicht mehr gebrauche).

Letter to Émile Baudin

The question of how to understand and respond to naturalism has been of
concern to phenomenology since its commencement. Within the last
couple of decades, much of the discussion has taken place in the border
area between phenomenology, cognitive science, and analytic philosophy
of mind. Recently, however, a new discussion partner has appeared on the
scene. One that very much wants to get non-human nature back on stage,
whose relation to naturalism is complicated, and whose attitude towards
phenomenology can only be described as deeply hostile. This new partner,
called 'speculative realism', is heralded (by its proponents) as one of the
most exciting and promising new currents in continental philosophy.

6.1 The end of phenomenology

In a recent book entitled *The End of Phenomenology*, Sparrow offers an
overview of speculative realism and highlights its relation to phenomenology. Sparrow's own explanation of his title is twofold. On the one hand,
he argues that the rise of speculative realism brings phenomenology to
a close. Why is that? Because speculative realism delivers what phenomenology always promised, but never provided: a wholehearted endorsement of realism (Sparrow 2014: xi). On the other hand, however,
Sparrow also argues that phenomenology never really got started. It
began and ended with Husserl. Since Husserl, according to Sparrow,
was never able to settle on what phenomenology should become, 'it is not
clear that it ever was anything at all' (Sparrow 2014: xi). In fact, the case

could be 'made that phenomenology never really existed' (p. 185), since no proponent of phenomenology has ever been able to 'adequately clarify its method, scope, and metaphysical commitments' (p. xiii). That many self-declared phenomenologists have failed to realize this merely attests to the fact that they are a kind of living dead. Sparrow even goes so far as to suggest that phenomenology is a form of 'zombie philosophy', 'extremely active, but at the same time lacking philosophical vitality and methodologically hollow' (p. 187).

The harshness of Sparrow's rhetoric is reminiscent of the work by Tom Rockmore, whom Sparrow often quotes as a source of authority. In his book *Kant and Phenomenology*, Rockmore maintains that Husserl never managed to make it clear precisely what he meant by phenomenology; that he was unable to clarify his basic account of the relationship between phenomenology and epistemology; that he repeatedly failed to address his own questions, and often just obscured the issues at stake. Thus, for Rockmore, Husserl's methodology, as well as most of his central concepts, including notions such as intuition, essence, representation, constitution, noesis, noema, and phenomenological reduction, remain fundamentally obscure (Rockmore 2011: 116, 127, 131).

Sparrow's own interpretation is as tendentious as Rockmore's.[1] To select just one example among many, consider Sparrow's claim that Merleau-Ponty in *Phénoménologie de la perception* 'affirms that yes, phenomenology is impossible' (Sparrow 2014: 48). How does Sparrow reach such a conclusion? In his preface to *Phénoménologie de la perception*, Merleau-Ponty characterizes phenomenology as a perpetual critical (self-)reflection. It should not take anything for granted, least of all itself. It is, to put it differently, a constant meditation (Merleau-Ponty 2012: lxxxv). Merleau-Ponty's point is that phenomenology is always on the way, but Sparrow equates this anti-dogmatic attitude with the view that phenomenology can never get started. In addition, Sparrow also takes issue with Merleau-Ponty's famous assertion that 'the most important lesson of the reduction is the impossibility of a complete reduction' (2012: p. lxxvii), and interprets it as amounting to the claim that the

---

[1] One of Rockmore's claims is that one should reject the often-repeated 'myth' that Husserl is the inventor of phenomenology and instead credit Kant as the first true phenomenologist (Rockmore 2011: 8). In fact, Rockmore even questions whether Husserl, Heidegger and Merleau-Ponty deserve to be classified as phenomenologists (p. 210).

reduction is a methodological step that cannot be undertaken (Sparrow 2014: 48). If the reduction is crucial to phenomenology—as Husserl insists—it would again show that phenomenology is impossible. As a closer reading of the text will show, however, this is not what Merleau-Ponty is saying. The reduction must be seen as a particular reflective move, and Merleau-Ponty's point is that we as finite creatures are incapable of effectuating an absolute reflection that once and for all would allow us to cut our ties to our world-immersed life and permit us to survey it from a view from nowhere. Even the most radical reflection depends upon and is linked to an unreflected life that, as Merleau-Ponty puts it, remains its initial, constant, and final situation (Merleau-Ponty 2012: lxxviii). To say that the reduction cannot be completed is not to say that it cannot be carried out. After all, it is only by distancing ourselves, albeit ever so slightly, from our world-immersed life that we can describe it. It is only by slackening them slightly that we can make visible the intentional threads that connect us to the world (Merleau-Ponty 2012: lxxvii). But this procedure is something that has to be performed repeatedly, rather than completed once and for all. To that extent, Merleau-Ponty's remarks about the unfinished character of phenomenology and about the incomplete reduction are two ways of making the same point. None of this entails that Merleau-Ponty should affirm that phenomenology or the reduction is impossible, which, of course, is also why he can insist that Heidegger's analysis of being-in-the-world presupposes the reduction (p. lxxviii).

Sparrow's misinterpretation of Merleau-Ponty aside, his main criticism is directed at what he takes to be the ambiguities of the phenomenological method. Husserl's inability to come up with a definite account of his own method, the fact that he never bequeathed us with something like Descartes's *Regulae ad directionem ingenii*, is, according to Sparrow, a fatal vice and weakness, since it entails that it is entirely unclear how phenomenology is supposed to be carried out (Sparrow 2014: 5–6). That subsequent phenomenologists have rebelled against Husserl's methodological requirements only makes matters even worse. There is for Sparrow no consensus and no criteria that will allow us to differentiate what is phenomenological from what is not (pp. 3–4, 10).

At this point, Sparrow starts to vacillate between three different positions. The first is the one just mentioned, namely that phenomenology has no method and stable identity. The second is that phenomenology is indeed unified by its commitment to a transcendental method. As he writes,

for a philosophical description, study, or conclusion to count as phenomeno-logical—that is, to mark it as something other than everyday description, empirical study, or speculative metaphysics—that description must take place from within some form of methodological *reduction* that shifts the focus of description to the transcendental, or at least quasi-transcendental, level. (Sparrow 2014: 14)

According to Sparrow, however, the price for this methodologically unifying transcendental commitment is too high: it entails that phenom-enology has to abandon and prohibit metaphysics. But if that is the case, phenomenology cannot offer or provide a defence of full-blown metaphysical realism, or as Sparrow puts it: 'when this book proclaims the end of phenomenology, it means that phenomenology *as a method for realists* has worn itself out' (p. 13).

After having argued at length that the execution of the epoché and transcendental reduction prevents phenomenology from making any judgements regarding the existence of things, for which reason phenomenology has to remain metaphysically neutral or agnostic, Sparrow makes his final move and claims that phenomenology cannot remain neutral, but must ultimately align itself with a form of antirealism or idealism (Sparrow 2014: 26). It is not clear how Sparrow can reconcile the claim that phenomenology has no method, that it has a transcendental method that prohibits metaphysical commitments, and that its method commits it to idealism, but given his general interpretational tactics, it is no wonder that he faults the phenomenologists (rather than his own interpretation) for the inconsistency (cf. pp. 31, 80).

When discussing the question of whether a philosophical tradition is sufficiently unified to count as a tradition, it might be unwise to adopt such rigid criteria that one ultimately risks proving just about any philosophical tradition out of existence. Were one to accept Sparrow's approach, it is hard to see how critical theory, hermeneutics, pragma-tism, or analytic philosophy could survive. Indeed, if consensus concern-ing a fixed set of methodological tools is a necessary condition for the existence of a research program, hardly any would exist. A somewhat similar remark holds true in the case of individual figures. It is hard to point to any influential thinker in the history of philosophy whose work has not given rise to scholarly disagreements and conflicting interpretations. A purist might insist that such disagreement simply reveals that the thoughts of the philosopher under examination are fundamentally confused and unclear, and that they therefore ought to be rejected. A contrasting and more sensible view would be that any philosophical work worth discussing decades and centuries later has a scope and depth to it that allows for conflicting interpretations, and that the continuing critical engagement with the tradition is part of what philosophy is all about. Should one be so unwise as to choose the first option, however, one cannot then single out a few figures for condemnation; one should at the very least be consistent, and then reject the whole lot: Plato, Aristotle, Augustine, Aquinas, Descartes, Leibniz, Locke, Hume, Kant, Nietzsche, etc.

Let me not spend more time on Sparrow's interpretation and accusations. His main conclusion and objection is that phenomenology cannot yield metaphysical realism. Despite its promise of returning us to the 'things themselves', it keeps us chained to the phenomenal. To that extent, phenomenology remains committed to a form of Kantianism, rather than providing a real realist alternative (Sparrow 2014: 1). If we want to get out of 'Kant's shadow' we shouldn't turn to phenomenology, but to speculative realism, since only 'speculative realism returns us to the real without qualification and without twisting the meaning of realism' (p. xii).

6.2 Speculative realism

What is speculative realism? It takes its name from a conference held at Goldsmiths College, University of London, in April 2007. The conference featured presentations by Ray Brassier, Iain Hamilton Grant, Graham Harman, and Quentin Meillassoux (Brassier et al. 2007). As quickly became apparent, these four protagonists diverged rather significantly when it came to their own positive proposals. Their philosophical progenitors included such diverse figures as Whitehead, Latour, Heidegger, Churchland, Metzinger, Sellars, Nietzsche, Levinas, Badiou, and Schelling, but they were united by what they opposed. They all had one common enemy: correlationism.

As we have already seen, correlationism is the view that subjectivity and objectivity cannot be understood or analysed apart from one another because both are intertwined and internally related. It is the view that we only ever have access to the correlation between thinking (theory) and being (reality) and never to either in isolation from or independently of the other. On this view, thought cannot get outside itself in order to compare the world as it is 'in itself' with the world as it is 'for us'. Indeed, we can neither think nor grasp the 'in itself' in isolation from its relation to the subject, nor can we ever grasp a subject that would not always-already be related to an object.[2]

It was allegedly Kant who introduced this type of philosophy.[3] Prior to Kant, one of the principal tasks of philosophy was to comprehend the universe, whereas since Kant, its primary focus and locus has been the correlationist circle. Rather than engaging in straightforward metaphysics, the effort has in turn been devoted to investigations of intentional correlations, language games, conceptual schemes, and discourses.

The speculative realists are unequivocal in their criticism of this development, which is described as the 'Kantian catastrophe' (Meillassoux 2008: 124) that has enduringly 'poisoned philosophy' (Badiou 2009: 535). Their hostility towards phenomenology is partially explained by the fact that it very much is a tradition 'that seeps from the rot of Kant' (Bogost 2012: 4). That phenomenology is indeed a form of correlationism should have been amply demonstrated in the preceding chapters. But here are a few additional quotes:

The genuine transcendental epoché makes possible the 'transcendental reduction'—the discovery and investigation of the transcendental correlation between world and world-consciousness. (Hua 6/154 [151])

One should not, therefore, allow oneself to be deceived by talk of the transcendence of the thing over against consciousness or talk of a 'being in itself.' [...] *An object, being in itself, is never such that would not involve consciousness and ego-consciousness at all.* (Hua 3/101)

World exists—that is, it is—only if Dasein exists, only if there is Dasein. Only if world is there, if Dasein exists as being-in-the-world, is there understanding of being, and only if this understanding exists are intraworldly beings unveiled as extant and handy. World-understanding as Dasein-understanding is self-understanding. Self and world belong together in the single entity, the Dasein.

---

[2] Although Meillassoux is often credited with the coinage of the term (2008: 5), 'correlationism' was in fact used and defined much earlier (cf. p. 114 above).

[3] The fact that Kant maintained the idea of the *Ding an sich* was of course an affront to the German idealists, who saw it as an expression of his inability to carry through his own revolutionary project. Whether Kant's view commits him to a two-world theory is debated, however. For a recent rejection of this idea, see Allais (2015).

Self and world are not two beings, like subject and object, or like I and thou, but self and world are the basic determination of the Dasein itself in the unity of the structure of being-in-the-world. (Heidegger 1982: 297)

Speculative realists, by contrast, insist that the 'world in itself—the world as it exists apart from us—cannot in any way be contained or constrained by the question of our *access* to it' (Shaviro 2011: 2). Their aim is to break out of the correlationist circle and once more reach 'the *great outdoors*, the *absolute* outside of pre-critical thinkers: that outside which was not relative to us, [. . .] existing in itself regardless of whether we are thinking of it or not' (Meillassoux 2008: 7).

Kant warned us 'never to venture with speculative reason beyond the boundaries of experience' (Kant 1998: B xxiv). The speculative realists by contrast urge us to do exactly that: 'Pace Kant, we *must* think outside of our own thought; and we must positively conceive the existence of things outside our own conceptions of them' (Shaviro 2011: 2). Indeed, on Sparrow's view, only speculative realism offers 'the kind of speculation required for grounding realism in philosophical argument' (Sparrow 2014: 3). Although Sparrow does not explain why only speculation should be able to ground realism philosophically, let us follow his suggestion and see where these speculations lead us.

According to Graham Harman, the only way to reverse Kant's 'human–world duopoly' and the anthropocentric bias of phenomenology is by opting for equality. The human–world relation is just a special case of the relation between any two entities whatsoever, or, as Harman and Bogost phrase it:

[A]ll relations in the cosmos, whether it be the perceptual clearing between humans and world, the corrosive effect of acid on lime stone, or a slap-fight between orangutans in Borneo, are on precisely the same philosophical footing. (Harman 2005: 75)

[T]here is no reason to believe that the entanglement in which a noodle finds itself is any less complex than the human who shapes, boils, vends, consumes, or digests it. (Bogost 2012: 30)

At first sight, the claim that causal relations between non-human objects are no different in kind from subject–object relations (Harman 2011: 198) seems rather familiar. It is strongly reminiscent of various reductionist attempts to naturalize intentionality, i.e. attempts to account for intentionality in terms of non-intentional mechanisms. But appearances are (in this case) misleading. When insisting on equality, the aim is not to reduce the mind (and its cognitive and affective relation to the world) to mindless mechanics. No, if anything the aim seems the reverse: to finally recognize that all objects, including fireplaces, lawnmowers, or slices of rotting pork possess an inner infinity of their own (Morton 2012: 132). Indeed, as Harman insists, the real weakness of phenomenology has precisely been its failure to capture the '"I" of sailboats and moons' (Harman 2005: 104). Phenomenology has been too restrictive, and has failed to recognize that it is entirely appropriate to ask 'What's it like to be a computer, or a microprocessor, or a ribbon cable? [. . .] What do they *experience*? What's their proper phenomenology? In short, what is it like to be a thing?' (Bogost 2012: 9–10).

Panpsychism (or, as Harman prefers to label it, polypsychism) emerges, on his view, 'directly from rejection of the Kantian Revolution' (Harman 2011: 120). One might wonder how direct and necessary that link is. On closer consideration, however, one might also wonder whether such a move really undermines correlationism, or whether it supports and expands it. Such worries also seem to have troubled Harman, since in other publications he has argued that panpsychism and human exceptionalism share a common feature: the idea that the psyche is one of the key building blocks in the universe (Harman 2005: 220). This is the fundamental assumption that has to be rejected. There might indeed be a difference between human beings and pieces of wood, but there is also a difference between the hum of a refrigerator and a bucket of yellow paint, and ultimately, we just have to face up to the fact that consciousness is simply one type of object among many others. There is no reason to prioritize it. If anything has to be prioritized, it is *sincerity*. As Harman writes, '[R]ocks and dust must be every bit as sincere as humans, parrots, or killer whales' (Harman 2005: 220). Some readers will undoubtedly be puzzled by now. But there is more puzzlement in store for us. As Harman also declares, 'philosophy's sole mission is *weird realism*. Philosophy must be realist because its mandate is to unlock the structure of the world itself; it must be weird because reality is weird' (p. 334). Indeed, one reason to be dissatisfied with Husserl is that he is 'neither weird, nor a realist, and even looks like the opposite: a "non-weird antirealist"' (p. 348).

Despite his criticism of correlationist subjectivism, Harman is no friend of naturalism. In fact, on his account, naturalism is itself a form of correlationism. It is merely another attempt to squeeze and conform reality to our (current scientific) mindset: '[T]he thing as portrayed by the natural sciences is the thing made dependent on our knowledge, and not the thing in its untamed, subterranean reality' (Harman 2011: 54). But if science does not reveal or disclose the mind-independent uncorrelated objects, how do we then gain access or knowledge about them? We do not. We can only know the appearance of the thing and never its true being. On Harman's account, the real objects, the things-in-themselves, forever remain inaccessible. As he remarks polemically against Heidegger: 'To use a hammer and to stare at it explicitly are both distortions of the very reality of that hammer as it goes about just being itself, unleashed in the world like a wild animal' (p. 74). Importantly, this inaccessibility of the in-itself is not due to some specific human cognitive flaw or incapacity, since Harman also holds the view that objects are hidden from and inaccessible to each other. The wind blowing on the banana, the hail hitting the tent, the rock colliding with the window, the flame consuming the cotton—in each case, the objects recede and withdraw from each other (Harman 2005: 19). Everything is isolated from everything else; nothing is ever in direct contact with anything else. This principle holds not only at the inter-objective level but even at the intra-objective level: an object also withdraws from and has no direct contact with its constituent parts (Harman 2005: 94, 172).

Harman criticizes phenomenology for its alleged anti-realism and argues that it chains us to the phenomenal. Whatever merit there is to this criticism, it certainly seems like a rather fitting description of his own position. Harman's fervent endorsement of realism goes hand in hand with a radical global scepticism that forever makes reality inaccessible to us—a fact that has not prevented him from making various claims about the structure and nature of this inaccessible realm.

Not all speculative realists share Harman's scepticism, however. Some of them have a far more positive view of science. In *After Finitude*, for instance, Meillassoux argues that phenomenology, because of its commitment to correlationism, is unable to accept the literal truth of scientific statements concerning events happening prior to the emergence of consciousness. When faced with a statement like 'The accretion of the Earth happened 4.56 billion years ago', phenomenology is forced to adopt a two-layered approach. It has to insist on the difference between the immediate, realist meaning of the statement and a more profound, transcendental interpretation of it. It can accept the truth of the statement, but only by adding the codicil that it is true 'for us'. Meillassoux finds this move unacceptable, and claims that it is dangerously close to the position of creationists (Meillassoux 2008: 18; see also Brassier 2007: 62). He insists that fidelity to science demands that we take scientific statements at face value and that we reject correlationism. No compromise is possible. Either scientific statements have a literal realist sense and only a realist sense, or they have no sense at all (Meillassoux 2008: 17). To put it differently, science gives us access to a reality that cannot be contained in or captured by any correlationist framework. More specifically, Meillassoux endorses a kind of Cartesian rationalism and rehabilitates the distinction between primary and secondary qualities. The former are mathematically graspable features of the things-in-themselves. Mathematics is consequently able to describe a world where humanity is absent; it can describe the great outdoors; it can give us absolute knowledge from a view from nowhere (Meillassoux 2008: 26). In the course of his argumentation, Meillassoux also defends the view, however, that everything is without reason and therefore capable of becoming otherwise without reason. Meillassoux takes this ultimate absence of reason to be an absolute ontological property (p. 53), and describes it as 'an extreme form of chaos, a *hyper-Chaos*, for which nothing is or would seem to be, impossible, not even the unthinkable' (p. 64). As he admits, it is quite a task to reconcile this view, which maintains that the laws of nature can change at any time for no reason whatsoever (p. 83), with an attempt to secure the scientific discourse and the idea that mathematical science can describe the in-itself and permit knowledge of the ancestral (p. 65).

An even more extreme form of anti-correlationist scientism can be found in the work of Brassier.[4] On his account, the ultimate aim and true consummation of the Enlightenment project is a radical demolishment of the manifest image (Brassier 2007: 26). Brassier consequently lauds

---

[4] Despite being sympathetic to Meillassoux's criticism of correlationism, Brassier has argued that the former's focus on ancestrality and on arch-fossils (materials indicating the existence of events anterior to terrestrial life) is unfortunate. To 'insist that it is only the ancestral dimension that transcends correlational constitution, is to imply that the emergence of consciousness marks some sort of fundamental ontological rupture, shattering the autonomy and consistency of reality, such that once consciousness has emerged on the scene, nothing can pursue an independent existence any more. The danger is that in privileging the arche-fossil as sole paradigm of a mind-independent reality, Meillassoux is ceding too much ground to the correlationism he wishes to destroy' (Brassier 2007: 60).

Churchland's eliminativist criticism of folk psychology, and sees speculative realism as a metaphysical radicalization of eliminativism (p. 31)—a
radicalization that ultimately leads to nihilism:

> [N]ihilism [. . .] is the unavoidable corollary of the realist conviction that there
> is a mind-independent reality, which, despite the presumptions of human
> narcissism, is indifferent to our existence and oblivious to the 'values' and
> 'meanings' which we would drape over it in order to make it more hospitable.
> (Brassier 2007: xi)

The world as it is in itself is inherently devoid of intelligibility and
meaning. To realize this, to realize the senselessness and purposelessness
of everything, is a mark of intellectual maturity (Brassier 2007: xi, 238).
This realization has also implications for our assessment of the value
of philosophical thinking. As Brassier concludes in *Nihil Unbound*:
'[P]hilosophy is neither a medium of affirmation nor a source of justification, but rather the organon of extinction' (p. 239). One inevitably
wonders how such a verdict affects the assessment of Brassier's own
philosophy, just as one might wonder whether one can consistently
celebrate the virtue of intellectual maturity at the same time as one denies
the reality of sense, meaning, intelligibility and purpose.

6.3 Forms of realism

How fatal is this criticism of phenomenology? How much of a threat to
phenomenology does it constitute? It is striking that some of Harman's
ideas are reminiscent of ideas found elsewhere, namely in phenomenology.[5]
Consider, for instance, that Merleau-Ponty, despite being a fervent correlationist (Merleau-Ponty 2012: 454) also insisted that idealism and construct-
ivism deprive the world of its transcendence. Had the former positions
been true, had the world really been a mere projection, the world would
have appeared in full transparency: it would only have possessed the
meaning we ascribed to it, and would have had no hidden aspects. In
truth, however, the world is an infinite source of richness, it is a mystery
and a gift (Merleau-Ponty 2012: lxxv, lxxxv). Consider also Levinas's claim
that object-intentionality cannot provide us with an encounter with true

---

[5] For an in-depth engagement with and criticism of Harman's Heidegger interpretation,
see Wolfendale (2014).

otherness. When I study or utilize objects, I am constantly transforming the foreign and different into the familiar and same, thereby making them lose their strangeness. This is also why, according to Levinas, Husserlian phenomenology cannot accommodate and do justice to the transcendence of the other. The other cannot be conceptualized or categorized. Any attempt to grasp or know the other necessarily domesticates and distorts what is ultimately an ineffable and untotalizable exteriority (Levinas 1969). It is debatable whether Merleau-Ponty's criticism of idealism is a criticism of Husserlian idealism, or whether it is instead targeting Kant and French neo-Kantians like Brunschvicg. It is also a matter of dispute whether Levinas's criticism of Husserl is justified (Derrida 2001; Overgaard 2003; Zahavi 2014). In either case, however, it is important to realize that the criticism in question is an internal criticism, preempted by and developed within phenomenology.

Consider next the following statement of Harman:

We have seen that one of the worst effects of phenomenology [. . .] was to cement the notion that the dispute between realism and anti-realism is a 'pseudo-problem.' Since intentionality is always directed toward something outside itself, perceiving or hating some object, phenomenology supposedly gives us all the realism we will ever need, and without falling into the 'naive' realism that posits entities beyond all possible perception. The problem is that the objects of intentionality are by no means real, as proven by the fact that we hate, love, or fear many things that turn out not to exist in the least. By confining itself to sensual objects and leaving no room for real ones, phenomenology is idealist to the core, and cannot get away with dismissing as a 'pseudo-problem' a difficulty that happens to threaten its own views about the world. (Harman 2011: 139)

This criticism is unconvincing. It is a non sequitur to argue that since some objects of intentionality are non-existing, all objects of intentionality are non-existing (or unreal). Furthermore, already in *Logische Untersuchungen* Husserl rejected any facile distinction between intentional objects (which Harman terms sensual objects) and real objects, and argued that '*the intentional object of a presentation is the same as its actual object, and on occasion as its external object, and that it is absurd to distinguish between them*' (Hua 19/439 [II/127]). This is not to say that all intentional objects are real, but only that if the intended object really exists, then it is this real object, and no other, which is our intentional object.

What about Harman's claim that the recurrent attempt by phenomenology to dismiss the dispute between realism and anti-realism as a pseudo-problem is disingenuous, since phenomenology is idealist to its core? This is potentially a more interesting claim, and one that needs to be discussed in detail. Initially, it is bound to strike many as historically incorrect. Even if Husserl seems an unremitting idealist, many of the early phenomenologists (including members of the Munich and Göttingen circles of phenomenology, i.e. figures like Reinach, Pfänder, Scheler, Stein, Geiger, Hildebrand, and Ingarden) were committed realists who were quite disappointed by Husserl's turn towards transcendental idealism. They considered this turn a betrayal of the realist thrust of phenomenology, and very much saw themselves as defending realism (Smith 1997). One might argue, however, that correlationism is one of the defining features of phenomenology, that correlationism has idealist implications, and that any early (or late) phenomenologist who is unwilling to accept correlationism is not a real phenomenologist. Considerations like these would then lead us towards the crucial question: how anti-realist is the phenomenological idealism? Or, to put it differently, how many of our realist intuitions can transcendental idealism accommodate? And conversely, how many of those intuitions can speculative realism honour?

Let me approach this set of questions by first conceding that the speculative realists are right in their assessment of how widespread correlationism is. It has indeed been 'the reigning *doxa* of post-metaphysical philosophy' (Brassier 2007: 50), and although Husserl in *Krisis* claims to have been the first to investigate the correlation philosophically (Hua 6/168), correlationism cannot be dismissed as a Husserlian idiosyncrasy. To illustrate its presence also in recent analytic philosophy, consider the case of Putnam.[6]

According to a traditional take on perception, our mind cannot on its own reach all the way to the objects themselves, and the typical claim has therefore been that we need to introduce some kind of interface between the mind and the world if we are to understand and explain intentionality. To put it differently, the claim has been that our cognitive access to the world is mediated by mental representations. Putnam takes this classical conception, which gained prominence with the British

---

[6] Over the years, Putnam has changed his view on a number of occasions. In some of his most recent publications, he has distanced himself from the position I am about to outline, and declared that he now endorses a form of metaphysical realism and rejects his former internal realism (Putnam 2015: 312).

Empiricists, to be fundamentally flawed (Putnam 1999: 20, 23). In his view, we can and do in fact experience the external world, and he insists that we need to develop a theory of perception that recovers, as he puts it, the natural realism of common man (p. 24). 'Winning through to natural realism is seeing the *needlessness* and the *unintelligibility* of a picture that imposes an interface between ourselves and the world' (p. 41). We should stop conceiving of perceptual experience as some kind of internal movie screen that confronts us with mental representations. Instead, perceptual experience should be understood in transactional terms, as (in successful cases) an acquaintance with the genuine properties of external objects (p. 169). We are *zunächst und zumeist* directed at real existing objects, and this directedness is not mediated by any intra-mental objects. The so-called qualitative character of experience, the taste of a lemon, the smell of coffee, the coldness of an ice cube, are not at all qualities belonging to some spurious mental objects, but qualities of the presented objects. Rather than saying that we experience *representations*, we should say that our experiences are *presentational*, and that they *present* the world as having certain features (p. 156).

What is the relation between Putnam's natural realism and metaphysical realism? One way to characterize the latter is by saying that it first distinguishes how things are for us from how they are *simpliciter* and then insists that the investigation of the latter is the truly important one. Another way of characterizing it is by saying that it is guided by a certain conception of knowledge. Knowledge is taken to consist in a faithful mirroring of a mind-independent reality. It is taken to be of a reality that exists independently of that knowledge, and indeed independently of any thought and experience (Williams 2005: 48). One can illustrate this way of thinking by way of the following metaphor. Whereas reality as it is in itself, independently of us, can be compared to a dough, our conceptual contribution can be compared to the shape of a cookie cutter. The world itself is fixed and stable, but we can conceive of it in different ways. If we want to know true reality, we should aim at describing the way the world is, independently of all the ways in which it happens to present itself to us human beings. But as Putnam insists, this view suffers from an intolerable naivety:

What the Cookie Cutter Metaphor tries to preserve is the naive idea that at least one Category—the ancient category of Object or Substance—has an absolute interpretation. The alternative to this idea is not the view that, in some inconceivable way, it's all *just* language. We can and should insist that some facts are there to be discovered and not legislated by us. But this is something to be said when one has adopted a way of speaking, a language, a 'conceptual scheme.' To talk of 'facts' without specifying the language to be used is to talk of nothing; the word 'fact' no more has its use fixed by Reality Itself than does the word 'exist' or the word 'object'. (Putnam 1987: 36)

To think that science can provide us with an *absolute* description of reality, i.e. a description from a view from nowhere, where all traces of ourselves have been removed; to think that science simply mirrors the way in which Nature classifies itself, is—according to Putnam—illusory. Putnam is not denying that there are 'external facts'; he even thinks that we can say what they are; but as he writes, what 'we *cannot* say—because it makes no sense—is what the facts are *independent of all conceptual choices*' (Putnam 1987: 33). We cannot hold all our current beliefs about the world up against the world and somehow measure the degree of correspondence between the two. It is, in other words, nonsensical to suggest that we should try to peel our perceptions and beliefs off the world, as it were, in order to compare them in some direct way with what they are about (Stroud 2000: 27). This is not to say that our conceptual schemes create the world, but, as Putnam writes, they do not just mirror it either (Putnam 1978: 1). Ultimately, what we call 'reality' is so deeply suffused with mind- and language-dependent structures that it is altogether impossible to make a neat distinction between those parts of our beliefs that reflect the world in itself and those parts of our beliefs that simply express our conceptual contribution. As he argues, the 'epistemological' and the 'ontological' are intimately related, and any serious philosophical work must respect their interconnection (Putnam 1988: 120). The very idea that our cognition should be nothing but a representation of something mind-independent consequently has to be abandoned (Putnam 1990: 28; 1981: 54; 1987: 77): '[T]he time has come for a moratorium on the kind of ontological speculation that seeks to describe the Furniture of the Universe and to tell us what is Really There and what is Only a Human Projection' (Putnam 1990: 118). All we can say is that 'the mind and the world jointly make up the mind and the world' (Putnam 1981: xi).

Putnam conceives of his own alternative—which he originally dubbed 'internal realism', but which he has later given various other names such as 'natural realism', 'pragmatic realism', or 'common sense realism'—as an attempt to find a third way beyond classical realism and subjective idealism, and between 'reactionary metaphysics and irresponsible relativism' (Putnam 1999: 5). He consequently sees no conflict between his rejection of metaphysical realism and his endorsement of a kind of empirical realism. Despite their attempt to monopolize the term 'realism', metaphysical realists have often made the idealist move of making a certain restricted theoretical outlook the measure of what counts as real. Occasionally the claim has been that science is the sole legitimate source of empirical knowledge. As a result, the existence of such everyday objects as tables, chairs, nations, marriages, economic crises, and civil wars have been denied with the argument that none of these entities figures in the account of reality provided by science (Putnam 1987: 3–4). Although metaphysical realism was once heralded as a strong antidote to idealism and scepticism, Putnam consequently argues that it has joined forces with what it was supposed to combat, and that we are ultimately confronted with one of those cases where the medicine has turned out to be part of the sickness it was supposed to cure, and in the end just as deadly.

When Putnam insists that the (scientistically minded) metaphysical realists do not take realism sufficiently seriously, and when he argues that it is the philosophers traditionally accused of idealism, namely the Kantians, the Pragmatists, and the Phenomenologists, who actually respect and honour our natural realism (Putnam 1987: 12), he is unwittingly following in the footsteps of Husserl. As Husserl wrote in a famous letter to Émile Baudin in 1934: 'No ordinary "realist" has ever been so realistic and so concrete as I, the phenomenological "idealist" (a term that I incidentally do not use anymore' (Hua Dok 3-VII/16).

Husserl's last claim is not entirely correct. But it is noteworthy that although Husserl in *Krisis* does use the term 'idealism', he only uses it when characterizing previous positions in the history of philosophy (primarily German Idealism and the idealism of Berkeley and Hume) and not when describing his own position. It would be a mistake to think, however, that this testifies to a decisive change in Husserl's view. Husserl remained a committed transcendental idealist to the end. We are merely dealing with a terminological choice. Husserl often insisted that his own idealism differed radically from traditional forms of idealism (Hua 5/149–53; 17/178; 1/33–4, 118), which—precisely in their opposition to realism—betrayed their inadequacy (Hua 5/151, Hua Dok 3-II/10). In *Krisis*, he also writes that all previous discussions of idealism and realism have failed to get to the bottom of matters (Hua 6/266). Husserl's terminological decision is best seen as a late realization of the fact that his transcendental idealism has so little in common with any garden variety of idealism, that the very term 'transcendental *idealism*' might be ill-chosen and also susceptible to frequent misinterpretation.

Levinas once remarked that Husserl's idealism is not a theory about how the subject is closed in upon itself and only knows its own states, but a theory about how the subject, qua intentional, is open to everything (Levinas 1998: 69). If idealism is the view that when the subject is aware of objects, it is only aware of its own subjective states, and if realism is the view that the world has a determinate nature that does not causally depend upon a creating subjectivity, Husserl might be more of a realist than a traditional idealist. Ultimately, Husserl's own view is that the transcendental reduction enables us to understand and account for the realism that is intrinsic to the natural attitude:

> The transcendent world; human beings; their intercourse with one another, and with me, as human beings; their experiencing, thinking, doing, and making, with one another: these are not annulled by my phenomenological reflection, not devalued, not altered, but only understood. (Hua 17/282)

> There can be no stronger realism than this, if by this word nothing more is meant than: 'I am certain of being a human being who lives in this world, etc., and I doubt it not in the least.' But the great problem is precisely to understand what is here so 'obvious'. (Hua 6/190–91 [187])

> That the world exists, that it is given as existing universe in uninterrupted experience which is constantly fusing into universal concordance, is entirely beyond doubt. But it is quite another matter to understand this indubitability which sustains life and positive science and to clarify the ground of its legitimacy. (Hua 5/152–3)

This is why Husserl would also write that his 'transcendental idealism' contains natural realism within itself (Hua 9/254), since it is an explication of the sense that the world has for all of us 'prior to any philosophizing' (Hua 1/36). Indeed, there is nothing wrong with the natural attitude and with our natural realism; what Husserl takes exception to is the philosophical absolutizing of the world that we find in metaphysical realism (Hua 3/120).

Although the main speculative criticism of phenomenology concerns its alleged failure to be sufficiently realist, although Sparrow insists that speculative realism 'returns us to the real without qualification and without twisting the meaning of realism' (Sparrow 2014: xii), it should have become clear by now that the realism on offer is of a rather peculiar kind. Harman defends a radical scepticism that denies us any glimpse of reality (while making various claims about the character of this ungraspable reality-in-itself); and whereas Meillassoux seeks to reconcile an old-style rationalism according to which only that which is amenable to mathematization counts as real with the idea that chaos is the primary absolute, Brassier opts for a nihilist eliminativism. How robustly realist are these divergent positions? If realism is about affirming the reality of everyday objects, the speculative realists fail miserably.

6.4 Cognitive neuroscience and neo-Kantianism

Speculative realism is not the only contemporary position whose realist credentials are somewhat dubious, its own declarations to the contrary notwithstanding. The field of naturalized epistemology provides another example.

Recently, a number of neuroscientists and philosophers including Frith, Metzinger, and Hohwy have defended different versions of the 'predictive coding approach' (also sometimes referred to as 'predictive processing theory' or 'prediction error minimization theory') and argued that it supports a form of radical neuro-representationalism—radical because the claim isn't simply that our access to the external world is mediated by neural representations, but rather that the world of experience is itself a representational construct. A central claim is that the brain doesn't process all the information it receives, but rather focuses its resources on unexpected input. To minimize costly surprises, however, the brain constantly seeks to anticipate what signals its sensory organs will be receiving. To do this as efficiently as possible, the brain constructs internal models of the possible causes of those inputs. These models allow the brain to better predict likely inputs, and these predictions are then continuously compared with the actual incoming sensory inputs. In case of error, i.e. if there is a large discrepancy between the predicted and actual inputs, the model is revised and improved (Frith 2007: 126–7). On this view, the brain is seen as a hypothesis-testing organ. However, the only data the brain can work on are the internal effects of the stimulated sense organs. Their external causes remain hidden. Whatever evidence the brain has access to is consequently evidence available on the inside, so to speak. As Hohwy puts it, we can never crawl outside our brains and directly compare our representations and predictions with the external state of affairs (Hohwy 2016: 265). The content of our conscious experiences must therefore be considered a neural construct, a brain-generated simulation. As Frith puts it, 'My perception is not of the world, but of my brain's model of the world' (2007: 132). Whatever we see, hear, touch, smell, etc. is all contained in the brain, but projected outwards and externalized, such that in normal life we fail to recognize it as a construct and mistake it for reality itself (Metzinger 2009: 6–7). Colours often serve as the relatively innocent starting point:

The apricot-pink of the setting sun is not a property of the evening sky; it is a property of the internal *model* of the evening sky, a model created by your brain. The evening sky is colorless. The world is not inhabited by colored objects at all. [. . .] Out there, in front of your eyes, there is just an ocean of electromagnetic radiation, a wild and raging mixture of different wavelengths. (Metzinger 2009: 20)

But what holds true of colours also holds true for other familiar objects. The immediate objects of perception are in fact mental constructs. The visually appearing rose, the touched ice-cube, the heard melody, etc. are all brain-generated representations, are all internal to and contained in the brain.

Given that we never have direct contact with external states of affairs—after all, the latter remains hidden behind the representational veil—we should reject all claims concerning the existence of a seamless, tight coupling between mind and world. Hohwy speaks of the strict and absolute division between inner and outer, and of the 'evidentiary boundary' that secludes and separates the brain from everything beyond its boundary (Hohwy 2016). This even includes our own bodies, which are as hidden to us, as 'very distal causes of sensory input such as the receding galaxies' (Hohwy 2016: 275).

Epistemically speaking, dualism reigns. But although the account on offer, as Hohwy admits, 'entails skepticism' (Hohwy 2016: 265), although our representational filters 'prevent us from seeing the world as it is' (Metzinger 2009: 9), this is not considered a serious cause of worry. As Metzinger reassures us, 'an external world does exist, and knowledge and action do causally connect us to it' (2009: 23). Taking an instrumentalist line, Frith dismisses the concern that we can never know whether our internal model really matches with the external world. What is crucial is the possibility of prediction and control, i.e. that the model works. Whether it truthfully describes reality or not is irrelevant (Frith 2007: 136).

Intriguingly, one historical reference that keeps reoccurring in these recent writings is a reference to the work of Hermann von Helmholtz (e.g. Frith 2007: 41, 102; Clark 2013: 182; Hohwy 2013: 5; Hobson and Friston 2014: 8). A central reason for this is that Helmholtz is seen as an early defender of the view that the task of perception is to infer the cause of sensation, and that perception to that extent amounts to a form of hypothesis testing (Hohwy 2013: 77). Helmholtz was also a neo-Kantian, however, who argued that natural science had vindicated some of Kant's central insights (see De Kock 2014; 2016). Helmholtz found an important source of inspiration for this claim in the work of the physiologist Johannes Müller, who had claimed that the properties of the external causes are not transmitted in a faithful and accurate manner to consciousness by our nerves. Indeed, so many intermediary steps and transformations occur on the way between the external cause and the experienced effect that any similarity or resemblance between the two can safely be ruled out. When we are cut by a knife, we do not feel an external object, but an internal pain. Likewise, when we see something, what we sense depends not only on the external causes, but also and far more significantly on our own physiological constitution.

That which through the medium of our senses is actually perceived by the sensorium, is indeed merely a property or change of condition of our nerves; but the imagination and reason are ready to interpret the modifications in the state of the nerves produced by external influences as properties of the external bodies themselves. (Müller 1842: 1059)

Helmholtz accepted this reasoning, and likewise argued that since the information about the external object is transformed beyond recognition on its way through the nervous system, what we end up perceiving is strictly speaking the internal effect rather than the external cause:

The result of [scientific] examination, as at present understood, is that the organs of sense do indeed give us information about external effects produced on them, but convey those effects to our consciousness in a totally different form, so that the character of a sensuous perception depends not so much on the properties of the object perceived as on those of the organ by which we receive the information. (Helmholtz 1995: 13)

I would interpret the sensation only as a sign of the object's effect. To the nature of a sign belongs only the property that for the same object the same sign will always be given. Moreover, no type of similarity is necessary between it and its object, just as little as that between the spoken word and the object that we designate thereby. (Helmholtz 1995: 408)

In the end, Helmholtz took Müller's theory and the evidence he presented as a scientific confirmation of Kant's basic claim in *Kritik der reinen Vernunft* concerning the extent to which 'we can have cognition of no object as a thing in itself, but only [...] as an appearance' (Kant 1998: B xxvi), and he argued that contemporary science on the basis of physiological evidence was reaching the same kind of insights as Kant had reached by a priori considerations. Our knowledge concerns reality as it is represented within ourselves, and not mind-independent reality as it is in itself, which remains unknowable. Although we are only ever presented with internal sensations, we can however infer that there must be an external world, since there has to be a 'cause of our nerve excitation; for there can be no effect without a cause' (Helmholtz 1855: 41). The internal sensation is consequently referred to the external object as its hypothesized cause, through an (unconscious) process of inference to best explanation.

Let us for a moment return to Kant. It has recently been claimed that Kant in his work on perception and cognition anticipated several core aspects of predictive coding theory, and that the latter theory's insistence on the active and hypothesis-driven character of perception might even be seen as an updated version of Kant's 'Copernican revolution' (Swanson 2016: 1, 4).[7] Already early on, however, Kant's theory was subjected to criticism. One of the early highly influential objections to *Kritik der reinen Vernunft* was formulated by Jacobi in 1787. Jacobi argued that Kant's appeal and reference to the things in themselves were violating his own critical system. We can, according to Kant, have no knowledge of the things in themselves, yet we are supposedly justified in asserting their existence. And although causality for Kant is a category of understanding,

---

[7] Swanson further argues that predictive coding theory can be 'seen as a major step in the evolution of Kant's transcendental psychology' (2016: 10), though he also acknowledges that the former's evolutionary, computational and neuroscientific approach 'goes beyond Kant's insights in ways that Kant could not have imagined' (p. 11). One might wonder, though, whether the naturalism of predictive coding theory is not ultimately incompatible with Kant's transcendental framework. For a critical take on the possibility of naturalizing Kant, see Allison (1995).

whose applicability is restricted to the realm of the phenomena, he still ascribes it to the things in themselves, which, although they neither exist in space and time (which are pure forms of intuition), are still taken to affect us and thereby cause us to have the representations we do. As Jacobi then concludes,

however contrary to the spirit of the Kantian philosophy it may be to say that objects make impressions on the senses, and in this way produce representations, it is hard to see how the Kantian philosophy could find an entry point for itself without this presupposition, and make any kind of presentation of its doctrine. [. . .] [W]ithout this presupposition, I could not find my way into the system, whereas with it I could not stay there. (Jacobi 2000: 173)

Jacobi's critical observation was shared by Fichte, who in an early 1796 text wrote with approval of Jacobi's complaint (Fichte 1988: 325). Fichte considered the notion of *das Ding an sich* inimical to Kant's system, as did other German idealists such as Hegel, who would go on to claim that the distinction between the thing in itself and the thing for us is a distinction we make, a distinction *for us*. As Hegel puts it in §44 of *Wissenschaft der Logik*:

The *thing-in-itself* [. . .] expresses the object insofar as one *abstracts* from everything that it is for consciousness, i.e. from all determinations of sensation as well as from all determinate thoughts of it. It is easy to see what remains, namely the *complete abstractum*, something entirely *empty*, determined only as a *beyond* [. . .]. Equally simple, however, is the reflection that this *caput mortuum* is itself merely *the product* of thought, more specifically, [the product] of thought that has progressed to pure abstraction. (Hegel 2010: 89)

Interestingly, we find a somewhat similar development regarding the status of the thing in itself among the physiological neo-Kantians. This is particularly evident in Friedrich Albert Lange's monumental and hugely influential *Geschichte des Materialismus und Kritik seiner Bedeutung in der Gegenwart* (1865). Lange initially endorses Helmholtz's view that a scientific investigation of the physiology of the sense organs has provided partial confirmation of Kant's fundamental claims, and can be interpreted as a corrected and improved form of Kantianism (Lange 1925: iii. 202–3). The senses only provide us with access to the internally occurring effects of things, and not to the external things themselves. Accordingly, the world we experience must be seen as a product of our constitution. But, as Lange then points out, if we think this through, it has some implications that are often overlooked. After all, the point just made also holds true for our bodily organs. Our body, our sensory organs, our nerves, and our very brain all figure as elements in the world of experience, and are consequently nothing but unfaithful images and signs of something unknown (Lange 1925: iii.219, 230). As Lange writes,

> The eye, with which we believe we see, is itself only a product of our ideas; and when we find that our visual images are produced by the structure of the eye, we must never forget that the eye too with its arrangements, the optic nerve with the brain and all the structures which we may yet discover there as causes of thought, are only ideas, which indeed form a self-coherent world, yet a world which points to something beyond itself. (Lange 1925: iii.224)

Ultimately, however, it is not only our sensations but also our conceptions that depend upon our physiological constitution and organization. That is, the internal mechanisms that give rise to our sensations are equally responsible for producing our concept of physical matter and of an external reality (Lange 1925: iii.204). Just as a fish swims in the pond and cannot go beyond its limit, we live within the realm of our conceptions and representations. Even when speaking of the things in themselves, we are not moving beyond our own realm (p. 226). The natural sciences have achieved immense progress and there is no reason to doubt their accomplishments, but eventually one has to engage with the fundamental epistemological questions, and when doing so, one will come to the realization that the realism of the materialists is mistaken. The physiological investigation of our sense organs might seem to offer a thoroughly materialist account of knowledge acquisition, but in truth it undermines our belief in material, self-subsistent, objects, which is why materialism, when thought through sufficiently radically reveals itself as a form of idealism (p. 223).

In the end, Lange remained somewhat ambivalent about the thing in itself. Sometimes he seemed to claim that, since appearances exist and since we need an explanation for their existence, we are entitled on the basis of an inference to best explanation to posit things in themselves as the external causes of these appearances. Sometimes he argued that the valid application of the concept of cause is restricted to experience and that we are consequently not entitled to employ causal explanations beyond the limits of experience. And sometimes he held the view that while the concept of a thing in itself is intelligible, it is a concept that might well remain empty, and that we will never know whether it actually has a referent (Edgar 2013: 107–8).

Whereas Lange somewhat ambiguously kept referring to the things themselves, Mach, who had been taught by students of Müller, took the final step a few years later. In publications from the 1880s, Mach also argued that a physiological investigation of the sense organs provided the foundations for a theory of knowledge, but on his view it was safe to eliminate the things in themselves. The objects of experience are not (unfaithful) representations of a world beyond experience; rather, all that exists are complexes of sensations (Mach 1895: 200–1)—a view that in turn has been interpreted as either amounting to a form of neutral monism or as a robust form of phenomenalism.

With this overview in mind, let us return to the contemporary neuro-representationalists, who with some justification might be labelled neo-neo-Kantians (cf. Anderson and Chemero 2013: 204). One lesson to draw is that it can be hard to preserve the existence of an external world the moment one embarks on the representationalist journey. It is not altogether clear how Metzinger can so confidently declare that, whereas the world of experience is a brain-generated illusion, the world as described by physics, the world of electromagnetic radiation, is the world as it truly is. How are scientists able to transcend their internal world simulation and reach reality itself? How do they manage to pull off this epistemic achievement? Scientists are human cognizers, and are presumably as encapsulated in their brains and as limited by their neural machinery as the rest of us allegedly are. So how can we know that our scientific theories, which are offered as explanations of the world of experience, really capture external reality? Why are they not merely elaborate cognitive extrapolations that remain as brain-generated and as internal to our constitution as everything else?

It might here be tempting to appeal to evolutionary considerations. Human beings inhabit a pre-existing natural world. To survive in that world, we have to have the capacity to acquire genuine knowledge of that world, since that is what enables us to undertake actions that can promote our survival. To put it differently, our cognitive machinery would never have evolved the way it did, would never have withstood selective pressure, unless it allowed our internal representations to match and track external reality. But this line of reasoning is hardly convincing. We cannot establish the reliability of our representations by appealing to evolutionary theory, since the latter presupposes the former.

Another strategy might be to point to the role of intersubjectivity. We do not develop our scientific theories individually; rather, they are the result of a collaborative effort. They are constructed over time by the scientific community, and can to that extent precisely be said to transcend our individual world simulation. The problem with this argument, however, should also be straightforward. Given the neurocentric disembodied framework, intersubjectivity is hardly something that can be taken for granted. The very existence of other subjects is as much in doubt as the existence of external objects.

At this point, it might be argued that we should just face up to the fact that our cognition is limited, that absolutely secure knowledge of the external world is unattainable, that we employ abductive reasoning throughout, and that the findings of science remain our best bet. To argue in this way, however, is to miss the point. What is currently being questioned is not whether we are fallible cognizers, or whether science is a worthwhile enterprise, but rather whether the position in question can so confidently embrace scientific realism.

Ultimately, however, this is not the main worry. As we can learn from Lange, there is a much more troublesome problem, one that threatens to undermine the whole setup. Why are we in the first place considering the possibility that our objects of perception are internally generated constructs rather than real spatio-temporal objects? Because this is what our neuroscientific investigation of the brain suggests. But if this theory is to be taken seriously, it has to be consistent. It cannot merely be the visually appearing hammer, orange, and passport which are part of a brain-generated fantasy or virtual reality; the same holds true of the visually appearing brain, regardless of whether we perceive it 'directly' when performing brain surgery or when looking at the colourful brain scans. After all, my empirical knowledge of brains (and neurophysiology) must be perceptually informed, and if we are to distrust the deliverance of the senses, then surely that must also hold for whatever they tell us about the brain. To put it in slightly different terms, it is hard to understand how one can motivate a general worry about perceptual experience on the basis of neuroscientific findings, since the latter—to some extent at least—presuppose the validity of the former. The main challenge, in short, is not how we can epistemically get out of the brain, but how we could possibly get into it in the first place. How do we know at all that there really is a brain? In order to enjoy any kind of initial plausibility, the neuro-representationalist account that we have been presented with must necessarily be half-baked. It asks us to abandon our naive realism, our confidence in the objective existence of ordinary objects of experience, but it only does so half-heartedly. As Slaby and Heilinger rightly point out, since the whole theory is constructed around the workings of the brain, the model must presuppose that one worldly object is exempt from its sceptical concerns and that we can indeed observe, describe, and explain the brain as it really is. But

if indeed the brain as discovered by science is 'real' in the transcendent sense of the term, then it is hardly convincing that we stop there, claiming that of all we can see and perceive, *only* one single object, the brain, is 'truly real' and not just a representation, perceived as it is in itself. (Slaby and Heilinger 2013: 89)

On the proposal in question, the world of experience is a representational construct generated by the brain. But this proposal is faced with an obvious dilemma. Either it also considers the brain a part of the world of experience, i.e. as a representational construct, and if so the account appears to be circular and explanatorily vacuous. After all, in explaining how representations come about, the account appeals to a representation. The other option is to hold that the brain is not a representational construct. But not only is it unclear how the theory could be entitled to hold that view, it is also unclear why the brain should then be the sole exception.

If we really were cognitively confined in the way proposed by recent neuroscience, it is difficult to understand how the position in question could be coherently formulated, let alone justified.

It is important to distinguish between the neuroscientific models and the theoretical interpretations they are subjected to. Friston's theoretical work (e.g. 2010) constitutes an important source of inspiration for recent discussions of predictive coding, and has been heralded as a 'theory that is set to dominate the science of mind and brain in the years to come' (Hohwy 2016: 259). But whereas Hohwy has argued that the theory entails the existence of a strict boundary between cognitive systems and the environment and therefore rules out certain hypotheses concerning the mind's extended, embodied, and enactive character (p. 259), Clark has insisted that the theory is compatible with and supports a situated, embodied and distributed approach to cognition, and that the prediction error minimization theory introduces no worrisome barrier between mind and world (Clark 2013: 195, 198; 2016). As Clark puts it, rather than saying that what we perceive is some internal representation, it is more correct to say that the brain's complex flow of sub-personal processing allows for a tight mind–world linkage and enables us to be perceptually open to the world itself (2013: 199). Clark, in turn, has subsequently been criticized for not going far enough in his criticism of representationalism, and recently proposals have been made that more directly seek to align Friston's core ideas with enactivism (Bruineberg, Kiverstein, and Rietveld 2016; Gallagher and Allen 2016).[8] I will not here take a stand on what is the correct interpretation of Friston's work, nor on whether the predictive coding paradigm is necessarily committed to neuro-representationalism. But it should be obvious that the worries presented above are primarily directed against the representationalist construal, and should be less troublesome for any non-representationalist alternative.

The naturalized epistemology presented to us by the neuro-representationalists might be driven by scientific findings, and to that extent appear to be on much firmer ground than the idealism of Husserl. But it doesn't really do a very good job of securing or preserving the reality of the ordinary world, let alone the world as described by science. Most of us want to be realists. But it isn't always that straightforward to determine what theory is best able to accommodate our realist intuitions. In fact, the neuro-representionalism just presented seems rather neatly to fit Kant's own definition of 'empirical idealism': 'Idealism is the opinion that we immediately experience only our own existence, but can only infer that of outer things (which inference from effect to cause is in fact uncertain)' (Kant 2005: 294).

Despite his commitment to transcendental idealism, Husserl was not opposed to empirical realism. Indeed, not unlike Kant, Husserl did not merely think that transcendental idealism and empirical realism are

---

[8] One reason for these continuing disagreements is not only that people tend to employ notions such as 'direct', 'indirect', and 'immediate' in quite different ways, but also that there has been a tendency to conflate epistemic, experiential, and causal understanding of these terms. The presence of causal intermediaries does not necessarily entail that perception is experientially and/or epistemically indirect. Likewise, the fact that our perceptual access to spatio-temporal objects in the world is enabled and underpinned by various sub-personal mechanisms and non-conscious cognitive processes does not necessarily entail that we therefore fail to see the objects as they are in themselves. Rather, one might view the cognitive processing as that which makes it possible for us to experience those objects in the first place (Hopp 2011: 163).

compatible; he thought that the latter requires the former. By rejecting the Kantian notion of *das Ding an sich*, however, Husserl also removed any reason to demote the status of the reality we experience to being 'merely' for us. To that extent, his transcendental idealism can be seen as an attempt to redeem rather than renounce the realism of the natural attitude. For Husserl, the world that can appear to us—be it in perception, in our daily concerns, or in our scientific analyses—is the only real world. To claim that in addition to this world there exists a world-behind-the-scenes, which transcends every appearance and every experiential and theoretical evidence, and to identify this world with true reality, is for Husserl an empty and countersensical proposition.

Obviously, Husserl didn't know anything about contemporary neurophilosophy, but he was familiar with physiological neo-Kantianism and, as pointed out by the editors of the volume *Transzendentaler Idealismus*, he considered his objections against the (Helmholtzian) attempt to construe perception as an inferential representational relation between an immanent phenomenon and an external object to serve as an indirect argument for his own transcendental idealism (Hua 36/xiii).

One articulation of these objections can be found in §§42 and 52 of *Ideen I*. There Husserl discusses and rejects the proposal that the perceptually appearing object is something merely subjective, a mere sign or illusory depiction of its hidden cause, the really existing physically determined object. First of all, such a proposal fails to respect the categorical distinction between perceptual consciousness on the one hand and signitive and pictorial consciousness on the other. Perceptual intentionality presents us with the object itself. There is no consciousness of something else of which the perceived might function as a sign or picture. In the latter forms of intentionality, by contrast, we perceive something that then signifies or depicts something else. We are directed not at that which we perceive, but through it, at something else. Signitive and pictorial intentionality consequently presupposes perceptual intentionality and cannot explain it. Secondly, what the proposal also overlooks is the fact that it is the perceived everyday object, and nothing else, that the *physicist investigates and scientifically determines*' (Hua 3/111–12). It is the planetary bodies I observe in the sky, the water I drink, the flower I admire, etc. that the natural scientist is also investigating, and whose true nature he seeks to determine in as exact and objective a manner as possible:

The thing that he [the physicist] observes, that he experiments with, that he constantly sees, takes in hand, lays on the scales, brings into the melting oven—this and no other thing becomes the subject of the physical predicates, since weight, mass, temperature, electrical resistance, and so forth are there. (Hua 3/113)

There are, in short, not two ontologically different objects, the appearing (intra-mental) object and the physical (extra-mental) object. Rather, there is only one appearing (extra-mental) object that carries categorically distinct but compatible sensuous and theoretical determinations. This is also why the findings of science and everyday experience, the scientific image and the manifest image, do not have to contradict each other. They can both be true according to their own standards. More generally speaking, the difference between the world of perception and the world of science is not a difference between the world for us and the world in itself (falling into the provinces of phenomenology and metaphysics, respectively). It is a difference between two ways in which the world appears. The world of science is not an autonomous world, a world behind or below the manifest world. Rather, the world that science studies is the same world as that of everyday experience, namely manifest reality, but now enriched and enlarged in scientific terms. This is also why it is phenomenologically absurd, as Heidegger points out:

to speak of the phenomenon as if it were something behind which there would be something else of which it would be a phenomenon in the sense of the appearance which represents and expresses [this something else]. A phenomenon is nothing behind which there would be something else. More accurately stated, one cannot ask for something behind the phenomenon at all, since what the phenomenon gives is precisely that something in itself. (Heidegger 1985: 86)

For Husserl, physical nature makes itself known in what appears perceptually. To suggest that the investigated object is a mere sign of a distinct hidden object whose real nature must remain unknown, and which can never be apprehended according to its own determinations, is for Husserl nothing but a piece of mythologizing (Hua 3/114).[9] The very idea of defining the really real reality either as the unknown cause of our

[9] The confusion is further aggravated by the unfortunate tendency to conflate the perceptually appearing object with the act of perceiving, i.e. the heard bell with the hearing of the bell, or the perceived tomato with the perceiving of the tomato. Thereby the more or less hidden physically determined object is taken to be the cause not merely of the perceptually appearing object but also of the very perception of the object. Husserl rejects such an attempt to reduce intentionality to causality.

experience or as that which is given to us with no involvement from our side is, according to Husserl, misguided, and will inevitably lead to a sceptical conundrum rather than to a securing of objectivity. How should we ever ascertain that the objects we come to know by means of our epistemic powers really remain unmodified by our epistemic grasp? As has already been pointed out repeatedly, we cannot adopt a view from nowhere from which to compare the object as it appears to us with how the object was before it appeared to us. Rather than defining objective reality as what is there in itself (a definition that gives rise to the claim that we come to know reality by removing ourselves from the equation), Husserl urges us to face up to the fact that our access to as well as the very nature of objectivity involves both subjectivity and intersubjectivity. Indeed, rather than being the antipode of objectivity, rather than consti-tuting an obstacle and hindrance to scientific knowledge, (inter)subject-ivity is a necessary enabling condition. Husserl embraces a this-worldly conception of objectivity and reality, and thereby dismisses the kind of scepticism that would argue that the way the world appears to us (even under optimal conditions) is compatible with the world really being completely different.

6.5 Phenomenology and science

At this point, the critics might retort that I have just been sidetracking and avoiding the main challenge: I have not been responding to the ancestrality objection. Is correlationism really incompatible with the findings of science? And if yes, is that not a *reductio ad absurdum* of correlationism?

As we saw, Meillassoux urged us to retrieve a reality that exists in itself 'regardless of whether we are thinking of it or not' (2008: 7). But does this really contrast with the kind of correlationism defended by Husserl? As he writes in the *Encyclopaedia Britannica* article, 'what belongs *in and for itself* to the world, is how it is, whether or not I, or whoever, become by chance aware of it or not' (Hua 9/288). Husserl is certainly not commit-ted to the view that an object only exists if it is actually thought of or experienced. In some of his manuscripts, he even addresses the problem of ancestrality. Consider, for instance, a text from February 1932, where Husserl discusses the constitution of the prehistoric natural world (Hua 39/509–13). He asks: how to account for the findings of geology and paleontology? What about geological periods long past? The world that we know is not only constituted as actually existing here and now, it is also experienced as possessing a past that transcends our individual historicity and finitude. Indeed, natural history stretches back far beyond that which is generatively constituted. It includes not only distant ice ages, and periods where no organic life were possible, but even points back to a deep past prior to the birth of Earth (Hua 39/512–13). But how can we square such findings with the claim made by transcendental idealism concerning the correlational a priori? Husserl's answer is that, just as the reality of something does not depend upon it being actually cognized by a specific subject, it also does not presuppose the simultaneous existence of any subject. Thus, on Husserl's account, the notion of a deep past without subjects is perfectly coherent, as long as it remains the past of a world with subjects (Hua 36/144):

> A merely material world as substratum, and as the earliest stretch of the duration of the world, satisfies the conditions of knowability, if a subjectivity exists which, through experience and thinking, can rationally constitute this world, first as the surrounding world which is present to it. The earlier periods of the world, including a period of merely material nature, can then be constituted backwards in accordance with reason. (Hua 36/141)

Husserl is consequently not disputing that there are things even when we are not around, and that the universe existed prior to the emergence of consciousness and will continue to exist after the cessation of life (if we for now disregard the panpsychist option). Indeed, as he writes in a text from 1926, no scientist would make the absurd suggestion that all animal life, let alone the world itself, should be dependent upon man—a late phylogenetic arrival. Such an attempt to derive everything from the psychical is dismissed by Husserl as nothing but an absurd psychological idealism (Hua 39/666). But he would insist that the truth of such claims and the objectivity of such findings are correlated with consciousness.

It might at this point not be amiss to refer to two central and much debated statements in *Sein und Zeit*. As Heidegger writes,

> If Dasein does not exist, then there 'is' no 'independence' either, nor 'is' there an 'in itself'. Such matters are then neither comprehensible nor incomprehensible. Innerworldly beings, too, can neither be discovered, nor can they lie in concealment. *Then* it can neither be said that beings are, nor that they are not. (Heidegger 1996: 196, translation modified)

> *'There is' truth only insofar as Dasein is and so long as it is.* Beings are discovered *only* when Dasein is, and only as long as Dasein is are they disclosed. Newton's

laws, the law of contradiction, and any truth whatsoever, are true only as long as Dasein *is*. Before there was any Dasein, there was no truth; nor will there be any after Dasein is no more. For in such a case truth as disclosedness, discovering, and discoveredness *cannot* be. Before Newton's laws were discovered, they were not 'true.' From this it does not follow that they were false or even that they would become false if ontically no discoveredness were possible any longer. Just as little does this 'restriction' imply a diminution of the being true of 'truths'. (Heidegger 1996: 208, translation modified)

How to interpret these statements? One possibility favoured by Blattner and Braver would be as follows: from an empirical point of view, it makes perfect sense to talk of objects existing before and after us. From a transcendental point of view, however, the intelligibility of such talk depends on a correlationalist framework. Mind-independence is a constitutive accomplishment. In the absence of minds, there would be no mind-independence (Blattner 1999: 238; Braver 2007: 193).

Husserl would agree. When it comes to ancestral statements, the 'historically primary' is our own present (Hua 6/382 [373]). This doesn't mean that the claim that, say, the sun existed prior to the emergence of consciousness is meaningless. The idea is not that such a claim is not really true, or only halfway true, but that it is true for us, which is the only truth available. The truth of ancestral statements consequently doesn't somehow prove the insignificance of consciousness. We cannot reach a position from which we can compare the world as it is for us with the world as it is in itself. This holds true in everyday life and for perceptual experience, but it also holds true for our scientific practice. It is consequently quite naive to assume that if we merely engage in astrophysics or geology, we can somehow escape our own finite perspective and gain access to a view from nowhere.

It might be tempting to accuse the correlationists of committing hubris, by defining reality in terms of what we can have access to. But as Braver has pointed out, one might also reverse this particular criticism (Braver 2012: 261–2). Not only do the speculative realists make claims about that which transcends us, but they (at least some of them) are also the ones who aspire to absolute knowledge. It is no coincidence that Meillassoux's book is called *After Finitude*. By contrast, correlationism might be a way of acknowledging the finite and perspectival character of our knowledge.

Although there are different accounts available regarding Husserl's final view on the relation between the world of perceptual experience and the world as determined by the natural sciences (see e.g. Soffer 1990; Smith 2003; Wiltsche 2012; Hardy 2013),[10] there is agreement regarding Husserl's consistent rejection of the claim that the natural sciences can provide access to a separate transphenomenal reality, one that is disconnected from the intentional correlation (Hua 3/113). It is not possible to look at our experiences sideways on to see whether they match with reality. This is so not because such views are incredibly hard to reach, but because the very idea of such views is nonsensical. Any epistemic access to reality is by definition perspectival. Effacing our perspective, subtracting our cognitive involvement, does not bring us any closer to the world, does not suddenly allow us to understand the objects as they are in themselves. It merely prevents us from understanding anything about the world at all.

This should not be construed as an anti-scientific sentiment. Husserl is certainly not opposed to science. Depending on the definition, he might even be less opposed to scientific realism than one might initially assume. He would have no issue with its anti-sceptical commitment to the possibility of scientific knowledge, and to the idea that the progress of science constitutes an advance on the truth about reality. Indeed, insofar as scientific realism is committed to empirical realism, Husserl would be on board. He would, however, have considerably less sympathy for the core metaphysical commitment of scientific realism, namely the idea that the reality investigated by science is independent of the experiential and theoretical perspectives we bring to bear on it. And he would also object to any alliance between scientific realism and scientism and reject the claim that the methods of natural science provide the sole means of epistemic access to the world, and that entities that cannot be captured in terms accepted by natural science are simply non-existent.

In any case, speculative realists are left in an uncomfortable bind. If they simply defer to the authority of science, and claim that science is to be the final arbiter of deep philosophical questions, their criticism of

---

[10] One disagreement concerns whether Husserl is ultimately an instrumentalist when it comes to theoretically postulated entities that are in principle imperceptible. I cannot discuss this issue in detail here, but I am sympathetic to Smith's construal, according to which it is important to remember that sense-perceptions are not the only intuitive acts. When experimental results rationally motivate us to posit a theoretical entity, the latter can be said to be a '*Vernunftsgegebenheit*', and to that extent originally given (Smith 2003: 194–6).

phenomenology (and any other kind of correlationism) lacks novelty. Not only would they thereby simply be accepting the existing view of various scientists (cf. Hawking and Mlodinow 2010: 5), but they would also merely be repeating an argument previously made by Russell. Already he claimed that results from astronomy and geology could refute Kant and Hegel by showing that the mind is of a recent date, and that the processes of stellar evolution proceeded according to laws in which mind plays no part (Russell 1959: 16). If the speculative realists do not take that route, they would have to buttress their criticism with proper philosophical arguments—for instance, arguments taken from philosophy of science. But as Wiltsche has recently pointed out in a critical discussion of Meillassoux's work, the latter's treatment of and engagement with philosophy of science is astonishingly sparse (Wiltsche 2016). In *After Finitude*, Meillassoux seems to take it for granted that scientific realism is the only available option. That, however, is hardly correct (for an informative overview, see Chakravartty 2011). Furthermore, most standard textbooks in philosophy of science contain more arguments for—and against—scientific realism than *After Finitude* (cf. Sankey 2008).

Given the extent to which the rise of speculative realism has been linked by its proponents to the alleged decline of phenomenology, my focus in this chapter has primarily been on assessing the former's critical contribution. Let me conclude with a few remarks concerning the positive contribution of speculative realism, with the proviso that a definitive verdict would have to await (somebody else's) more exhaustive and thorough treatment and analysis:

- I find its realist credentials questionable, ranging from Harman's scepticism (with its paradoxical revival of something akin to Kant's noumenal realm) to Brassier's radical nihilism. It is an open question whether any of these positions are coherent.

- It is epistemologically underdetermined. Husserl was led to his view regarding the status of reality through a focused exploration and analysis of intentionality. Even when rejecting the correlationist claim that the ontological and the epistemological are deeply interconnected, many scientific realists would consider it of paramount importance to explain how human cognition can give rise to genuine knowledge of a mind-independent reality: how is knowledge possible? The speculative realists, by contrast, do not really offer much in terms of a theory of knowledge that could justify their metaphysical claims.

- Given the significant divergence between the positive views of Harman, Meillassoux, and Brassier, one might finally wonder whether it at all makes sense to employ the collective label 'speculative realism'. Sparrow obviously thinks so, although he does admit that the defenders of speculative realism do not actually share a critical method (Sparrow 2014: 19). 'What then legitimates its speculative claims?' (p. 19). The answer given by Sparrow is as brief as it is unsatisfactory. He writes that the speculative realists share 'a set of commitments', including a 'commitment to speculation' (p. 19). But this merely restates the problem. What is the justification for the various (outlandish) claims being made? How should we distinguish speculation from free phantasy? As Sparrow continues, to different degrees the speculative realists are committed to 'a blending of fiction and fact', they have 'a taste for the weird, the strange, the uncanny' (p. 20), and their aim 'is to clear the ground for new advances in the thinking of reality. This is, after all, the end of philosophy' (p. 20). Perhaps speculative realism does indeed constitute the end of philosophy, or perhaps it has merely reached its own dead end. If so, Sparrow's unfounded verdict on phenomenology would turn out to be an impressively accurate assessment of speculative realism: it never really got started and it is not clear that it ever was anything at all.

Conclusion

In the previous chapters, I have chartered Husserl's route from descriptive phenomenology to transcendental idealism. I have discussed how the latter is phenomenologically motivated, what kind of transcendental philosophy it amounts to, and what its metaphysical implications are. Let me by way of conclusion return to the last question. In Chapter 3, I distinguished various meanings of the term 'metaphysics'. Let me here simplify the options even further. We can define metaphysics, as

- a fundamental reflection on and concern with the status and being of reality. Is reality mind-dependent or not, and if yes, in what manner?

- a philosophical engagement with questions of facticity, birth, death, fate, immortality, etc.

In both cases, metaphysics goes beyond eidetic possibility to also engage with (f)actuality, but in each case it does so in rather different ways. When interpreters in the past have referred to Husserl's metaphysical neutrality, when they have insisted that metaphysical issues are off-limits to phenomenology, and when they have argued that the employment of the epoché and the reduction involves an abstention of positings, a bracketing of questions related to existence and being, they have primarily had in mind the first definition of metaphysics. Given the textual material at hand, however, I think it is undeniable that Husserl was engaged in both types of endeavour.

As for the latter, I recognize that Husserl sometimes speaks of something he calls 'metaphysics in a new sense', which he characterizes as an exploration of the irrationality of the transcendental fact (Hua 7/188). As Tengelyi has argued, whereas Husserl was initially adopting a fairly traditional approach, according to which the investigation of possibility had priority over the investigation of reality (cf. p. 49 above), Husserl eventually came to have doubts about such a neat distinction between the eidetic and the factual, and about his own initial conception of the relation between phenomenology and metaphysics (Tengelyi 2014: 180–1, 184). As we have seen, Husserl came to acknowledge that the very process of constitution relies on irreducible factual components, and that transcendental phenomenology itself consequently has to engage with the problem of facticity. Eventually, however, this realization made Husserl engage with questions pertaining to the ethical-religious domain (Hua 1/182)—an engagement that culminated in what has been called his 'philosophical theology' (Hart 1986). When it comes to this side of Husserl's work, which has not been of concern to me in the present book, I must admit that I tend to side with A. D. Smith, when he writes that he cannot explain how these ideas, 'which will strike most readers as somewhat speculative', could be derived from Husserl's transcendental phenomenology (Smith 2003: 210).

As for the former endeavour, which is the one I have been focusing on, it is an integral, central, and indispensable part of Husserl's transcendental project. Phenomenology investigates not merely how different types of objects are meant, but also whether the reality of these objects is mind-dependent or not. In its exploration of the phenomena, transcendental phenomenology cannot permit itself to remain neutral or indifferent regarding the relation between phenomena and reality. By having to take a stand on that relationship, phenomenology by necessity has metaphysical implications. To that extent, Husserl's transcendental idealism must be appreciated as an attempt to offer a philosophical account of reality. But what exactly does it amount to?

Sebold has recently argued that one can distinguish a metaphysical, a semantic, and an epistemological reading of Husserl's correlationism (Sebold 2014: 176), the first two of which come in both stronger and weaker versions.

The strong metaphysical interpretation of the correlation makes Husserl into a metaphysical idealist. Consciousness is taken to be the 'ontological ground for the existence of the world' (Sebold 2014: 185), where this is understood such that 'consciousness creates the world' (p. 186), i.e. where constitution is taken to amount to production (p. 186). The weak metaphysical reading, by contrast, argues that the existence of appearing objects is correlated with and dependent upon subjectivity (p. 190).

The strong semantic interpretation argues that phenomenology is not directly engaged in a metaphysical pursuit, but rather primarily concerned with understanding the *sense* of reality and objectivity (Sebold 2014: 197). It is the sense of reality, i.e. what it means for something to be real, rather than reality itself, that is constituted by and correlated with consciousness. Whereas the physical world is independent of consciousness, the meaning of the physical world would be relative to and dependent upon consciousness (p. 199). Although it is important to distinguish the semantic reading from the metaphysical reading, the former is not without metaphysical implications of its own. For one, by amounting to a form of semantic anti-realism, it rules out metaphysical realism as nonsensical (p. 200). The weak semantic interpretation differs from the strong semantic interpretation by arguing that subjectivity is disclosing rather than creating and producing meaning. In the absence of consciousness, no meaning could manifest itself, nothing could be given as real and objective (p. 206).

Epistemological correlationism finally holds that transcendental idealism is an epistemic doctrine according to which subjectivity plays an indispensable role for knowledge. Epistemic

correlationism claims that to be *justified* as being real is to be correlated with experience. This means that while an objective reality may be metaphysically independent of experience, in that consciousness is not its causal condition, and its sense may make no reference to it being experienceable, to be epistemically warranted in believing it to be real involves it being the object of a direct or indirect experience. That is, there must be evidence to accept something as real. (Sebold 2014: 237)

If we are to posit something as existing, we need an experiential justification, which is why the positing of a different world behind the appearing world is an idle hypothesis that should be avoided (Sebold 2014: 210). On this reading, Husserl's correlationism excludes metaphysical speculation devoid of any connection to experience and empirical evidence (p. 213).

According to Sebold, the strong metaphysical and semantic interpretations should be avoided since they are both incompatible with metaphysical realism. The weak metaphysical and semantic interpretations, by contrast, are both compatible with metaphysical realism, but they are also, on Sebold's reading, rather trivial and uninteresting claims. Sebold consequently ends up favouring the epistemic interpretation, since on his view it allows for a fairly interesting position that in no way undermines metaphysical realism (p. 213).

Throughout the book, we have encountered proponents of various positions listed by Sebold. Whereas Philipse would count as a defender of a strong metaphysical interpretation, Hardy would defend the epistemological reading. Carr's and Crowell's deflationary non-metaphysical interpretations of Husserl might to some extent exemplify the weak semantic interpretation. What about my own interpretation? To the argument that transcendental subjectivity is only a necessary and not a sufficient transcendental condition, the best match might seem to be the weak semantic interpretation as well, with the only difference being that, on my reading, even the weak semantic interpretation has metaphysical implications. It is incompatible with metaphysical realism, for which reason it is not as weak or trivial as Sebold makes it out to be. Ultimately, however, I think one ought to reject Sebold's neat separation between an epistemic, semantic, and metaphysical interpretation of correlationism. Even if Husserl is certainly also driven by epistemic and evidential concerns, his transcendental idealism entails substantial metaphysical commitments concerning the mind-dependence of reality. Rather than amounting to a neutral classification, Sebold's distinction reveals his prior commitment to a realist metaphysics. For Husserl, as well as for many other post-Kantian thinkers, the epistemic, semantic, and metaphysical dimensions are intertwined. This is not to say that Husserl would necessarily have accepted the specific strong metaphysical and semantic interpretation discussed by Sebold; indeed, I have argued that he would not.

Sebold doesn't provide many arguments in favour of metaphysical realism. In fact, he seems to think that it is the only reasonable view, such that 'anyone who denies the mind-independent nature of the world is playing a hopelessly losing strategy' (Sebold 2014: 7). My aim in the foregoing text has been to elucidate and clarify Husserl's position, rather than to defend it or provide independent arguments for it. As I have argued, however, in opposing metaphysical realism, Husserl is very much a philosopher of the twentieth century. It is regrettable that Braver, in his otherwise admirable study of the development of continental anti-realism from Kant to Derrida, jumps from Nietzsche to Heidegger and fails to include a chapter on Husserl (Braver 2007). Husserl's significant broadening and transformation of the scope and nature of transcendental philosophy to include embodiment, intersubjectivity, and temporality must be appreciated as a decisive and influential contribution to twentieth-century philosophy. Indeed, on the interpretation I have been offering, Husserl's transcendental idealism is far more mainstream than has often been assumed, and has (at least in some respects) more in common with the position of figures like Heidegger, Merleau-Ponty, Wittgenstein, Dummett, Putnam, and Davidson than with the internalism of Descartes and Searle, let alone the introspectionism of Titchener. Husserl would have been in agreement with Davidson, when the latter in his *Dewey Lectures* writes that the position that truth is 'radically non-epistemic' and that all our best researched and established beliefs and theories may be false is an incomprehensible view (Davidson 1990: 308–9), and when in *Subjective, Intersubjective, Objective* he declares that a 'community of minds is the basis of knowledge; it provides the measure of all things. It makes no sense to question the adequacy of this measure, or to seek a more ultimate standard' (Davidson 2001: 218).

If Husserl's transcendental philosophical project today seems somewhat remote and removed from mainstream philosophy, this is primarily because of the massive onslaught of naturalism that we have witnessed in recent decades. What can be somewhat surprising, however, is that some forms of naturalism, as exemplified by my brief discussion of neuro-representationalism, are further removed from commonsense realism than Husserl's transcendental idealism. Indeed, depending on the definitions used, Husserl's transcendental idealism might have more in common with some forms of realism, than with traditional idealism. At the same time, one should not overlook, as pointed out in Chapter 5, the fact that Husserl's thinking can not only challenge but also productively engage with naturalism. When looking at current developments in cognitive science, there are even trends that have taken up and transformed some of Husserl's core ideas. Consider, for instance, *enactivism*. Enactivism has the stated goal of negotiating a middle path between the Scylla of cognition as a recovery of a pregiven outer world (realism), and the Charybdis of cognition as the projection of a pregiven inner world (idealism) (Varela, Thompson, and Rosch 1991: 172). Enactivism does not view cognition in terms of a faithful representation occurring between two separate and independent entities, mind and world, but instead views it as something that cuts across the divide between body, brain, and environment. Rather than seeing the world of the cognizer as an external realm that is represented (mirrored) internally in the brain, the enactive approach views it as a cognitive domain that is enacted, i.e. brought about or constituted by the coupling of the living organism (self) with its environment (Thompson 2007: 154, 158).

Yoshimi has recently argued that phenomenology ought to be neutral with respect to those aspects of metaphysics that go beyond consciousness. As he points out, this is not meant to entail that metaphysics has no relation to phenomenology, but merely that one's metaphysical commitments ought to be determined independently of phenomenology. We should, in short, simply think of phenomenological and metaphysical commitments as independently variable parameters. Yoshimi is careful to point out that this endorsement of metaphysical neutrality is not proposed as an interpretation of Husserl, but as a proposal of how Husserlian phenomenology ought to restrict itself if it is to stay within sensible parameters (Yoshimi 2015: 2). Whether we ought to follow Husserl all the way is certainly debatable, but we should not blind ourselves to the implications of Yoshimi's suggestion. To opt for the proposed restriction would be to classify phenomenology as a position in philosophy of mind, and at the same time break away from what I would consider one of its core claims, namely its insistence on the intertwining and interdependence of mind and world. It is this claim that constitutes the transcendental core of phenomenology and makes it incompatible with metaphysical realism. By short-circuiting the transcendental aspect of phenomenology, Yoshimi also subverts what Husserl would consider to be his major contribution to the study of the mind. After all, for Husserl, it is only by effectuating the transcendental turn that we can come to appreciate the full significance of consciousness and the first-person perspective.

As I pointed out at the beginning, when discussing Husserl's legacy, I think Husserl himself might have been more concerned with the continuing relevance of his transcendental project than with the extent to which the details of his concrete analyses were taken up by future generations of researchers. If we are to assess the strengths and weaknesses of his transcendental program, we first need to understand it properly, and hopefully the preceding studies have been able to offer some degree of clarification. Whether we should accept Husserl's assessment is, of course, another question. It is worth remembering, though, that Husserl also stressed the importance of providing minute and careful analyses at the expense of developing ambitious systems. As he wrote in a letter to Natorp, he remained unsatisfied 'as long as the large banknotes and bills are not turned into small change' (Hua Dok 3-V/56). A comprehensive appraisal of his philosophical impact would certainly also have to engage in a detailed study of his many concrete contributions to the study of the lifeworld, intentionality, time-consciousness, affectivity, embodiment, empathy, etc.

Even though parts of Husserl's program will remain controversial, let me in closing insist on the genuine merit of his philosophical questioning. Husserl is asking questions that we as philosophers need to ask. To that extent one can hardly overstate the difference between his approach and the philosophical sentiment expressed by Stove, when the latter claimed that the introduction of idealism into modern philosophy did more harm than the arrival of syphilis in Europe (Stove 1991: 109).

References

References to the Husserliana (Hua) edition are cited by volume number, with the page number(s) following a slash (e.g. Hua 25/104–5). Where an English translation exists, different conventions are used. In cases where the English edition includes the Husserliana page numbers in the margin, only the German page numbers are provided. But where no marginal page numbers are provided, the corresponding English page number is added in square brackets immediately following the Husserliana citation—for example, 18/87 [I/109–110], 6/154–5 [152]. For the most part, I have used the standard English translations of Husserl's works. Where no English translation was available, I have provided one myself (with the help of numerous colleagues), and in the few cases where Husserl's unpublished manuscripts are quoted, the original German text can be found in the notes. When referring to these latter manuscripts the last number always refers to the original shorthanded page.

Husserliana 1: *Cartesianische Meditationen und Pariser Vorträge*, ed. S. Strasser (The Hague: Martinus Nijhoff, 1950); pp. 3–39 trans. P. Koestenbaum as *The Paris Lectures* (The Hague: Martinus Nijhoff, 1964); pp. 43–183 trans. D. Cairns as *Cartesian Meditations: An Introduction to Phenomenology* (The Hague: Martinus Nijhoff, 1960).

Husserliana 2: *Die Idee der Phänomenologie: Fünf Vorlesungen*, ed. W. Biemel (The Hague: Martinus Nijhoff, 1950); trans. L. Hardy as *The Idea of Phenomenology* (The Hague: Martinus Nijhoff, 1999).

Husserliana 3, 1–2: *Ideen zu einer reinen Phänomenologie und phänomenologischen Philosophie. Erstes Buch: Allgemeine Einführung in die reine Phänomenologie*, ed. K. Schuhmann (The Hague: Martinus Nijhoff, 1976); trans. F. Kersten as *Ideas Pertaining to a Pure Phenomenology and to a Phenomenological Philosophy. First Book: General Introduction to a Pure Phenomenology* (The Hague: Martinus Nijhoff, 1982); trans. D. O. Dahlstrom as *Ideas for a Pure Phenomenology and Phenomenological Philosophy. First Book: General Introduction to Pure Phenomenology* (Indianapolis: Hackett, 2014).[1]

Husserliana 4: *Ideen zu einer reinen Phänomenologie und phänomenologischen Philosophie. Zweites Buch: Phänomenologische Untersuchungen zur Konstitution*, ed. M. Biemel (The Hague: Martinus Nijhoff, 1952); trans. R. Rojcewicz

---

[1] I have made use of both English translations of *Ideen I*.

and A. Schuwer as *Ideas Pertaining to a Pure Phenomenology and to a Phenomenological Philosophy. Second Book: Studies in the Phenomenology of Constitution* (Dordrecht: Kluwer Academic, 1989).

Husserliana 5: *Ideen zu einer reinen Phänomenologie und phänomenologischen Philosophie. Drittes Buch: Die Phänomenologie und die Fundamente der Wissenschaften*, ed. M. Biemel (The Hague: Martinus Nijhoff, 1952); pp. 1–137 trans. T. E. Klein and W. E. Pohl as *Ideas Pertaining to a Pure Phenomenology and to a Phenomenological Philosophy. Third Book: Phenomenology and the Foundations of the Sciences* (The Hague: Martinus Nijhoff, 1980); pp. 138–62 trans. R. Rojcewicz and A. Schuwer as *Ideas Pertaining to a Pure Phenomenology and to a Phenomenological Philosophy. Second Book: Studies in the Phenomenology of Constitution* (Dordrecht: Kluwer Academic, 1989), 405–30.

Husserliana 6: *Die Krisis der europäischen Wissenschaften und die transzendentale Phänomenologie: Eine Einleitung in die phänomenologische Philosophie*, ed. W. Biemel (The Hague: Martinus Nijhoff, 1954); pp. 1–348, 357–86, 459–62, 473–5, 508–16 trans. D. Carr as *The Crisis of European Sciences and Transcendental Phenomenology: An Introduction to Phenomenological Philosophy* (Evanston, Ill.: Northwestern University Press, 1970).

Husserliana 7: *Erste Philosophie (1923/24). Erster Teil: Kritische Ideengeschichte*, ed. Rudolf Boehm (The Hague: Martinus Nijhoff, 1956).

Husserliana 8: *Erste Philosophie (1923/24). Zweiter Teil: Theorie der phänomenologischen Reduktion*, ed. Rudolf Boehm (The Hague: Martinus Nijhoff, 1959).

Husserliana 9: *Phänomenologische Psychologie: Vorlesungen Sommersemester 1925*, ed. W. Biemel (The Hague: Martinus Nijhoff, 1962); pp. 3–234 trans. J. Scanlon as *Phenomenological Psychology: Lectures, Summer Semester, 1925* (The Hague: Martinus Nijhoff, 1977); pp. 237–349, 517–26 ed. and trans. T. Sheehan and R. E. Palmer as *Psychological and Transcendental Phenomenology and the Confrontation with Heidegger (1927–1931)* (Dordrecht: Kluwer Academic, 1997).

Husserliana 10: *Zur Phänomenologie des inneren Zeitbewusstseins (1893–1917)*, ed. R. Boehm (The Hague: Martinus Nijhoff, 1966); trans. J. B. Brough as *On the Phenomenology of the Consciousness of Internal Time (1893–1917)* (Dordrecht: Kluwer Academic, 1991).

Husserliana 11: *Analysen zur passiven Synthesis: Aus Vorlesungs- und Forschungsmanuskripten 1918–1926*, ed. M. Fleischer (The Hague: Martinus Nijhoff, 1966); trans. A. Steinbock as *Analyses Concerning Passive and Active Synthesis: Lectures on Transcendental Logic* (Dordrecht: Kluwer Academic, 2001).

Husserliana 13: *Zur Phänomenologie der Intersubjektivität: Texte aus dem Nachlass. Erster Teil: 1905–1920*, ed. I. Kern (The Hague: Martinus Nijhoff, 1973).

Husserliana 14: *Zur Phänomenologie der Intersubjektivität: Texte aus dem Nachlass. Zweiter Teil: 1921–1928*, ed. I. Kern (The Hague: Martinus Nijhoff, 1973).

Husserliana 15: *Zur Phänomenologie der Intersubjektivität: Texte aus dem Nachlass. Dritter Teil: 1929–1935*, ed. I. Kern (The Hague: Martinus Nijhoff, 1973).

Husserliana 16: *Ding und Raum. Vorlesungen 1907*, ed. U. Claesges (Den Haag: Martinus Nijhoff, 1973); trans. R. Rojcewicz as *Thing and Space: Lectures of 1907* (Dordrecht: Kluwer Academic, 1997).

Husserliana 17: *Formale und transzendentale Logik: Versuch einer Kritik der logischen Vernunft*, ed. P. Janssen (The Hague: Martinus Nijhoff, 1974); pp. 5–335 trans. D. Cairns as *Formal and Transcendental Logic* (The Hague: Martinus Nijhoff, 1969).

Husserliana 18: *Logische Untersuchungen. Erster Band: Prolegomena zur reinen Logik*, ed. E. Holenstein (The Hague: Martinus Nijhoff, 1975); trans. J. N. Findlay as *Logical Investigations I* (London: Routledge, 2001), 1–161.

Husserliana 19, 1–2: *Logische Untersuchungen. Zweiter Band: Untersuchungen zur Phänomenologie und Theorie der Erkenntnis*, ed. Ursula Panzer (The Hague: Martinus Nijhoff, 1984); trans. J. N. Findlay as *Logical Investigations I–II* (London: Routledge, 2001), 162–331, 1–364.

Husserliana 20, 1: *Logische Untersuchungen: Ergänzungsband. Erster Teil: Entwürfe zur Umarbeitung der VI. Untersuchung und zur Vorrede für die Neuauflage der Logischen Untersuchungen (Sommer 1913)*, ed. U. Melle (Dordrecht: Kluwer Academic, 2002).

Husserliana 20, 2: *Logische Untersuchungen: Ergänzungsband. Zweiter Teil: Texte für die Neufassung der VI. Untersuchung. Zur Phänomenologie des Ausdrucks und der Erkenntnis (1893/94–1921)*, ed. U. Melle (Dordrecht: Springer, 2005).

Husserliana 22: *Aufsätze und Rezensionen (1890–1910)*, ed. B. Rang (The Hague: Martinus Nijhoff, 1979).

Husserliana 24: *Einleitung in die Logik und Erkenntnistheorie: Vorlesungen 1906/07*, ed. U. Melle (Dordrecht: Martinus Nijhoff, 1984); trans. C. O. Hill as *Introduction to Logic and Theory of Knowledge: Lectures 1906/07* (Springer: Dordrecht, 2008).

Husserliana 25: *Aufsätze und Vorträge (1911–1921)*, ed. T. Nenon and H. R. Sepp (Dordrecht: Martinus Nijhoff, 1987).

Husserliana 27: *Aufsätze und Vorträge (1922–1937)*, ed. T. Nenon and H. R. Sepp (Dordrecht: Kluwer Academic, 1989).

Husserliana 29: *Die Krisis der europäischen Wissenschaften und die transzendentale Phänomenologie: Ergänzungsband. Texte aus dem Nachlass 1934–1937*, ed. R. N. Smid (Dordrecht: Kluwer Academic, 1993).

Husserliana 32: *Natur und Geist: Vorlesungen Sommersemester 1927*, ed. M. Weiler (Dordrecht: Kluwer Academic, 2001).

Husserliana 34: *Zur phänomenologischen Reduktion: Texte aus dem Nachlass (1926–1935)*, ed. S. Luft (Dordrecht: Kluwer Academic, 2002).

Husserliana 35: *Einleitung in die Philosophie: Vorlesungen 1922/23*, ed. B. Goossens (Dordrecht: Kluwer Academic, 2002).

Husserliana 36: *Transzendentaler Idealismus: Texte aus dem Nachlass (1908–1921)*, ed. R. Rollinger (Dordrecht: Kluwer Academic, 2003).

Husserliana 39: *Die Lebenswelt. Auslegungen der vorgegebenen Welt und ihrer Konstitution: Texte aus dem Nachlass (1916–1937)*, ed. R. Sowa (New York: Springer, 2008).

Husserliana 42: *Grenzprobleme der Phänomenologie. Analysen des Unbewusstseins und der Instinkte. Metaphysik. Späte Ethik. Texte aus dem Nachlass 1908–1937*, ed. R. Sowa and T. Vongehr (New York: Springer, 2014).

Husserliana Dokumente 3: *Briefwechsel I–X*, ed. Karl Schuhmann and E. Schuhmann (Dordrecht: Kluwer Academic, 1994).

Husserliana Materialien 8: *Späte Texte über Zeitkonstitution (1929–1934): Die C-Manuskripte*, ed. D. Lohmar (Dordrecht: Springer, 2006).

Husserl, E. (1939). Entwurf einer 'Vorrede' zu den *Logischen Untersuchungen* (1913). *Tijdskrift voor Philosophie* 1: 105–33, 319–39.

Husserl, E. (1981). *Shorter Works*, ed. P. McCormick and F. A. Elliston (Notre Dame, Ind.: University of Notre Dame Press).

Husserl's unpublished manuscripts: Ms. A VI 21 (1928 and 1933), Ms. B III 12 IV (1922). Husserl Archives Leuven.

Ali, R. (2017). Does hallucinating involve perceiving? *Philosophical Studies*, doi 10.1007/s11098-017-0884-7.

Allais, L. (2015). *Manifest Reality: Kant's Idealism and his Realism* (Oxford: Oxford University Press).

Allison, H. E. (1983). *Kant's Transcendental Idealism: An Interpretation and Defense* (New Haven, Conn.: Yale University Press).

Allison, H. E. (1995). On naturalizing Kant's transcendental psychology. *Dialectica* 49(2–4): 335–56.

Anderson, M. L., and Chemero, T. (2013). The problem with brain GUTs: conflation of different senses of 'prediction' threatens metaphysical disaster. *Behavioral and Brain Sciences* 36: 204–5.

Badiou, A. (2009). *Logics of Worlds: Being and Event 2*, trans. A. Toscano (London: Continuum).

Beck, M. (1928). Die Neue Problemlage der Erkenntnistheorie. *Deutsche Vierteljahrsschrift für Literaturwissenschaft und Geistesgeschichte* 6: 611–39.

Bennett, M. R., and Hacker, P. M. S. (2003). *Philosophical Foundations of Neuroscience* (Oxford: Blackwell).

Benoist, J. (1997). *Phénoménologie, sémantique, ontologie* (Paris: PUF).

Bergson, H. (1910) [1889]. *Time and Free Will: An Essay on the Immediate Data of Consciousness*, trans. F. L. Pogson (Whitefish, Mont.: Kessinger).

Bernet, R. (1990). Husserls Begriff des Noema. In S. Isseling (ed.), *Husserl-Ausgabe und Husserl-Forschung* (Dordrecht: Kluwer Academic), 61–80.

Bernet, R., Kern, I., and Marbach, E. (1993). *An Introduction to Husserlian Phenomenology* (Evanston, Ill.: Northwestern University Press).

Beyer, C. (1997). Ideen zu einer reinen Phänomenologie der empirischen Bedeutung. *Phänomenologische Forschungen. Neue Folge* 2(2): 167–76.

Bitbol, M., and Petitmengin, C. (2011). On pure reflection. *Journal of Consciousness Studies* 18(2): 24–37.

Bitbol, M., and Petitmengin, C. (2013a). A defense of introspection from within. *Constructivist Foundations* 8(3): 269–79.

Bitbol, M., and Petitmengin, C. (2013b). On the possibility and reality of introspection. *Kairos* 6: 173–98.

Blackburn, S. (2016). *The Oxford Dictionary of Philosophy* (Oxford: Oxford University Press).

Blattner, W. D. (1999). *Heidegger's Temporal Idealism* (Cambridge: Cambridge University Press).

Boehm, R. (1968). *Vom Gesichtspunkt der Phänomenologie* (The Hague: Martinus Nijhoff).

Boehm, R. (2000) [1959]. Husserl's concept of the absolute. Trans. R. O. Elveton. In R. O. Elverton (ed.), *The Phenomenology of Husserl: Selected Critical Readings*, 2nd edn (Seattle, WA: Noesis Press), 164–91.

Bogost, I. (2012). *Alien Phenomenology, or What it's Like to be a Thing* (Minneapolis: University of Minnesota Press).

Borrett, D., Kelly, S., and Kwan, H. (2000). Bridging embodied cognition and brain function: the role of phenomenology. *Philosophical Psychology* 13(2): 261–6.

Brassier, R. (2007). *Nihil Unbound: Enlightenment and Extinction* (New York: Palgrave Macmillan).

Brassier, R., Grant, I. H., Harman, G., and Meillassoux, Q. (2007). Speculative realism. *Collapse* 3: 306–449.

Braver, L. (2007). *A Thing of This World: A History of Continental Anti-Realism* (Evanston, Ill.: Northwestern University Press).

Braver, L. (2012). A brief history of Continental Realism. *Continental Philosophy Review* 45(2): 261–89.

Bruineberg, J., Kiverstein, J., and Rietveld, E. (2016). The anticipating brain is not a scientist: the free-energy principle from an ecological-enactive perspective. *Synthese*, doi:10.1007/s11229-016-1239-1.

Caputo, J. D. (1992). The question of being and transcendental phenomenology: reflections on Heidegger's relationship to Husserl. In C. Macann (ed.), *Martin Heidegger: Critical Assessments I* (London: Routledge), 326–44.

Carman, T. (2003). *Heidegger's Analytic: Interpretation, Discourse and Authenticity in Being and Time* (Cambridge: Cambridge University Press).

Carr, D. (1999). *The Paradox of Subjectivity: The Self in the Transcendental Tradition* (Oxford: Oxford University Press).

Chakravartty, A. (2011). Scientific Realism. In E. N. Zalta (ed.), *The Stanford Encyclopedia of Philosophy*, http://plato.stanford.edu/entries/scientific-realism/

Clark, A. (2013). Whatever next? Predictive brains, situated agents, and the future of cognitive science. *Behavioral and Brain Sciences* 36(3): 181–204.

Clark, A. (2016). Busting out: predictive brains, embodied minds, and the puzzle of the evidentiary veil. *Noûs* doi:10.1111/nous.12140.

Cole, J. D. (1995). *Pride and a Daily Marathon* (Cambridge, Mass.: MIT Press).

Courtine, J.-F. (1990). *Heidegger et la phénoménologie* (Paris: Vrin).

Crick, F. (1995). *The Astonishing Hypothesis* (London: Touchstone).

Crowell, S. (2001). *Husserl, Heidegger and the Space of Meaning* (Evanston, Ill.: Northwestern University Press).

Crowell, S. (2008). Phenomenological immanence and semantic externalism: a rapprochement. *Synthese* 160: 335–54.

Crowell, S. (2015). Phenomenology and transcendental philosophy: making meaning thematic. In S. Gardner and M. Grist (eds), *The Transcendental Turn* (Oxford: Oxford University Press), 244–63.

Damasio, A. (1999). *The Feeling of What Happens* (San Diego, Calif.: Harcourt).

Davidson, D. (1990). The structure and content of truth. *Journal of Philosophy* 87 (6): 279–328.

Davidson, D. (2001). *Subjective, Intersubjective, Objective* (Oxford: Oxford University Press).

De Boer, T. (1978). *The Development of Husserl's Thought* (The Hague: Martinus Nijhoff).

De Kock, L. (2014). Hermann von Helmholtz's empirico-transcendentalism reconsidered: construction and constitution in Helmholtz's psychology of the object. *Science in Context* 27(4): 709–44.

De Kock, L. (2016). Helmholtz's Kant revisited (once more). The all-pervasive nature of Helmholtz's struggle with Kant's *Anschauung*. *Studies in History and Philosophy of Science Part A*, 56: 20–32.

De Palma, V. (2015). Eine peinliche Verwechselung. *Metodo* 1(1): 13–45.

Dennett, D. C. (1982). How to study human consciousness empirically, or, nothing comes to mind. *Synthese* 53: 159–80.

Dennett, D. C . (1987). *The Intentional Stance* (Cambridge, Mass.: MIT Press).

Dennett, D. C. (1991). *Consciousness Explained* (Boston, Mass.: Little, Brown).

Dennett, D. C. (1994). Tiptoeing past the covered wagons: a response to Carr. https://ase.tufts.edu/cogstud/dennett/papers/tiptoe.htm.

Dennett, D. C. (2007). Philosophy as naïve anthropology: comment on Bennett and Hacker. In M. Bennett, D. Dennett, P. Hacker, and J. Searle, *Neuroscience and Philosophy: Brain, Mind, and Language* (New York: Columbia University Press), 73–95.

Depraz, N., Varela, F., and Vermersch, P. (2003). *On Becoming Aware: A Pragmatics of Experiencing* (Amsterdam: John Benjamins).

Derrida, J. (1982) [1972]. *Margins of Philosophy*, trans. A. Bass (Brighton: Harvester Press).

Derrida, J. (2001) [1967]. *Writing and Difference*, trans. A. Bass (London: Routledge).

Dillon, M. C. (1988). *Merleau-Ponty's Ontology*, 2nd edn (Evanston, Ill.: Northwestern University Press).

Dreyfus, H. L. (1982). Husserl's perceptual *noema*. In H. L. Dreyfus and H. Hall (eds), *Husserl, Intentionality and Cognitive Science* (Cambridge, Mass.: MIT Press), 97–123.

Dreyfus, H. L. (1988). Husserl's epiphenomenology. In H. R. Otto and J. A. Tuedio (eds), *Perspectives on Mind* (Dordrecht: D. Reidel), 85–104.

Dreyfus, H. L. (1991). *Being-in-the-World* (Cambridge, Mass.: MIT Press).

Dreyfus, H. L., and Hall, H. (1982). Introduction. In H. L. Dreyfus and H. Hall. (eds), *Husserl, Intentionality and Cognitive Science* (Cambridge, Mass.: MIT Press), 1–27.

Dreyfus, H. L., and Kelly, S. D. (2007). Heterophenomenology: heavy-handed sleight-of-hand. *Phenomenology and the Cognitive Sciences* 6(1–2): 45–55.

Dreyfus, H. L., and Rabinow, P. (1983). *Michel Foucault: Beyond Structuralism and Hermeneutics* (Chicago: Chicago University Press).

Drummond, J. J. (1990). *Husserlian Intentionality and Non-Foundational Realism* (Dordrecht: Kluwer Academic).

Drummond, J. J. (1992). An abstract consideration: de-ontologizing the noema. In J. J. Drummond and L. Embree (eds), *The Phenomenology of the Noema* (Dordrecht: Kluwer Academic), 89–109.

Drummond, J. J. (2012). Intentionality without representationalism. In D. Zahavi (ed.), *The Oxford Handbook of Contemporary Phenomenology* (Oxford: Oxford University Press), 115–33.

Dwyer, P. (1990). *Sense and Subjectivity: A Study of Wittgenstein and Merleau-Ponty* (Leiden: Brill).

Edgar, S. (2013). The limits of experience and explanation: F. A. Lange and Ernst Mach on things in themselves. *British Journal for the History of Philosophy* 21(1): 100–21.

Fichte, J. G. (1988) [1796]. *Early Philosophical Writings*, trans. D. Breazeale (Ithaca, NY: Cornell University Press).

Findlay, J. N. (1972). Phenomenology, realism and logic. *Journal of the British Society for Phenomenology* 3(3): 235–44.

Fink, E. (1981) [1939]. The problem of the phenomenology of Edmund Husserl. Trans. R. M. Harlan. In W. McKenna, R. M. Harlan, and L. E. Winters (eds), *Apriori and World: European Contributions to Husserlian Phenomenology* (The Hague: Martinus Nijhoff), 21–55.

Fink, E. (1995) [1932]. *Sixth Cartesian Meditation: The Idea of a Transcendental Theory of Method*, trans. R. Bruzina (Bloomington: Indiana University Press).

Fink, E. (2000) [1933]. The phenomenological philosophy of Edmund Husserl and contemporary criticism. Trans. R. O. Elveton. In R. O. Elveton (ed.), *The Phenomenology of Husserl: Selected Critical Readings*, 2nd edn (Seattle, WA: Noesis Press), 70–139.

Flanagan, O. (1992). *Consciousness Reconsidered* (Cambridge, Mass.: MIT Press).

Føllesdal, D. (1974). Husserl's theory of perception. *Ajatus* 36: 95–103.

Foucault, M. (2002). *The Order of Things* (London: Routledge).

Friedman, M. (2002). Exorcising the philosophical tradition. In N. H. Smith (ed.), *Reading McDowell on Mind and World* (London: Routledge), 25–57.

Friston, K. (2010). The free–energy principle: A unified brain theory? *Nature Reviews: Neuroscience* 11(2): 127–38.

Frith, C. (2007). *Making up the Mind: How the Brain Creates Our Mental Worlds* (Oxford: Blackwell).

Gadamer, H.-G. (1972). *Kleine Schriften III* (Tübingen: J. C. B. Mohr).

Gallagher, S. (1997). Mutual enlightenment: recent phenomenology in cognitive science. *Journal of Consciousness Studies* 4(3): 195–214.

Gallagher, S. (2003). Phenomenology and experimental design: toward a phenomenologically enlightened experimental science. *Journal of Consciousness Studies* 10(9–10): 85–99.

Gallagher, S., and Allen, M. (2016). Active inference, enactivism and the hermeneutics of social cognition. *Synthese*, doi.org/10.1007/s11229-016-1269-8.

Gallagher, S., and Zahavi, D. (2012). *The Phenomenological Mind*, 2nd edn (London: Routledge).

Gallese, V. (2001). The shared manifold hypothesis: from mirror neurons to empathy. *Journal of Consciousness Studies* 8(5–7): 33–50.

Gardner, S., and Grist, M. (eds) (2015). *The Transcendental Turn* (Oxford: Oxford University Press).

Hanna, R. (2014). Husserl's crisis and our crisis. *International Journal of Philosophical Studies* 22(5): 752–70.

Hardy, L. (2013). *Nature's Suit: Husserl's Phenomenological Philosophy of the Physical Sciences* (Athens: Ohio University Press).

Harman, G. (2005). *Guerrilla Metaphysics: Phenomenology and the Carpentry of Things* (Chicago: Open Court).

Harman, G. (2008). On the horror of phenomenology: Lovecraft and Husserl. *Collapse* 4: 333–64.

Harman, G. (2011). *The Quadruple Object* (Alresford, Hants: Zero Books).

Hart, J. G. (1986). A precis of a Husserlian phenomenological theology. In S. C. Laycock and J. G. Hart (eds), *Essays in Phenomenological Theology* (Albany, NY: SUNY), 89–168.

Hawking, S., and Mlodinow, L. (2010). *The Grand Design* (New York: Bantam).

Hegel, G. W. F. (2010) [1817]. *Encyclopedia of the Philosophical Sciences in Basic Outline. Part I: Science of Logic*, trans. K. Brinkmann and D. O. Dahlstrom (Cambridge: Cambridge University Press).

Heidegger, M. (1972) [1969]. *On Time and Being*, trans. J. Stambaugh (New York: Harper and Row).

Heidegger, M. (1982) [1927]. *The Basic Problems of Phenomenology*, trans. A. Hofstadter (Bloomington: Indiana University Press).

Heidegger, M. (1985) [1925]. *History of the Concept of Time*, trans. T. Kisiel (Bloomington: Indiana University Press).

Heidegger, M. (1993). *Grundprobleme der Phänomenologie (1919/1920)* (Frankfurt am Main: Vittorio Klostermann).

Heidegger, M. (1996) [1927]. *Being and Time*, trans. J. Stambaugh (Albany, NY: SUNY).

Heidegger, M. (1998) [1976]. *Pathmarks*, ed. W. McNeill (Cambridge: Cambridge University Press).

Heidegger, M. (2010) [1920]. *Phenomenology of Intuition and Expression*, trans. T. Colony (London: Continuum).

Heinämaa, S. (2014). The animal and the infant: from embodiment and empathy to generativity. In S. Heinämaa, M. Hartimo, and T. Miettinen (eds), *Phenomenology and the Transcendental* (London: Routledge), 129–46.

Heinämaa, S., Hartimo, M., and Miettinen, T. (eds) (2014). *Phenomenology and the Transcendental* (London: Routledge).

Helmholtz, H. v. (1855). *Das Sehen des Menschen* (Leipzig: Leopold Voss).

Helmholtz, H. v. (1995) [1853–1892]. *Science and Culture: Popular and Philosophical Lectures*, ed. D. Cahan (Chicago: Chicago University Press).

Henry, M. (1973) [1963]. *The Essence of Manifestation*, trans. G. Etzkorn (The Hague: Martinus Nijhoff).

Hobson, J. A., and Friston, K. J. (2014). Consciousness, dreams, and inference: the Cartesian theatre revisited. *Journal of Consciousness Studies* 21(1–2): 6–32.

Hohwy, J. (2013). *The Predictive Mind* (Oxford: Oxford University Press).

Hohwy, J. (2016). The self evidencing brain. *Noûs* 50(2): 259–85.

Holenstein, E. (1972). *Phänomenologie der Assoziation: zu Struktur und Funktion eines Grundprinzips der passiven Genesis bei E. Husserl* (The Hague: Martinus Nijhoff).

Hopp, W. (2011). *Perception and Knowledge: A Phenomenological Account* (Cambridge: Cambridge University Press).

Hume, D. (2007) [1739–40]. *A Treatise of Human Nature* (Oxford: Clarendon Press).

Iacoboni, M. (2009). *Mirroring People: The Science of Empathy and How We Connect with Others* (New York: Picador).

Ingarden, R. (1994). *Gesammelte Werke, Band 6: Frühe Schriften zur Erkenntnistheorie* (Tübingen: Max Niemeyer).

Jacobi, F. H. (2000) [1787]. On transcendental idealism. In B. Sassen (ed.), *Kant's Early Critics: The Empiricist Critique of the Theoretical Philosophy* (Cambridge: Cambridge University Press), 169–75.

Journal of Consciousness Studies (1997). Editorial: The future of consciousness studies. Vols 4(5–6): 385–8.

Kant, I. (1998) [1781/1789]. *Critique of Pure Reason*, trans P. Guyer and A. W. Wood (Cambridge: Cambridge University Press).

Kant, I. (2005) [1785–9]. *Notes and Fragments*, trans. C. Bowman, P. Guyer, and F. Rauscher (Cambridge: Cambridge University Press).

Keller, P. (1999). *Husserl and Heidegger on Human Experience* (Cambridge: Cambridge University Press).

Kern, I. (1964). *Husserl und Kant: Eine Untersuchung über Husserls Verhältnis zu Kant und zum Neukantianismus* (The Hague: Martinus Nijhoff).

Korsgaard, C. M. (2009). *Self-Constitution: Agency, Identity, and Integrity* (Oxford: Oxford University Press).

Lafont, C. (2005). Was Heidegger an externalist? *Inquiry* 48(6): 507–32.

Lange, F. A. (1925) [1865]. *The History of Materialism and Criticism of its Present Importance*, trans. E. C. Thomas (London: Kegan Paul).

Lawlor, L. (2009). Becoming and auto-affection (Part II): Who are we? Invited lecture, ICNAP. Published at: http://www.icnap.org/lawlor%20-%20paper.pdf (accessed 3 March 2012).

Lee, N. (1993). *Edmund Husserls Phänomenologie der Instinkte* (Dordrecht: Kluwer).

Levinas, E. (1969) [1961]. *Totality and Infinity: An Essay on Exteriority*, trans. A. Lingis (Pittsburgh, Penn.: Duquesne University Press).

Levinas, E. (1995) [1930]. *The Theory of Intuition in Husserl's Phenomenology*, trans. A. Orianne (Evanston, Ill.: Northwestern University Press).

Levinas, E. (1998). *Discovering Existence with Husserl*, trans. R. A. Cohen and M. B. Smith (Evanston, Ill.: Northwestern University Press).

Levine, J. (1983). Materialism and qualia: the explanatory gap. *Pacific Philosophical Quarterly* 64: 354–61.

Lewis, M. (2003). The development of self-consciousness. In J. Roessler and N. Eilan (eds), *Agency and Self-Awareness* (Oxford: Oxford University Press), 275–95.

Lutz, A. (2002). Toward a neurophenomenology as an account of generative passages: a first empirical case study. *Phenomenology and the Cognitive Sciences* 1: 133–67.

Lutz, A., Lachaux, J.-P., Martinerie, J., and Varela, F. J. (2002). Guiding the study of brain dynamics by using first-person data: synchrony patterns correlate with ongoing conscious states during a simple visual task. *Proceedings of the National Academy of Sciences* 99(3): 1586–91.

Lutz, A., and Thompson, E. (2003). Neurophenomenology: integrating subjective experience and brain dynamics in the neuroscience of consciousness. *Journal of Consciousness Studies* 10: 31–52.

Mach, E. (1895) [1882]. The economical nature of physical inquiry. In *Popular Scientific Lectures*, trans. Thomas J. McCormack (Chicago: Open Court).

Malpas, J. (2002). *From Kant to Davidson: Philosophy and the Idea of the Transcendental* (London: Routledge).

Marion, J.-L. (1998) [1989]. *Reduction and Givenness*, trans. T. A. Carlson (Evanston, Ill.: Northwestern University Press).

McClamrock, R. (1995). *Existential Cognition: Computational Minds in the World* (Chicago: University of Chicago Press).

McDowell, J. (1992). Putnam on mind and meaning. *Philosophical Topics* 20(1): 35–48.

McDowell, J. (1994). *Mind and World* (Cambridge, Mass.: Harvard University Press).

McDowell, J. (2002). Responses. In N. H. Smith (ed.), *Reading McDowell on Mind and World* (London: Routledge), 269–305.

McIntyre, R. (1982). Intending and referring. In H. L. Dreyfus and H. Hall (eds), *Husserl, Intentionality and Cognitive Science* (Cambridge, Mass.: MIT Press), 215–31.

McIntyre, R. (1986). Husserl and the representational theory of mind. *Topoi* 5: 101–13.

Meillassoux, Q. (2008) [2006]. *After Finitude: An Essay on the Necessity of Contingency*, trans. R. Brassier (London: Continuum).

Meixner, U. (2010). Husserl transzendentaler Idealismus als Supervenienzthese: ein interner Realismus. In M. Frank and N. Weidtmann (eds), *Husserl und die Philosophie des Geistes* (Berlin: Suhrkamp), 178–208.

Merleau-Ponty, M. (1963) [1942]. *The Structure of Behavior*, trans. A. Fisher (Pittsburgh, Penn.: Duquesne University Press).

Merleau-Ponty, M. (1964) [1948]. *Sense and Non-Sense*, trans. H. Dreyfus and P. Dreyfus (Evanston, Ill.: Northwestern University Press).

Merleau-Ponty, M. (2004) [1948]. *The World of Perception*, trans. O. Davis (London: Taylor and Francis).

Merleau-Ponty, M. (2010). *Child Psychology and Pedagogy: The Sorbonne Lectures 1949-1952*, trans. T. Welsh (Evanston, Ill.: Northwestern University Press).

Merleau-Ponty, M. (2012) [1945]. *Phenomenology of Perception*, trans. D. A. Landes (London: Routledge).

Metzinger, T. (2003). *Being No One* (Cambridge, Mass.: MIT Press).

Metzinger, T. (2009). *The Ego Tunnel* (New York: Basic Books).

Mohanty, J. (1985). *The Possibility of Transcendental Philosophy* (Dordrecht: Martinus Nijhoff).

Moran, D. (2016). Sinnboden der Geschichte: Foucault and Husserl on the structural a priori of history. *Continental Philosophy Review* 49(1): 13–27.

Moran, R. (2001). *Authority and Estrangement: An Essay on Self-Knowledge* (Princeton, NJ: Princeton University Press).

Morton, T. (2012). Art in the age of asymmetry: Hegel, objects, aesthetics. *Evental Aesthetics* 1(1): 121–42.

Müller, J. (1842) [1838]. *Elements of Physiology II*, trans. W. Baly (London: Taylor and Walton).

Murray, A. (2002). Philosophy and the 'anteriority complex'. *Phenomenology and the Cognitive Sciences* 1(1): 27–47.

Neisser, U. (1976). *Cognition and Reality* (San Francisco, Calif.: W. H. Freeman).

O'Murchadha, F. (2008). Reduction, externalism and immanence in Husserl and Heidegger. *Synthese* 160(3): 375–95.

Oksala, J. (2011). Post-structuralism: Michel Foucault. In S. Overgaard and S. Luft (eds), *The Routledge Companion to Phenomenology* (London: Routledge), 528–39.

Overgaard, S. (2003). On Levinas' critique of Husserl. In D. Zahavi, S. Heinämaa, and H. Ruin (eds), *Metaphysics, Facticity, Interpretation* (Dordrecht: Kluwer), 115–38.

Overgaard, S. (2004). *Husserl and Heidegger on Being in the World* (Dordrecht: Kluwer Academic).

Overgaard, S. (2010). Royaumont revisited. *British Journal for the History of Philosophy* 18: 899–924.

Papineau, D. (2015). Naturalism. In E. N. Zalta (ed.), *The Stanford Encyclopedia of Philosophy* (Fall 2015 edn): http://plato.stanford.edu/archives/fall2015/entries/naturalism/

Parnas, J., Møller, P., Kircher, T., Thalbitzer, J., Jansson, L., Handest, P., and Zahavi, D. (2005). EASE: examination of anomalous self-experience. *Psychopathology* 38: 236–58.

Peirce, C. S. (1955). *Philosophical Writings of Peirce*, ed. J. Buchler (New York: Dover).

Petitmengin, C. (2006). Describing one's subjective experience in the second person: an interview method for the science of consciousness. *Phenomenology and the Cognitive Sciences* 5: 229–69.

Petitmengin, C., and Bitbol M. (2009). The validity of first-person descriptions as authenticity and coherence. *Journal of Consciousness Studies* 16: 363–404.

Petitot, J., Varela, F. J., Pachoud, B., and Roy, J.-M. (eds) (1999). *Naturalizing Phenomenology* (Stanford, Calif.: Stanford University Press).

Philipse, H. (1995). Transcendental idealism. In B. Smith and D. W. Smith (eds), *The Cambridge Companion to Husserl* (Cambridge: Cambridge University Press), 239–322.

Putnam, H. (1975). *Mind, Language and Reality* (Cambridge: Cambridge University Press).

Putnam, H. (1978). *Meaning and the Moral Sciences* (London: Routledge and Kegan Paul).

Putnam, H. (1981). *Reason, Truth and History* (Cambridge: Cambridge University Press).

Putnam, H. (1987). *The Many Faces of Realism* (LaSalle, Ill.: Open Court).

Putnam, H. (1988). *Representation and Reality* (Cambridge, Mass.: MIT Press).

Putnam, H. (1990). *Realism with a Human Face* (Cambridge, Mass.: Harvard University Press).

Putnam, H. (1999). *The Threefold Cord: Mind, Body, and World* (New York: Columbia University Press).

Putnam, H. (2015). Naturalism, realism, and normativity. *Journal of the American Philosophical Association* 1(2): 312–28.

Ramstead, M. J. D. (2015). Naturalizing what? Varieties of naturalism and transcendental phenomenology. *Phenomenology and the Cognitive Sciences* 14(4): 929–71.

Ratcliffe, M. (2006). Phenomenology, neuroscience, and intersubjectivity. In H. L. Dreyfus and M. A. Wrathall (eds), *A Companion to Phenomenology and Existentialism* (Oxford: Blackwell), 329–45.

Rochat, P., and Zahavi, D. (2011). The uncanny mirror: a re-framing of mirror self-experience. *Consciousness and Cognition* 20(2): 204–13.

Rockmore, T. (2011). *Kant and Phenomenology* (Chicago: University of Chicago Press).

Rowlands, M. (2003). *Externalism: Putting Mind and World Back Together Again* (Montreal: McGill-Queen's University Press).

Roy, J.-M., Petitot, J., Pachoud, B., and Varela, F. J. (1999). Beyond the gap: an introduction to naturalizing phenomenology. In J. Petitot, F. J. Varela, B. Pachoud, and J.-M. Roy (eds), *Naturalizing Phenomenology* (Stanford, Calif.: Stanford University Press), 1–83.

Rudd, A. (2003). *Expressing the World: Skepticism, Wittgenstein, and Heidegger* (Chicago: Open Court).

Russell, B. (1959). *My Philosophical Development* (New York: Simon and Schuster).

Ryckman, T. (2005). *The Reign of Relativity: Philosophy in Physics 1915–1925* (New York: Oxford University Press).

Sankey, H. (2008). *Scientific Realism and the Rationality of Science* (Aldershot: Ashgate).

Sartre, J.-P. (1970) [1939]. Intentionality: a fundamental idea of Husserl's phenomenology. *Journal of the British Society for Phenomenology* 1(2): 4–5.

Sartre, J.-P. (1981) [1975]. Interview with Michel Rybalka, Oreste Pucciani, and Susan Gruenheck. In P. Schilpp (ed.), *The Philosophy of Jean-Paul Sartre* (La Salle, Ill.: Open Court), 5–51.

Sartre, J.-P. (2003) [1943]. *Being and Nothingness*, trans. H. E. Barnes (London: Routledge).

Scheler, M. (1973) [1913/1916]. *Formalism in Ethics and Non-Formal Ethics of Values: A New Attempt Toward a Foundation of an Ethical Personalism*, trans M. S. Frings and R. L. Funk (Evanston, Ill.: Northwestern University Press).

Schutz, A. (1967) [1932]. *The Phenomenology of the Social World*, trans. G. Walsh and F. Lehnert (Evanston, Ill.: Northwestern University Press).

Sebold, R. (2014). *Continental Anti-Realism: A Critique* (London: Rowman and Littlefield International).

Sellars, W. (1963). *Science, Perception and Reality* (London: Routledge and Kegan Paul).

Shaviro, S. (2011). Panpsychism and/or eliminativism. Retrieved 5 Oct. 2015 from: http://www.shaviro.com/Blog/?p=1012.

Siewert, C. (2007). In favour of (plain) phenomenology. *Phenomenology and the Cognitive Sciences* 6: 201–20.

Slaby, J., and Heilinger, J.-C. (2013). Lost in phenospace: questioning the claims of popular neurophilosophy. *Metodo* 1(2): 83–100.

Smith, A. D. (2003). *Routledge Philosophy Guidebook to Husserl and the Cartesian Meditations* (London: Routledge).

Smith, A. D. (2008). Husserl and externalism. *Synthese* 160(3): 313–33.

Smith, B. (1997). Realistic phenomenology. In L. Embree (ed.), *Encyclopedia of Phenomenology* (Dordrecht: Kluwer), 586–90.

Smith, D. W. (2013). *Husserl*, 2nd edn (New York: Routledge).

Smith, D. W., and McIntyre, R. (1982). *Husserl and Intentionality* (Dordrecht: D. Reidel).

Soffer, G. (1990). Phenomenology and scientific realism: Husserl's critique of Galileo. *Review of Metaphysics* 44(1): 67–94.

Sokolowski, R. (1970). *The Formation of Husserl's Concept of Constitution* (The Hague: Martinus Nijhoff).

Sokolowski, R. (1977). On the motives which led Husserl to transcendental idealism. *Journal of Philosophy* 74(3): 176–80.

Sokolowski, R. (1984). Intentional analysis and the noema. *Dialectica* 38(2–3): 113–29.

Sokolowski, R. (1987). Husserl and Frege. *Journal of Philosophy* 84: 521–8.

Sparrow, T. (2014). *The End of Phenomenology: Metaphysics and the New Realism* (Edinburgh: Edinburgh University Press).

Spaulding, S. (2015). Phenomenology of social cognition. *Erkenntnis* 80: 1069–89.

Spiegelberg, H. (1965). *The Phenomenological Movement* (The Hague: Martinus Nijhoff).

Staiti, A. (2015). On Husserl's alleged Cartesianism and conjunctivism: a critical reply to Claude Romano. *Husserl Studies* 31(2): 123–41.

Stern, R. (2000). *Transcendental Arguments and Scepticism: Answering the Question of Justification* (Oxford: Oxford University Press).

Stove, D. C. (1991). *The Plato Cult and Other Philosophical Follies* (Oxford: Blackwell).

Straus, E. (1958). Aesthesiology and hallucinations. In R. May et al. (eds), *Existence: A New Dimension in Psychiatry and Psychology* (New York: Basic Books), 139–69.

Strawson, G. (2008). *Real Materialism, and Other Essays* (Oxford: Oxford University Press).

Strawson, P. (1992). Discussion of Strawson's *Analysis, Science, and Metaphysics*. In R. M. Rorty (ed.), *The Linguistic Turn: Essays in Philosophical Method* (Chicago: University of Chicago Press), 321–30.

Ströker, E. (1987). *Husserls transzendentale Phänomenologie* (Frankfurt am Main: Vittorio Klostermann).

Stroud, B. (2000). *The Quest for Reality* (Oxford: Oxford University Press).

Swanson, L. R. (2016). The predictive processing paradigm has roots in Kant. *Frontiers in Systems Neuroscience* 10(79): 1–13. doi: 10.3389/fnsys.2016.00079

Taipale, J. (2014). *Phenomenology and Embodiment: Husserl and the Constitution of Subjectivity* (Evanston, Ill.: Northwestern University Press).

Taylor, C. (1964). Review of *La philosophie analytique*. *Philosophical Review* 73: 132–5.

Tengelyi, L. (2015). *Welt und Unendlichkeit: Zum Problem phänomenologischer Metaphysik* (Freiburg: Karl Alber).

Thomasson, A. L. (2005). First-person knowledge in phenomenology. In D. W. Smith and A. L. Thomasson (eds), *Phenomenology and Philosophy of Mind* (Oxford: Clarendon Press), 115–38.

Thomasson, A. L. (2007). In what sense is phenomenology transcendental? *Southern Journal of Philosophy* 45(S1): 85–92.

Thompson, E. (2007). *Mind in Life: Biology, Phenomenology, and the Sciences of Mind* (Cambridge, Mass.: Harvard University Press).

Thompson, K. (2016). From the historical a priori to the *dispositif*: Foucault, the phenomenological legacy, and the problem of transcendental genesis. *Continental Philosophy Review* 49(1): 41–54.

Titchener, E. B. (1910). *A Textbook of Psychology* (New York: Macmillan).

Tugendhat, E. (1970). *Der Wahrheitsbegriff bei Husserl und Heidegger* (Berlin: de Gruyter).

Twardowski, K. (1982) [1894]. *Zur Lehre vom Inhalt und Gegenstand der Vorstellungen* (Vienna: Philosophia).

Van Breda, H. L. (1959). Die Rettung von Husserls Nachlaß und die Gründung des Husserl-Archivs. In H. L. Van Breda and J. Taminiaux (eds), *Husserl und das Denken der Neuzeit* (The Hague: Martinus Nijhoff), 1–41.

Van Breda, H. L. (1992). Merleau-Ponty and the Husserl Archives at Louvain. In H. J. Silverman and J. Barry, Jr (eds), *Merleau-Ponty, Texts and Dialogues* (Atlantic Highlands, NJ: Humanities Press), 150–61, 178–83.

Varela, F. J. (1996). Neurophenomenology: a methodological remedy for the hard problem. *Journal of Consciousness Studies* 3(4): 330–49.

Varela, F. (1997). The naturalization of phenomenology as the transcendence of nature: searching for generative mutual constraints. *Alter* 5: 355–81.

Varela, F. J., Thompson, E., and Rosch, E. (1991). *The Embodied Mind: Cognitive Science and Human Experience* (Cambridge, Mass.: MIT Press).

Velmans, M. (2000). *Understanding Consciousness* (London: Routledge).

Vermersch, P. (1994). *L'entretien d'explicitation* (Paris: ESF).

Vermersch, P. (2009). Describing the practice of introspection. *Journal of Consciousness Studies* 16(10–12): 20–57.

Vermersch, P. (2011). Husserl the great unrecognized psychologist! A reply to Zahavi. *Journal of Consciousness Studies* 18(2): 20–3.

Waldenfels, B. (2000). *Das leibliche Selbst: Vorlesungen zur Phänomenologie des Leibes* (Frankfurt am Main: Suhrkamp).

Wilkes, K. V. (1988). *Real People: Personal Identity without Thought Experiments* (Oxford: Clarendon Press).

Willard, D. (2011). Realism sustained? Interpreting Husserl's progression into idealism. Paper presented at the Early Phenomenology Conference held at Franciscan University of Steubenville, 29–30 April 2011. http://www.dwillard.org/articles/artview.asp?artID=151.

Williams, B. (2005) [1976]. *Descartes: The Project of Pure Enquiry* (London: Routledge).

Wiltsche, H. A. (2012). What is wrong with Husserl's scientific anti-realism? *Inquiry* 55(2): 105–30.

Wiltsche, H. A. (2016). Science, realism, and correlationism: a phenomenological critique of Meillassoux' argument from ancestrality. *European Journal of Philosophy*, doi: 10.1111/ejop.12159.

Wolfendale, P. (2014). *Object-Oriented Philosophy: The Noumenon's New Clothes* (Falmouth: Urbanomic).

Yoshimi, J. (2015). The metaphysical neutrality of Husserlian phenomenology. *Husserl Studies* 31(1): 1–15.

Zahavi, D. (1999). *Self-awareness and Alterity: A Phenomenological Investigation* (Evanston, Ill.: Northwestern University Press).

Zahavi, D. (2001). *Husserl and Transcendental Intersubjectivity: A Response to the Linguistic-Pragmatic Critique*, trans. E. A. Behnke (Athens: Ohio University Press).

Zahavi, D. (2003a). Inner time-consciousness and pre-reflective self-awareness. In D. Welton (ed.), *The New Husserl: A Critical Reader* (Bloomington: Indiana University Press), 157–80.

Zahavi, D. (2003b). How to investigate subjectivity: Heidegger and Natorp on reflection. *Continental Philosophy Review* 36(2): 155–76.

Zahavi, D. (2003c). *Husserl's Phenomenology* (Stanford, Calif.: Stanford University Press).

Zahavi, D. (2004). Back to Brentano? *Journal of Consciousness Studies* 11(10–11): 66–87.

Zahavi, D. (2005). *Subjectivity and Selfhood: Investigating the First-Person Perspective* (Cambridge, Mass.: MIT Press).

Zahavi, D. (2014). *Self and Other: Exploring Subjectivity, Empathy, and Shame* (Oxford: Oxford University Press).

Zahavi, D., and Stjernfelt, F. (eds) (2002). *One Hundred Years of Phenomenology: Husserl's Logical Investigations Revisited* (Dordrecht: Kluwer Academic).

Index of names

Index of subjects

Printed and bound by CPI Group (UK) Ltd, Croydon, CR0 4YY